Federalism and Regionalism in Australia

New Approaches, New Institutions?

Federalism and Regionalism in Australia

New Approaches, New Institutions?

Edited by A.J. Brown and
J.A. Bellamy

ANU
THE AUSTRALIAN NATIONAL UNIVERSITY

E PRESS

ANU
E PRESS

the Australia and New Zealand
School of Government

Published by ANU E Press
The Australian National University
Canberra ACT 0200, Australia
Email: anuepress@anu.edu.au
This title is also available online at: http://epress.anu.edu.au/fra_citation.html

---

National Library of Australia
Cataloguing-in-Publication entry

Federalism & Regionalism in Australia (2006 : Sydney,
N.S.W.).

Federalism and regionalism in Australia : new approaches,
new institutions?

Bibliography.
ISBN 9781921313417 (pbk.)
ISBN 9781921313424 (online)

1. Central-local government relations - Australia. 2.
Regionalism - Australia. 3. Federal government - Australia.
4. Australia - Politics and government. I. Brown, A. J.
(Alexander Jonathan). II. Bellamy, J. A. (Series : ANZSOG
series).

320.994

Cover design by John Butcher, based on the Interim Biogeographic Regionalisation of
Australia, Version 5.1., Commonwealth Department of Environment & Heritage (2000).

Funding for this monograph series has been provided by the Australia and New
Zealand School of Government Research Program.

John Wanna, *Series Editor*

Professor John Wanna is the Sir John Bunting Chair of Public Administration at the Research School of Social Sciences at The Australian National University. He is the director of research for the Australian and New Zealand School of Government (ANZSOG). He is also a joint appointment with the Department of Politics and Public Policy at Griffith University and a principal researcher with two research centres: the Governance and Public Policy Research Centre and the nationally-funded Key Centre in Ethics, Law, Justice and Governance at Griffith University. Professor Wanna has produced around 17 books including two national text books on policy and public management. He has produced a number of research-based studies on budgeting and financial management including: *Budgetary Management and Control* (1990); *Managing Public Expenditure* (2000), *From Accounting to Accountability* (2001) and, most recently, *Controlling Public Expenditure* (2003). He has just completed a study of state level leadership covering all the state and territory leaders — entitled *Yes Premier: Labor leadership in Australia's states and territories* — and has edited a book on Westminster Legacies in Asia and the Pacific — *Westminster Legacies: Democracy and responsible government in Asia and the Pacific*. He was a chief investigator in a major Australian Research Council funded study of the Future of Governance in Australia (1999-2001) involving Griffith and the ANU. His research interests include Australian and comparative politics, public expenditure and budgeting, and government-business relations. He also writes on Australian politics in newspapers such as *The Australian*, *Courier-Mail* and *The Canberra Times* and has been a regular state political commentator on ABC radio and TV.

Table of Contents

Acknowledgements

The Symposium on which this volume is based, held on 8 May 2006, was supported by Griffith University, the NSW Farmers' Association, and CSIRO Sustainable Ecosystems as part of three research initiatives coordinated by the Griffith University Federalism Project – see www.griffith.edu.au/federalism.

Particular thanks go to the NSW Farmers' Association, including Mal Peters, Shaugn Morgan, Anand Sugrim and Margaret McCullough, for their ongoing support for research to quantify the economic and financial benefits of regional devolution within Australia's federal system, and for development of an overall framework for evaluating new spatial approaches to governance, to help contextualise and guide this research. The Symposium marked the release of this framework in the form of the Appendix to this volume: the NSW Farmers' Association discussion paper '*Reform of Australia's Federal System – Identifying the Benefits*', launched by Professor Kenneth Wiltshire AO at the end of proceedings. This paper provides a roadmap to the objectives of new spatial approaches to governance in Australia, and identifies evaluation methods that can establish whether their intended benefits are being achieved or alternatively, which alternative approaches might better deliver on outcomes.

Special thanks also to CSIRO Sustainable Ecosystems, particularly Associate Professor Tim Smith (now with University of the Sunshine Coast), for chairing and other support through the joint *Regional Governance Futures* project between Griffith University and CSIRO; to Professor Frank Stilwell, University of Sydney, for chairing and ongoing support and involvement; and to the Institute of Public Administration Australia, NSW Division (especially Liz Thomas) for symposium organisation. The symposium was also an important contribution to the Australian Research Council-funded Discovery Project, *Towards Sustainable Regional Institutions* (DP0666833). Final acknowledgements to Professor John Wanna and John Butcher, Australia and New Zealand School of Government, for respectively chairing the final session, including these proceedings in the ANZSOG publication series, and associated editorial support.

Contributors

Professor Andrew Beer researches and teaches in the School of Geography, Population and Environmental Management at Flinders University, South Australia. He is an expert in regional and local economic development, regional policy and institutional regulation theory, urban geography and public policy, and Australian Housing. He is Director of the Australian Housing and Urban Research Institute's Southern Research Centre, and a Visiting Professor at the University of Ulster, Northern Ireland. He has edited the national journal *Sustaining Regions*, and his recent books with colleagues include *Developing Australia's Regions: Theory and Practice* (University of NSW Press, 2003), and *Developing Locally: Lessons in Economic Development from Four Nations* (Policy Press, Bristol, 2003).

Cr Paul Bell AM is President of the Australian Local Government Association and of the Local Government Association of Queensland. He has been a councillor of Emerald Shire Council, Queensland, since 1985, where he was mayor from 1991-2000. He chairs Australian Local Government Training Limited, a national industry training advisory board, and is Deputy Chair of Queensland Rail and a Director of the Ergon Energy Corporation of Queensland. Cr Bell was appointed as a Member of the Order of Australia in January 2005 for service to local government, regional development and tourism, vocational education and training, and the community. In February 2005 he was awarded an Honorary Bachelor of Business Administration degree by the University of Central Queensland.

Jennifer Bellamy is a Principal Research Fellow in the School of Natural and Rural Systems Management, University of Queensland, St. Lucia. Formerly a Principal Research Scientist (Resource Governance) CSIRO Sustainable Ecosystems, she has over 30 years experience in research on regional resource use management and planning, both in Australia and overseas. In particular, she has lead a number of major interdisciplinary research projects on the social and institutional aspects of regional natural resource management and planning including the evaluation of natural resource management governance within the framework of regional sustainable development.

Cr Mike Berwick has been Mayor of Douglas Shire Council, Far North Queensland since 1991, and is a current member of the National Sea Change Task Force. He has wide ranging experience in local and regional governance and is also currently chair of the Wet Tropics Regional Natural Resource Management Board and the Australian Tropical Forest Institute. He is a member of the Ministerial Advisory Committee for Vegetation Management (MACVM) as well as having served on many past boards and committees, and as a media advisor to the Commonwealth Minister for the Environment, Graham Richardson.

Dr A. J. Brown is a Senior Lecturer and Senior Research Fellow in the Socio-Legal Research Centre, Griffith University; and a Visiting Fellow with The Australian National University College of Law in Canberra. He has worked or consulted in public law, policy and accountability issues for all levels and branches of government, as well as in the non-government sector. He has worked as Senior Investigation Officer for the Commonwealth Ombudsman; Associate to Justice Tony Fitzgerald AC, President of the Queensland Court of Appeal; and as ministerial policy advisor to the Hon Rod Welford MLA, Queensland Minister for Environment Heritage and Natural Resources. His recent publications include *Restructuring Australia: Regionalism, Republicanism and Reform of the Nation State* (Federation Press, 2004). He currently leads several research projects on the future of federalism through the Griffith University Federalism Project.

Professor Brendan Gleeson is Professor of Urban Management and Policy, and Director of the Urban Research Program at Griffith University. Prior to joining Griffith University in 2003, he was Deputy Director of the Urban Frontiers Program, University of Western Sydney. He has researched, published and consulted widely on planning and urban governance, the political economy of planning, social policy and the city, and environmental policy and theory. His recent books include *Australian Urban Planning: New Challenges, New Agendas* (with Nicholas Low, Allen & Unwin, 2000) and the inaugural winner of the Iremonger Award for Writing on Public Issues, *Australian Heartlands: Making space for hope in the suburbs* (Allen & Unwin, 2006).

Associate Professor Ian Gray is Head of the School of Sociology at Charles Sturt University, Wagga Wagga, NSW, and Deputy Director of the Centre for Rural Social Research. He has many years experience in research related to rural sociology, rural resource management, sustainability, transport and regional development. His recent publications include *A Future for Regional Australia: Escaping Global Misfortune* (with Professor Geoff Lawrence, Cambridge University Press, 2001).

Professor Brian Head is Director of the Institute for Social Research at the University of Queensland. He was formerly Professor of Governance at Griffith University, and the Chief Executive Officer of the Australian Research Alliance for Children and Youth, based in Canberra. After working as a senior researcher in government and policy studies at several Australian universities, Professor Head spent 13 years in the Queensland public service where he held senior positions in a range of government agencies, including as Queensland Public Service Commissioner. His current research interest is in public sector governance issues including new network models for regional and environmental planning. Professor Head has extensive experience in leading interdisciplinary teams to address major policy issues, especially those involving cross-agency and intergovernmental considerations.

Mal Peters is the Immediate Past President of NSW Farmers' Association, having completed four terms as President in July 2005. He currently Chairs the NSW Farmers' Association Non Metropolitan State Taskforce and has been a driving force within the Association on Federalism and Regionalism in Australia. He was appointed as a member of Ministerial Agricultural Advisory Committee in 2005 and he is also a member of Native Vegetation Review Committee. He has served as Chairman of Farmsafe NSW, Primary Industry training Board. He has also served on the Wool, Economics, Rural Affairs, Insurance Review and Executive Committees of the Association. In partnership with his wife Anne, Mal runs 6,000 sheep and 200 head of cattle on 7,500 acres near Ashford in Northern NSW.

Andrew Podger AO is National President of the Institute of Public Administration Australia. He retired from the Australian Public Service after 37 years in 2005, and is now a consultant and also Adjunct Professor at The Australian National University. His most recent role in the Australian Public Service was to chair a task force for the Prime Minister on the delivery of health services in Australia. Prior to that, he was the Public Service Commissioner for three years following six years as Secretary to the Department of Health and Aged Care. He has also headed the Departments of Housing and Regional Development and Administrative Services. In 2004 he was made an Officer in the General Division of the Order of Australia.

Professor Christine Smith is a Professor of Economics at Griffith University and a long term Council member of the Australian and New Zealand Regional Science Association. She has research interests in the areas of regional and urban economics with an emphasis on quantitative modelling. She has published extensively in these areas and is the editor of the Australasian Journal of Regional Studies, and on the Editorial Board of Papers in Regional Science. She has over 20 years experience in applied research and consulting work for various levels of government and with non-government organisations including Queensland Treasury, Brisbane City Council (Office of Economic Development), the Darwin Committee (a joint Federal /Northern Territory Government initiative), the Commission of Inquiry into the Future of the Conversation, Management and Use of Fraser Island and the Great Sandy Region, the United States National Academy of Science, trade unions and private companies.

Professor Kenneth Wiltshire AO is the J.D. Story Professor of Public Administration at the University of Queensland Business School. He served as a member of the Commonwealth Grants Commission 1995-2004, was a Founding member of the Constitutional Centenary Foundation, and a consultant to the Australian Advisory Council on Intergovernment Relations, the Economic Planning Advisory Council, and the NSW and Queensland Premier's Departments. He is the author of many books on comparative federalism in Australia, North

America and Europe. Professor Wiltshire served as Australia's Representative on the Executive Board of UNESCO 1996-2005, and is a National Fellow of the Institution of Public Administration Australia, and an Honorary Trustee of the Committee for Economic Development of Australia.

Part 1. Setting the Scene: Old Questions or New?

Chapter 1: Introduction

A. J. Brown and Jennifer Bellamy

The symposium

Australia's federal system of governance is in a state of flux, and its relevance in a globalised world is being challenged. After decades of debate about different possibilities for institutional reform – some of them predating Federation itself – dramatic shifts are occurring in the way in which power and responsibility are shared between federal, state and local governments, and in the emergence of an increasingly important 'fourth sphere' of governance at the regional level of Australian society. For those who fear a continuing growth in the power of the Commonwealth Government, the shifting state of federalism may seem unwelcome; but whether we see state governments as in decline or a new ascendancy, the fact remains that in the early 21st century, subnational regionalism is a live issue amid the practical realities of Australian public policy. Far from simple questions of local administration, the effectiveness, legitimacy and efficiency of new regional approaches are 'big ticket' issues on the contemporary political landscape. The management of our cities, of our sea-change regions, of natural resources through regions of every type, of hospitals and health services across the Australian community; these are all issues focussing the attention of decision-makers and communities from the top to the bottom of our system of government.

In May 2006, around 100 experts with diverse experiences in public policy, academic research and community arenas from across eastern Australia came together in Parliament House, Sydney, New South Wales, to discuss current shifts in the relationship between federalism and subnational regionalism, their implications for existing institutions of government, and the directions in which public institutions could and should evolve as a result of these new approaches. The symposium '*Federalism and Regionalism in Australia: New Approaches, New Institutions?*',[1] resulted in a broad consensus that traditional institutional frameworks are indeed changing, in response to the quest for more adaptive, effective, legitimate and efficient forms of governance. The main question put to the symposium, was whether it was also time to start addressing how new regional approaches fitted into overall trends in institutional restructuring and reform affecting the Australian public sector, rather than simply noting and tracking a plethora of developments that otherwise remain fundamentally *ad hoc*. The consensus arising was, again, that the answer was 'yes'. The policy 'drivers' behind new governance approaches were identified as not simply national, but also, at the same time, fundamentally local and regional in nature.

As a result, this volume, based on papers and presentations given to the symposium, is intended as a first step towards understanding these new trajectories of Australian federalism and regionalism.

The purpose of the volume is to test – and confirm – two basic propositions about the future of Australian federalism. The first is that the evolution of state, regional and local institutions has become a vital issue for the future of federal governance. In other words, making federalism work is not simply a matter of continual improvement in public administration, or fine-tuning intergovernmental relations between the Commonwealth and existing State governments, but a question of structural reform involving the distribution of roles, responsibilities and governance capacities throughout our system of government. The second proposition is that this question needs to be addressed in a conscious and concerted way, through a program of informed restructuring, if the federal system is to be made adequately legitimate, effective, adaptive and efficient in the medium to long term.

These propositions immediately inspire a lot of questions. What do we mean by adequacy, when it comes to goals such as legitimacy, effectiveness, adaptiveness, and efficiency? What types of reform are we talking about? What path of reform are we on already, if we are on one? What research is needed to better inform that path? The chapters in this volume provide the basis for a more informed debate by fleshing out these questions and, in many cases, providing clearer answers. While a variety of suggestions are made, no specific institutional prescription arises from this discussion about how federalism should be reformed. Indeed, it is a strength of these chapters that all the contributors argue, directly or indirectly, for a new debate which better establishes the common principles that reform proposals need to address, in order to establish a more coherent direction for the federal system. Together these chapters set out multiple examples of the current 'drivers' for reform, including a range of new approaches and imperatives in regional policy, against a background of old and new institutional options for the strengthening of local and regional governance in Australian federalism. Drawing on the diverse experience of a disparate group of people, collected from many corners of the country, walks of life and areas of government, the discussion sets the scene for the development of more concrete ideas about options, future directions and methods for generating better information and higher quality debate about our federal system.

Part 1: Setting the scene

In the remainder of this first part of the book, we seek to further outline the scope and content of these issues by placing them in the context of existing political history, and current public attitudes. After this introduction, the next two chapters together frame some of the existing case for institutional reform to deliver more legitimate, effective and efficient forms of regional governance.

In Chapter 2, *'Federalism, regionalism and the reshaping of Australian governance'*, A. J. Brown discusses the importance of current pressures for reform with reference to five key facts about the place of 'regionalism' in the culture and practice of Australian federalism, and five key lessons from constitutional and political history that form the context of current challenges. He also briefly reviews past reform ideas including attempts to create new states and some of the arguments underpinning calls for devolution reform.

Further evidence supporting the currency of reform demands is found in Chapter 3, Ian Gray and A. J. Brown's paper, *'The political viability of federal reform: interpreting public attitudes'*. This chapter presents some empirical evidence of the extent to which the Australian community considers reform of Australia's federal system of governance to be an issue, and why. These social surveys confirm the importance of the question of reforming the federal system, not simply due to the historical, theoretical and policy rationales set out in Chapter 2, but from the perspective of the average citizen. The level of public interest in a wider debate appears to be such that, depending on how the debate is conducted, institutional reform may well be more politically viable than often assumed by experts and policy-makers.

Part 2: Drivers for change

The six chapters in Part 2 of this volume chart some of the major policy imperatives driving current institutional experimentation, across different social and geographic contexts and in different policy sectors.

The first three of these chapters deal with governance challenges confronting the quite different social-demographic policy contexts in which Australians live – urban, rural and coastal – and the responses needed in terms of improved approaches to regional and federal governance. Chapter 4, Mal Peters' presentation *'Towards a wider debate on federal and regional governance: the rural dimension'*, highlights rural dissatisfaction with current Australian federalism and the issues underpinning the perceived 'city-country divide'. It argues the case for a change in the structure of Australia's governments in the long term, including the possibility of new states or regional governments. In Chapter 5, *'Rescuing urban regions: the federal agenda'*, Brendan Gleeson makes the parallel argument that, of course, 'regionalism' is not just a rural issue, emphasising that urban regions face their own governance challenges which similarly, albeit differently, mitigate in favour of new institutional strategies for recognising the role of urban regions within national discussions and frameworks on regional policy.

Chapter 6, Mike Berwick's presentation, *'The challenge of coastal governance: federalism and regionalism in Australia'*, addresses the failure of Australia's current dysfunctional federal, state and local system of governance to deal effectively with the 'seachange' phenomenon. It highlights the complex impacts of high growth rates on coastal communities and explores priorities for a more responsive federal-regional-local system that embodies stronger principles of participatory democracy.

The next three papers shift from the geographic context to contemporary challenges of governance seen from the perspective of different policy sectors: environmental management, economic development and human services. In Chapter 7, '*Adaptive governance: the challenge for regional natural resource management*', Jenny Bellamy examines the current complexity of Australian federal-state-regional institutional arrangements in response to the rapidly growing pressures for sustainable natural resource management. The paper argues the case for a national shift in the focus of these reforms from 'top-down' administrative approaches towards the development of a more participative, deliberative and adaptive governance system. It proposes essential attributes of this adaptive governance system to deal with the long-term challenges of inevitable environmental and societal change. In Chapter 8, '*Regionalism and economic development: achieving an efficient framework*', Andrew Beer reveals equivalent challenges in the way in which national and state policies aimed at regional economic development – in particular, regionally-specific structural adjustment – fail to achieve their goals in practice at the local and regional level. The paper identifies the tensions between centrally-driven regional initiatives and regional needs, especially in the current context of neoliberalism, and argues the case for institutional reforms to deliver more effective regional development.

In Chapter 9, '*Reconceiving federal-state-regional arrangements in health*', Andrew Podger deals with the governance challenges facing Australia's health system. He explores the applicability of the subsidiarity principle and the relevance of whole-of-government approaches in the Australian health system, emphasising that the essential attributes of a successful long-term Commonwealth-funded public health system include a transition to new national-regional arrangements. Here, a specific model is suggested for discussion, further setting the scene for the institutional questions confronted by the next part of the volume, but also highlighting that these are 'here and now' practical issues in the short term, and not simply questions for debates about long-term constitutional reform.

Together, Chapters 7 to 9 demonstrate that across all three dimensions of sustainability – environmental, economic and social – the quest for effective policy capacity is increasing pressure for institutional reform both on a national scale and at the regional level.

Part 3: New institutions?

The third and final part of the volume turns toward options for structural reform of Australian federalism to meet these challenges. It takes as its starting point a view from each existing tier or 'sphere' of government, and concludes with more detailed analysis of how the task of reform should be approached, taking into account how the potential costs and benefits of change might best be estimated, as well as more general principles.

In Chapter 10, *'Taking subsidiarity seriously: what role for state government?'*, Brian Head commences with a general review of major recent arguments for structural reform of Australian federalism, highlighting the difference between radical and incremental reform options. As a former senior State official, he argues against radical reform – assuming this is even possible – but emphasises this provides no excuse for a 'do nothing' approach, or a reversion to archaic notions of 'states' rights'. On the contrary, the conclusion reached is that state and federal governments alike must take principles of subsidiarity and devolution far more seriously within agreed national policy frameworks, which may still require a commitment to long-term institutional reform and new forms of local and regional power-sharing. By implication, if state governments are unprepared to do this, they may face the prospect of continuing encroachments on their power and yet more pressure for radical reform.

Chapter 11, Paul Bell's paper on *'How local government can save Australia's federal system'*, demonstrates the importance of the local government sector in the response to contemporary governance challenges. Adding bite to Head's analysis, this chapter argues that, notwithstanding substantial reform over the last 20 years, there has indeed been a failure in national arrangements to enable local government to play its full role in the design and delivery of public programs, compounded by structural problems in the national system of public finance, and inappropriate 'piecemeal' approaches to local government reform itself. The extent of necessary reform is dramatic, even limiting institutional reform to the future of the existing three tiers, requiring a revised national approach to the roles and resources of local government, supported if necessary by federal constitutional recognition. Whether pursued in tandem with more coordinated approaches to region-level institution-building, or as a stand alone program, the imperative for major devolution to the local and regional levels is clear.

Presenting a general, national perspective, in Chapter 12 *'Reforming Australian governance: old states, no states or new states?'*, Ken Wiltshire argues that whatever is done in the short and medium term to streamline and redistribute roles and responsibilities, can and should also be reinforced by Australia's federal constitutional arrangements. In other words, a new phase of cooperative federalism incorporating stronger elements of devolution, and action to address the present under-capacity and under-utilisation of local government, do not obviate the need to look at more general, permanent reform. Reviewing the history of Australian federalism and recent trends towards centralism, the chapter outlines basic principles for reform and examines the constitutional paths to achieving it, concluding in favour of not simply the desirability, but the inevitability of major reform within Australia's existing federal traditions.

Together these chapters emphasise the importance of better research into new options for governance, in particular into the economic and financial costs and benefits of meaningful reform. Christine Smith accepts this challenge in Chapter 13, '*Quantifying the costs and benefits of change: towards a methodology*'. Taking a detailed look at existing attempts to estimate the costs of existing federal arrangements and those of alternative approaches, the chapter notes that estimates of potential public finance savings from reform vary wildly, from as low as $1-2 billion per annum, to up to $20-30 billion. The result is a proposal for a new approach to the quantification of the costs and benefits of change in structural and/or financial arrangements of the current Australian federal system, building on existing lessons but taking a more comprehensive and functional approach than so far attempted.

In Chapter 14, '*Where to from here: common ground in the new federal reform debate*', we draw on all chapters and key elements of discussion from the floor of the symposium to present a new analysis of the growing points of consensus around the need for reform of Australian federalism. The chapter briefly summarises key next steps for a more robust debate about institutional reform to deliver better long-term public policy outcomes at national and regional levels. In addition, the Appendix to the volume includes an abridged version of the discussion paper, '*Reform of the Australian Federal System: Identifying the Benefits*', which was launched at the symposium, and which contains a suggested evaluation framework for all options for institutional restructuring.

Previously, debate about reform of Australia's federal system has tended to be sharply divided between the immediately practicable and long-term 'dreams'; between those with a deep sense of federalism's dynamic history and those who presume nothing can substantially change; between institutional actors presumed only to be concerned with preserving the status-quo and protecting their own immediate self-interest; and between different assessments of the challenges of federalism, with no relationships drawn between the centralising drift in federal-state relations and the growing pressures for improved governance capacity at the local and regional levels. The analyses in this volume bridge all of these gaps, setting out with new clarity some of the unifying imperatives for institutional reform and basic principles for new institutional design, without prescription as to the result. Federal systems of governance are meant, in theory, to be all about delivering quality governance at the regional level of political community, as well as achieving national goals – how this is to be achieved in practice in contemporary Australia is now a vital question of public administration and political development, underscored by community preferences and public demand. The pursuit of improved institutional arrangements is an increasingly necessary task, and one for which this volume will help equip a wide range of decision-makers from all professional disciplines and all walks of life.

ENDNOTES

[1] Held on 8 May 2006 – see www.griffith.edu.au/federalism.

Chapter 2: Federalism, Regionalism and the Reshaping of Australian Governance

A. J. Brown

Introduction

For at least a generation, Australia has been regarded as, 'constitutionally speaking', a frozen continent (Sawer 1967). In the face of social and economic change and diverse pressures for adaptation in the structures of government, there has been little change, since 1901, in the formal structures of our federal system or success in updating the formal text of the federal Constitution. In reality, however, Australia's systems of government and public administration have been anything but static. Indeed, since the times of Australia's Indigenous political geography – particularly over the 10,000 years since the last ice age – systems of social governance across the 'island continent' have been extremely adaptive. Ever since British colonisation began in earnest in the 1820s, movements for the political separation of colonies and blueprints for local, district and provincial government have produced a rich tapestry of options for postcolonial governance, many of them still fundamental in enduring institutions (Brown 2005, 2006). Administrative innovation to cope with Australian demography and economic geography has been ongoing since before the advent of responsible government in the 1850s, and accelerated by Federation in 1901 and the rise of the modern federal welfare state through the late 20th century.

More recently, pressures of economic, environmental and social sustainability in the face of a globalising world have introduced entirely new interactions between politics and administration, government and the community, and the different levels of government. Although formal changes in intergovernmental power-sharing have been minimal, massive practical shifts have occurred on the back of changing judicial interpretations of Commonwealth and state power. Most recently, the High Court's invalidation of many state taxes in 1997 (Ha 1997) led directly to a New Tax System based on the new federally-collected Goods and Services Tax (GST), and the Court's 2006 interpretation of federal power to regulate corporations has changed the landscape of federal and state industrial relations (WorkChoices 2006), with further areas of regulation set to follow. Federal proposals to take over the regulation of water rights across the nation's largest river system, the Murray-Darling Basin, are indicative of the appetite for change in the fundamentals of who runs what within our system of government. When it comes to the politics and practice of Australian federalism, we live in very interesting times.

Many Australians regard the main direction of change in Australia's systems of government, since the 1940s, as primarily one of centralisation – the growth of federal power, and the progressive decline in influence of the once-powerful state governments (Craven 2005, 2006). However the picture is not so simple, especially when the extent of public support for change, and the causes of this growing federal influence, are closely analysed. With the strong trend to more uniform and consistent national regulation of business and the economy, state governments have bounced back with innovation in the design and delivery of social services (see Twomey and Withers 2007). Local government, always the poor cousin if not 'lame duck' in the Australian federal system, has grown rapidly in capacity and importance. Pressure for increased federal spending and intervention on matters such as environmental management, are indicative not only of public demands for more coordinated, national approaches, but for more action and greater flexibility 'on the ground'. More decentralised governance approaches have evolved, not only economically through privatisation and contracting-out of services, but in the form of new strategies of community engagement and place management (e.g. Beer, Bellamy, Podger, this volume). Despite the lack of change in the formal structures of federalism, unprecedented attention is being given to how Australia can progress towards a more responsive, adaptive system of government. Within the pressures for stronger central action lie at least as many pressures for *devolution* in the resources and capacity to deal with today's pressing social, economic and environmental challenges.

This chapter seeks to frame an important new set of questions confronting Australian governance, by seeking to reconcile these apparently inconsistent trends in public policy – dramatic centralisation in federal-state relations on one hand, yet on the other, a major new interest in improved policy and service delivery capacities at decentralised levels. Why is Australia experiencing both of these trends at the same time, and are they as inconsistent as they superficially appear? The answers are interrelated. By positing five key facts about the nature of Australian federalism, and eliciting five lessons from Australian political and constitutional history about the relationship between federalism and regionalism, the chapter seeks to demonstrate that it is perfectly logical that centralising and decentralising pressures should be found operating together within contemporary governance debates. Indeed, as many chapters in this book reinforce, it appears to be at least partly because of public dissatisfaction with Australia's strong history of centralised governance at the state level, that successive federal governments have come under such strong pressure (or viewed another way, have been given the political opportunity) to intervene and interfere in so many policy areas traditionally lying at state and local levels. But if *state* governments are perceived as having had such trouble, historically, in delivering quality governance outcomes in an effective, efficient and responsive way, then what hope does an increasingly interventionist *national* government have for doing so, or even for finally forcing change in long-established patterns of state government behaviour? If the effort is to yield sustainable outcomes, it is now important to better chart the institutional implications of these shifting relationships between the different levels – formal and informal – of the Australian federation.

Ships in the night? 'State-regionalism' and 'region-regionalism'

As background to the key facts and lessons relevant to current institutional choices, it is important to confront the difficult relationship between concepts of federalism and regionalism in Australia. We need look no further than the standard international political science definition of federalism, to be reminded that federalism and regionalism are fundamentally intertwined, in theory and practice. According to this definition, federalism is 'a system of government in which authority is constitutionally divided between central and regional governments' (Gillespie 1994). In Australia, the constitutionally-recognised 'regions' of the federation are the six States, being the former British colonies as they stood in 1900. However the force given to 'state-regionalism' under the 1901 Constitution immediately raises a tension, because our normal understanding of a 'region' – in political life, in economic life, in biogeographic terms and so on – is very different. For the most part, it rarely and sometimes never aligns with our concepts of state government.

Occasionally, we find commentators trying to make Australian federalism fit the mould of the international definition, by describing the 19th century process of colonial subdivision as one in which British political authority was fragmented between 'six regional centres' (Holmes and Sharman 1977: 12-14). However such descriptions are rare, because as an *ex post facto* justification of Australia's current structure they are, from a historical perspective, grossly inaccurate (see Brown 2004a, b; 2005; 2006). Since at least the late 1960s, when the legitimacy of federal principles began to revive among Australian experts, much of the debate about the practical realities of federalism has, consequently, resembled two ships passing in the night. Many experts and policy actors have based their analyses on the constitutionally-recognised assumption that 'state-regional' differences are the only ones that matter, when it comes to trying to make the federal system work (see Holmes and Sharman 1977: 34-101, 172-80; Galligan 1986: 245-55). In the real world of public policy and popular political culture, however, the vast bulk of citizens operate on an entrenched assumption that Australia has many more than six regions (as also recognised by Holmes and Sharman 1977: 86, 129).

Does this definitional conflict matter in practice, as opposed to theory? The answer is sometimes presumed to be 'no', because the concept of 'regionalism' in Australian public policy itself takes at least four different forms. First, the concern to map trends in globalisation sees the term 'region' often used in a supra-national sense, as meaning groupings of the nations of the globe (e.g. 'the Asia-Pacific region'). Without exception, 'regionalism' is not used in this sense in this book, even though globalisation does have importance for the concepts of subnational regionalism here discussed. Second, as we already see above, many experts in federalism need to see regionalism expressed in direct, political, geographically-specific ways before it can potentially take on constitutional significance. This is true at subnational, supra-national and trans-national levels alike. From this view, credible movements for secession are perhaps the easiest way to identify a 'region' in this way (e.g. the Basque region in Spain, Scotland in Britain, or Quebec in Canada), although less militant forms of cultural regionalism are also generally recognised (e.g. regional differences within France, Italy or Switzerland, and indeed between regions such as Ticino that effectively span 'national' borders).

However, for reasons associated with the history of the introduction of the term into Australia, at a subnational level regionalism is also defined in a third way – as a reference to 'administrative' or 'scientific' regionalism, a top-down concept used by experts for purposes of planning, bureaucratic organisation, funding distribution, service delivery or, more recently, community engagement (see Brown 2005: 19-27). This third concept operates independently of regionalism as a bottom-up political or constitutional phenomenon, because it can be used by any government as an administrative strategy for recognising and dealing with the spatial layout of society, whatever the formal political structure. Indeed, because different public programs have different spatial objectives, economies, consumers and stakeholders even within the same community, this concept of regionalism tends to lead to multiple, overlapping definitions of what is a 'region' in any given area; as well as multiple, overlapping and sometimes conflicting regional institutions of various kinds.

These regions are actually more accurately described as a product of top-down 'regionalisation', than bottom-up 'regionalism' based on political self-identification and/or cultural expression (for more on the difference, see Ford 2001: 204-8; Bellamy et al 2003; Gray 2004). Just because many conceptions of 'the region' are generated from the top-down, however, does not mean that they do not also provide an accurate description of the social, economic, political and cultural demography of the nation. Regionalisations may be normative, such as Australia's first official national regionalisation in 1949, setting out 97 'regions for development and decentralisation' (see Brown 2005: 20); and there are important debates over the effects of the different ways in which regional boundaries are drawn, or revised, in public policy (e.g. Brunckhorst and Reeve 2006). However, many regionalisations are purely descriptive, and indeed sometimes also reflect 'bottom-up' political realities. From the web of regional boundaries drawn by federal and/or state and/or local governments, broad patterns emerge which confirm that for the vast majority of public purposes and programs – at all levels of governance – we operate according to agreed understandings of 'region-regionalism' with little or no relationship with the 'state-regionalism' embedded in the Constitution. Currently, key national regionalisations include:

- the 85 biogeographic regions of Australia, identified cooperatively by federal and state government scientists since the early 1990s (DEH 2000);
- the 69 statistical divisions, based on agreed definitions of a 'region', identified cooperatively by federal and state statisticians and used by the Australian Bureau of Statistics since 1969-1973 (ABS 2006);
- the 64 regions identified by the formation of voluntary Regional Organisations of Councils (ROCs), i.e. groupings of the approximately 700 local governments in Australia;
- the 57 regions of the federal-state natural resource management regional bodies administering the Natural Heritage Trust (NHT) and National Action Plan (NAP) on Water Quality and Salinity (DEH 2004); and
- the 54 regions of the nation's Area Consultative Committees (ACCs), administering Commonwealth regional development assistance funds (DOTARS 2005, 2007) – see Figure 2.1.

Figure 2.1. Australian Area Consultative Committees (2004-2005)

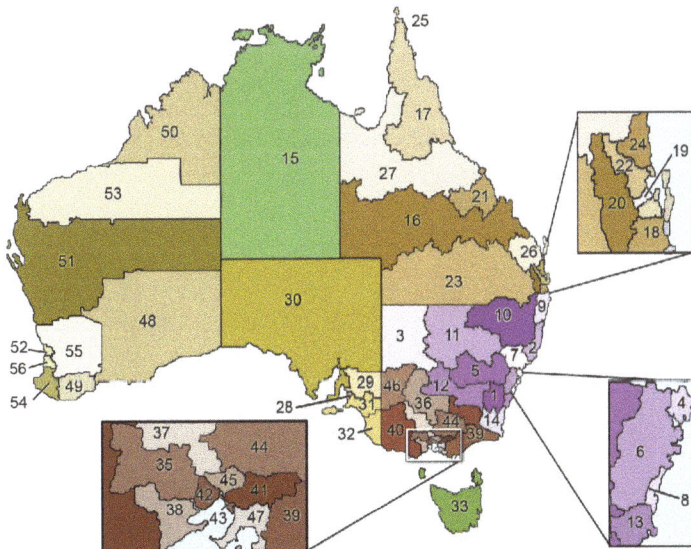

Source: DOTARS 2005

15

A fourth definition of regionalism has also arisen in Australian public debate since the mid-1990s, tending to further confuse the issue. Increasingly the phrase 'regional Australia' has become a bastardised political synonym for 'rural and remote regions' – that is, all regions outside the capital cities. The term 'rural and regional Australia' or 'RaRA' has become familiar (see Pritchard and McManus 2000; Commonwealth 2001). As Brendan Gleeson argues (this volume), this co-option of the term 'regional' has run the risk of slanting regional policy only towards rural regions, as if metropolitan regions do not exist, or do not require federal or national policy intervention. However, while a misleading way to approach regional policy, this particular reinvention of the term does demonstrate that 'regionalism' is not just a top-down administrative convenience, but also a live phenomenon in electoral politics. We know this because the renewed political interest in 'regional Australia' has arisen in response to a particular phase of political restiveness, or electoral instability, in rural regions – and indeed outer-metropolitan ones. Accordingly this bastardised definition reflects something of a hybrid between top-down and bottom-up concepts of regionalism. The response has also extended to a new suite of administrative initiatives in community engagement and place management, often targeted to less advantaged urban and peri-urban communities in addition to rural community renewal.

Rather than seeking a definitive reconciliation of these definitions, it is more important to note here that they exist, and that, on any of them, the place of the region in Australian federalism now matters enormously. It not only matters in immediate political and administrative terms, but raises questions about the evolution of institutional structures over the medium-term and into the future – especially if one accepts the following facts and lessons.

Why is regionalism a federal issue? Some facts

A centralised system

The first of five facts crucial to understanding the extent of the challenges faced by Australia's current federal system, is the unusually centralised nature of that system by comparison to most federations. Indeed Australian federalism is probably more centralised in its politics, finances and operations than many unitary, non-federal systems of government. This fact is important because it is often assumed that since federations tend, by their structure, to be more decentralised than unitary states, the decentralist benefits of being a federation necessarily flow in fair measure to Australian citizens (e.g. Saunders 2001: 130; Galligan 1995: 253; Twomey and Withers 2007: 6-7). While Australia can be safely presumed to be less centralised in its political structure with six states than if it had none, this does not mean that it is not highly centralised – and not only in the degree of national government control, described at the outset, but in the degree of political centralisation that also exists at state level.

In fact, seen in its totality, the history of Australian constitutional development makes the nation uniquely centralised. The historical weakness of local government, the size of most states in either population or geography (or both), and the history of large-scale state intervention and public bureaucracy at state level are all distinctive features of the Australian experience. One indicator of the stark contrast with other federations is provided in Figure 2.2, which shows the share of public expenditure that falls within the control of local government in Australia, by comparison with five other federations. This figure does not simply demonstrate the impoverished state of Australian local government by comparison with other countries, as further described later in this book by Paul Bell. It also demonstrates graphically that many of the functions and responsibilities undertaken by state governments in Australia – including many elements of education, policing, health and other social services – in most other federations would be controlled from a more localised level. In seeking explanations for why public dissatisfaction with state-administered services appears relatively high (see Gray and Brown this volume), and why so many political opportunities seem to exist for federal governments to intervene to correct or redirect state government policies, it behoves us to consider whether, structurally, it makes sense for so many areas of policy and service delivery to be controlled from the level of state governments.

Figure 2.2. Federal, state and local government 'own purpose' outlays as a share of total public outlays (2000-01)

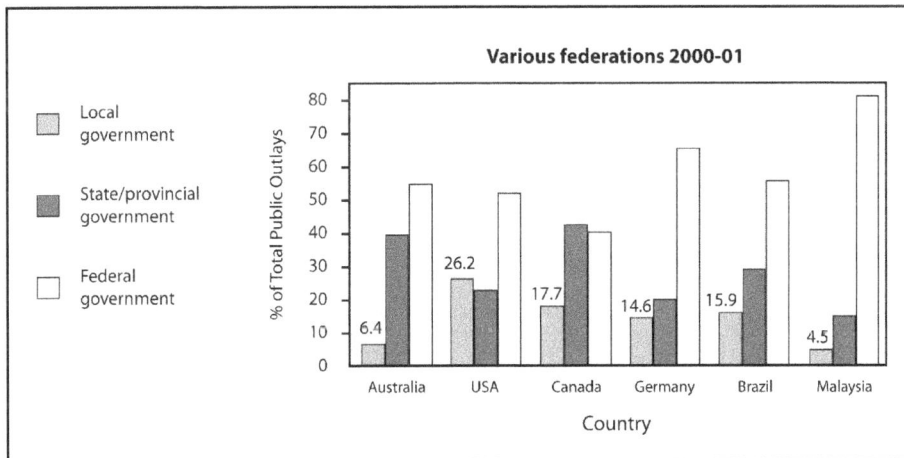

Source: International Monetary Fund *Government Finance Statistics Yearbook* (2002).

This situation also demonstrates graphically that all levels of government need to be considered if reform of Australian federalism is to be justified on the grounds of achieving greater 'subsidiarity'. Subsidiarity is the policy principle that government functions and services should be administered at the lowest level of government that can feasibly exercise that function, 'to the maximum extent possible consistent with the national interest' (Australian Premiers and Chief Ministers 1991, quoted in Galligan 1995: 205; Wilkins 1995; Twomey and Withers 2007: 28). In 1991 it was adopted by Australian governments as one of four key 'pillars' of modern intergovernmental relations – but chiefly in support of arguments against continued drift of responsibility upwards from the States to the Commonwealth, and/or return of responsibilities downwards from the Commonwealth to the States, rather than dealing with the at least equally important issue of governance deficits at the local and regional level (Brown 2002). How subsidiarity might be taken more seriously, is a key question throughout this book (see Podger, Head, Wiltshire and Smith, this volume).

Political legitimacy

A second, related fact is that our federal system has been historically dependent on institutions with weak – or indirect – political legitimacy. In other words, we have relied heavily on experts, officials and participating interest groups to help generate policy solutions, or direct services, rather than relying on elected officials to take direct responsibility for how programs are run. This is in part a corollary of the legacy of weak local government and large centralised state governments. While Australia has more legislators per capita than many countries, if local government representatives are included in the equation Australians actually have far less elected politicians working for them than the citizens of most countries (Brown and Drummond 2001; see also Twomey and Withers 2007: 20).

To respond to the diverse needs of large territories, state governments have instead responded to (and helped perpetuate) the weakness of local governance through the extension of large government departments, bureaucracies, commissions and statutory authorities, quasi-non-government organisations and, more recently, the engagement of non-government organisations and not-for-profit organisations in service delivery. From the time of its own first forays into regional policy, the Commonwealth Government has followed a similar pattern, with 'the prejudices and ambitions of individual officials and ministers' tending to be 'more influential than any general doctrine regarding the appropriate roles of central and provincial government authorities' (Walker 1947: 4-5, 89). While this experience resulted in strong public service traditions, it reduced popular expectation that elected officials should even be in place, let alone have the capacities, to take direct responsibility for the delivery of many services. Arguably, this state of affairs may have increased popular cynicism about the worth of those legislators we *do* have, relatively removed as they often are from the coalface of the programs for which they are notionally responsible. In any event, for most of the last 150 years we have tended to rely on large specialist bureaucracies more than general-purpose local, provincial or 'regional' government.

Political devolution not a newly identified problem

While we have had many decades to become inured to a system of governance based on these first two facts, a third fact is that Australian federalism would be quite different, institutionally, if many of our own federal founders' beliefs about the structure of the Federation had come to pass. Among the various provisions that allow for adaptation and change in the federal system, the founders of the 1890s included express provisions in Chapter VI of the Constitution contemplating structural or territorial change – in particular, decentralisation of the colonial-era structures through further territorial subdivision and the admission of new states. It is not often realised that federation coincided with a revival of the principle that the British colonies should be divided into a greater number, a process commenced but, according to many, not finished by the separation of the various existing colonies from New South Wales between 1825 and 1859.

In particular, with adoption of an American basis for the Australian Constitution in 1889-1890 came a rekindled awareness of the way in which the United States had grown in number, following their union a century earlier. This growth had taken place not only through subdivision of the Southern and Eastern territories acquired *after* federation, but reapportionment of the territory held (or claimed) by many of the original states themselves, between 1776 and 1861. Figure 2.3 sets out this aspect of American history, now dimly remembered, but better appreciated by Australia's federal founders. Just as Benjamin Franklin had predicted that federalism could work as a 'commonwealth for increase' through the subdivision of large territories within a federal union (1754; see Beer 1993: 155-8, 354-5), so too Henry Parkes adopted the rhetoric of an American-style commonwealth that would be 'great and growing' (Parkes 1890: 4, 28, 169; see also Parkes 1892: 603-10). It is no accident that in this book, both Mal Peters and Ken Wiltshire make further reference to Parkes.

Figure 2.3. How The Original 13 U.S. Colonies Became 25 States

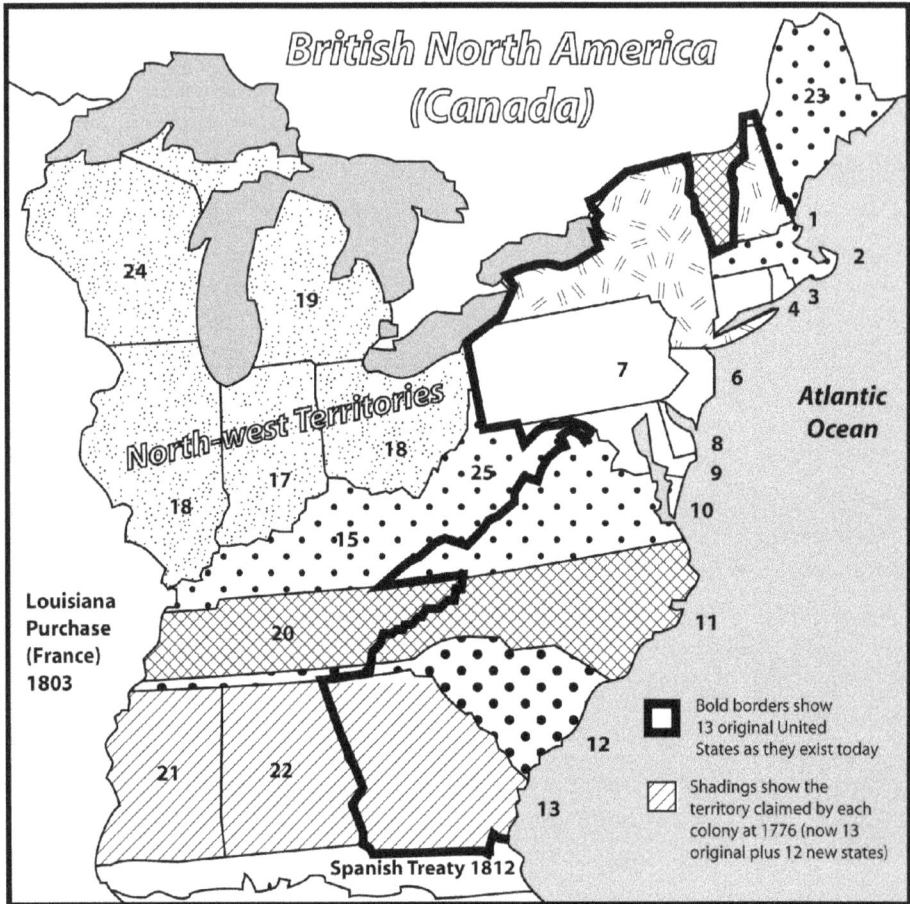

Source: Brown (2003: 151)

Here is not the place to recite the little known history of the new state provisions in Australia, their importance in securing popular support for federation particularly in Queensland and Western Australia, or the reasons why various movements for new states from the 1920s to the 1960s failed. Suffice to say, the provisions were not included simply through blind copying or accident. Similarly, whether successful or otherwise, the existence of such movements provides a tangible demonstration of political regionalism in Australia, at times commanding the support of a majority of the population in major regions, and again reinforcing the poor alignment between the 'state-regionalism' inherited at federation and regionalism as its exists in real political culture. It is striking that analysts of federalism still recall those expressions of regionalism which *did* succeed in gaining territorial self-government, such as the 18th century campaign for the separation of Victoria from New South Wales (see e.g. Twomey and

Withers 2007: 18) – but fail to remember the identical but unsuccessful movements that followed, or acknowledge the challenge present for the notion that 'state-regionalism' adequately reflects Australia's major subnational political identities.

Deliberative culture

A fourth fact worth noting, is that Australian federalism would also be institutionally different today, if the 20th century had seen the development of a more effective deliberative culture on constitutional questions – and in particular, a better party-political culture of constitutional bipartisanship. Without examining the technical flaws inherent in the Constitution's new state provisions, or whether the favoured solutions to these would have ever worked, it is important to recall that both major formal constitutional reviews of the 20th century did achieve a bipartisan consensus that the provisions should be adjusted so as to make it easier for new regions to be recognised and admitted to the federation. The first of these, the Peden Royal Commission on the Constitution (1927-1929) recommended unanimously to this effect, even as it voted only narrowly – by four members to three – to retain a federal system rather than abolish it in favour of a unitary one. A similar recommendation was reached by the federal parliamentary constitutional review committee of 1958, notwithstanding that at the time, the Labor members of that committee subscribed to a party platform which advocated total abolition of the States.

This curious history has its value as a reminder of past lost opportunities for better discussing and diagnosing the basis of widespread popular, expert and political criticism of the federal system. Not only have varying levels of popular disaffection with the spatial structure of federalism always been with us, but we have not been very proficient at realising when the different solutions being proposed by different groups, in fact relate to similar if not identical problems. For example, defenders of federalism tend to remember that new state advocates were explicitly pro-federal in principle, being pro-decentralisation, but not that they also advocated significant enlargement of federal power to deal with national issues (see e.g. Page 1917; 1963: 45). Instead, we prefer to associate pro-centralisation sentiments with the Labor or social-democratic interests that have made the most direct attacks on federalism in principle (see Galligan 1995: 91ff, 122) – ignoring the fact that most 20th century proposals for conversion to a unitary system closely resembled new state movements, in their embodiment of constitutional formulae for the structural devolution of power to 'regional' provincial governments (e.g. Figure 2.4; see Brown 2006).

Figure 2.4. Australia as 31 Provinces (Australian Labor Party, 1920)

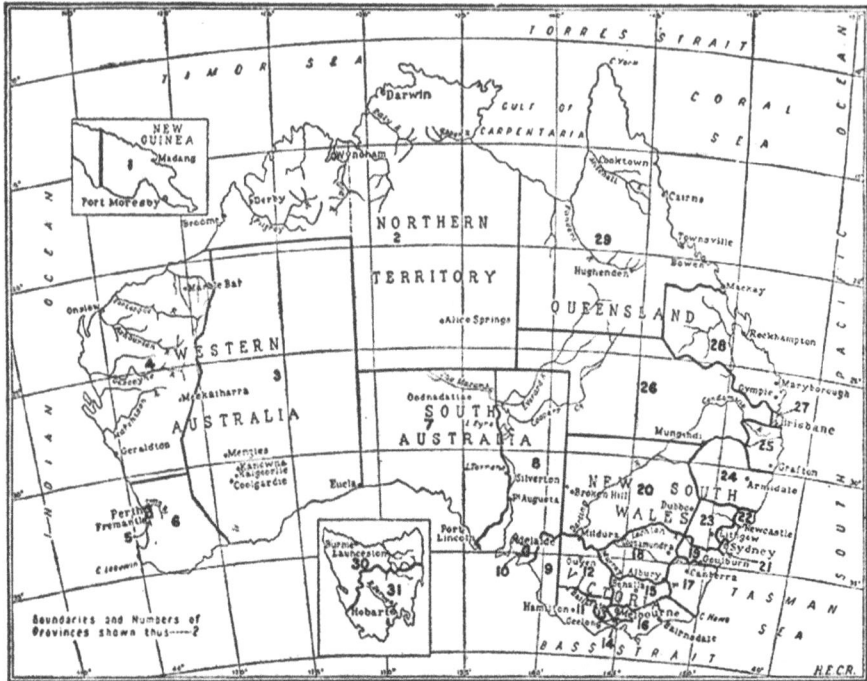

The Labor party scheme of 1920 proposed the subdivision of Australia into the 31 provinces shown in the map.

Source: Ellis (1933)

In recent years, a greater ability to look beyond party-political stereotypes and short-term political gains has been identified as an important need in all debates on constitutional development (e.g. Saunders 2000). This need clearly applies to questions concerning the relationship between regionalism and federalism under the present Constitution.

A dynamic and changing system

A fifth fact, as asserted at the outset of this chapter, is that the Australian federal system remains dynamic as we move forward into the 21st century, notwithstanding the gridlock affecting these past 19th and 20th century efforts to better accommodate regionalism within the national constitutional settlement. Notwithstanding the lack of productive outcome from these debates, there has been enormous past and current change in the dynamics of Australian federalism, including with respect to regionalism. In almost every aspect, the federation we have today is vastly different from the federation of 1901 or 1910. The growth in federal influence and financial control has been phenomenal, particularly in the recent period of 'pragmatic federalism' (Hollander and Patapan 2007), also described as 'regulatory federalism' (Parkin and Anderson 2007) or, less generously, 'opportunistic federalism' (Twomey and Withers 2007). While some people decry this trend, in other respects it has been clearly advantageous to national social and economic development, and holds further potential for nationally-coordinated approaches to improved policy making, service delivery and institutional restructuring at all levels of the system. When it comes to the quest for a more effective, responsive and efficient system overall, three examples will suffice:

- *Intergovernmental collaboration:* The way in which governments work together has changed enormously, and even if under pressure of centralisation, serious discussion is occurring around the need for more robust permanent systems of intergovernmental relations. For example, the Business Council of Australia (2006) and the Federal Labor party (McMullan 2007) are united in support for this path. As part of the movement to collaboration, we also see completely different relationships between existing governments. The idea that state governments were autonomous or sovereign within their sphere, and therefore intractably resistant to pressures for change from above or below, has largely gone away. State governments are now actively dealing other actors into what used to be their core business, and often actively dealing themselves out or reducing their role in particular areas of public policy. This is a very dynamic situation.

- *Growth in the role and capacity of local government:* Although local government remains structurally weak, it is on a growth path – much stronger, much more credible and better recognised by its citizens than 40 years ago (see Gray and Brown, Bell, this volume). In response to the intergovernmental cost-shifting affecting local government, consensus is growing that local government should be brought fully within the federal financial system, and receive a larger share of total public revenues in exchange for its growing role in many areas of policy and services. Local government is also again steeling for a campaign for federal constitutional recognition, despite referendum failures in 1974 and 1988. Whether or not this occurs, there is no reversing the trend towards local government taking on greater significance both for citizens, and for other levels of government, as the federal system as a whole continues to respond to the pressures of globalisation. Questions of how best to develop the capacity of local government to shoulder a greater burden, including its own structural reforms, have ceased to be purely state-level questions: they are also clearly national ones.

- *Regional governance:* The future of regional governance has become an unavoidable question for all existing levels of government, as they become progressively more collaborative and as the Commonwealth increasingly enters policy spheres that require action and implementation 'on the ground'.

Most obviously, this has occurred in environmental and natural resource management, where robust and sustainable regional arrangements are now pivotal, if problematic, for the success of well-entrenched national initiatives (see Bellamy, this volume). Moreover, this need for more robust regional governance systems is set to expand under initiatives such as the Commonwealth's proposed $10 billion Murray-Darling Basin water management plan. As set out through much of this book, however, the same needs exist in many policy areas for a review of how diverse new and old regional programs can best be constituted, rationalised, staffed and resourced into the medium-term. Concerns for whole-of-government cooperation in place management, community renewal and improved social service delivery raise the same questions. Even without any express ideology of 'devolution' to local and regional levels, the increasing reliance of all levels of government on regional bodies (including regionally-organised local bodies, and new regional configurations in traditional state administration) reveals an overall trend in this direction, however unplanned and messy the devolutionary trend may currently be.

Conclusions: five lessons for contemporary institutional design

From these historical relationships between the federal system and Australian regionalism, we can draw five key lessons about future approaches to the development of Australia's system of governance.

First, we must recognise that we have undervalued the idea of general-purpose government at local and regional levels, as an element of our national governance strategies. Whether we approach the quest for improved on-ground outcomes through the prism of collaborative federalism, or capacity-building in local government, or improved regional governance, we have to make active choices about whether – or how – we intend to strengthen local and/or regional governance as a sustainable constitutional player in the medium to long-term. Devolution in federal and state responsibilities is unlikely to be effective, or enduring, without dealing with the issue of general-purpose government capacity at local and regional levels to carry the burden, in a manner that is democratically accountable. Regional institutions cannot be further developed without a constructive debate about their political legitimacy, including dealing with the political reality of existing local government. The opportunities for meaningful reform are limited unless the strengthening of local and regional governance is accompanied by a strengthening of local and regional democracy.

A second key lesson is that while the current reform environment holds positive opportunities for a new reconciliation of federalism and regionalism, it is not currently fashionable to build governance capacity by enlarging the size of the public sector, at any level. This is implicit in recent theories of 'governance' as approaches to societal decision-making in which governments steer, but no longer necessarily row; and in which a range of networked policy actors take responsibility for policy formulation and on-ground action – including privatised, contracting and not-for-profit organisations, as well as interest and community groups (see Weller 2000). Despite the appearance of being a large, cumbersome system, comparative analysis suggests that federalism can help deliver government that is relatively small (Twomey and Withers 2007). Just as importantly, these arguments accompany a period in which Australian governments have withdrawn from direct public investment in economic development, and tend to prefer to let the market decide, as demonstrated by Andrew Beer's chapter. These trends raise important challenges for the task of strengthening local and regional capacity. Even if governance is now about partnerships, the facilities needed to develop and sustain effective partnerships are coming off an extremely low base. In short, if national and state governments intend to continue to put more back on to the community and onto business to 'do it itself', then without investment in some greater local-level governmental infrastructure to support this, the risks of policy failure are probably increasing rather than being reduced.

A third key lesson is the need for more productive debate about the problems and solutions inherent in the current federal system, both among experts and at a community level. As Gray and Brown (this volume) demonstrate, it is relatively easy to find evidence that citizens have problems with the existing system. It is more complex to identify the basis for differing views, and to reconcile these with historical experiences and institutional design principles in order to identify potential common ground for reform. There is every reason to be positive about the potential gains from reform of the federal system, to deliver more effective and responsive government both nationally and at the local and regional levels – and yet many of the arguments for reform continue to be presented negatively, as 'whinges' about the inadequacy of particular existing institutions. Painting federal governments as centralist, totalitarian or opportunistic 'monsters' does a disservice to many efforts of federal legislators and administrators to secure practical improvement in policy outcomes. It is similarly pointless to blame the State government of the day for 'ignoring the regions', as if today's legislators and administrators should take moral responsibility for the complex history that has left most state government operating at such problematic scales. In the survey described in Gray and Brown (this volume), two-thirds of the NSW State government employees captured within the respondent group expressed a preference for a scenario consistent with abolition of State government. If state government employees are indeed as cognisant as this of the potential merits of change, it makes little sense to hold them culpable for their own current predicament. Similarly, at a larger level, it makes little sense for reform advocates to campaign for the abandonment of federalism *in principle* when, plainly, the opportunities for improvement in our system of governance relate less to whether the system is federal or unitary in nature, than how our federal experience has panned out *in practice*. There are strong reasons why federalism makes sense as a constitutional system for Australia, even if there are also strong reasons why that system should evolve, either incrementally or dramatically.

Fourth, the key to a more productive debate may lie in the better alignment of thinking about short, medium and long-term approaches to reform. The last 20 years, in particular, have seen reform options approached competitively – in other words, if a short-term solution or 'quick fix' is presented, it tends to be grabbed as an alternative to investigating longer-term reform, and the potential gains from longer-term reform consequently dismissed altogether. This has tended to be true even when it makes sense to consider both, or to at least make short-term decisions in the context of an identified longer-term direction. Equally, the experience with collaborative federalism in the 1990s tends to indicate that even when something works, we are slow to consider mechanisms to institutionalise or constitutionalise the advance. Even when dramatic, the coercive use of federal legislative powers to reshape federalism, such as in the WorkChoices decision, may open up as many questions as it answers about the medium and long-term evolution of the system – after all, contrary to the government advertising that preceded it, the massive expansion of the Commonwealth industrial relations system nevertheless still leaves state industrial tribunals in place.

Similar considerations apply when considering the future of local and regional governance within the federal system. Despite being pursued as alternatives to long-term reform, the challenges encountered by many short-term initiatives simply increase the case for better thought-out, sustainable institutional investment. The more federal and state governments collaborate on the design and delivery of programs, the greater their need to also agree on how communities are to be engaged in the design, and how the delivery will be achieved, measured and monitored at the local level. Without agreement on this local-level engagement and delivery, all the political triggers remain for the collaboration to fail – for example, for dissatisfied regional communities to again take their issues directly to the federal level, and campaign for alternative programs or new interventions to correct poor implementation by state governments. This dynamic, as much as any fixation with power for power's sake, appears to explain much of the growth of federal intervention in many local and regional issues. To break this cycle, short-term program objectives and longer-term institutional development need to be pursued hand-in-hand. In other words, wherever it is acknowledged that design or delivery of programs will rely on action at lower local or regional levels, then initiatives in whole-of-government collaboration need to be supported by whole-of-government commitment to optimal devolution of responsibility to that level – even if this means substantial development in the capacity and direct accountability of regional frameworks. Without it, assuming the program is substantially delivered, there is little to prevent the inevitable conflicts over outcomes and performance from reinfecting federal-state relations, and jeopardising further collaboration.

On a positive note, the fifth and final lesson from this background is that the 21st century political landscape does appear to hold improved prospects for a productive approach – including a heightened capacity to make more informed short-term choices. There is little complacency about current arrangements, at any level of government. Instead there is widespread consensus that it is worth considering almost anything, if it can help contribute to more effective, responsive, adaptive and efficient governance. Many of the ideologies that dichotomised political debate over the size, role and structure of government in the 20th century have disappeared. So too have the more parochial 'states' rights' perspectives that once helped ensure that any constitutional debate was likely to degenerate immediately into a federal-state stand-off – it is difficult to imagine a state premier ever again telling Japanese hosts that he is 'not from Australia, but from Queensland', as Joh Bjelke-Petersen is once reputed to have done. On questions of regional institution-building, the destructive ideological deadlock of the Cold War era has long since receded, in which social progressives tended to fear new state ideas as an agenda of rural fascists, and conservatives opposed alternative regional or provincial bodies as some kind of centralised, urban Communist plot.

Instead, we have an environment in which all political parties tend to have equally minimalist commitments to any kind of constitutional development, and the focus is a pragmatic one, on simply making the existing system of government work better. While this scarcely sounds visionary, when the unproductive nature of past debates over regional devolution are considered, this new 'year zero' of thinking about federalism is, in fact, a safe place to start. If we get the next phase of federal reform wrong – for example, if the under-capacity of local and regional governance are not addressed, and 'subsidiarity' principles remain simply a rhetorical device in the tussles between national and state governments – then history is likely to lead us back to where we already are or have been. If we get it right, and find new ways to develop the practical machinery of federalism to recognise, empower and utilise local and regional action, we will not only have achieved a theoretical resolution of the relationship between federalism and regionalism in Australia; we will also have moved towards more durable solutions to some of the pressing policy challenges and problems set out in this book, in which we already know local and regional action to be vital. Whether strong or weak, transient or a symptom of something longer term, regionalism is alive and well in Australia today, and it matters in both political and public policy terms. As new national approaches unfold in most major policy areas, more and more we recognise these are unlikely to work without also growing the capacity of local and regional governance.

This chapter concludes with a picture from the cover of *The New State Magazine* of 1922 (Figure 2.5). This is not because the option of new state governments represents a solution to everything, but because the image helps reinforce the depth of our own historical capacity to think about these issues. While the map shows an alternative political structure for Australia, the magazine as a whole carries the motto 'For a Bigger Australia'. It may be that it is not actually practical to create a bigger Australia, but the reform of federalism is certainly motivated by a vision of a better Australia, and this remains the outcome we should expect from more informed, research-based policy and political discussion about the development of our institutions in the long term.

Figure 2.5. For A Bigger Australia

ice, 7d.

New Staters and the Prime Minister

SYDNEY.

The NewStateMagazine

FOR A BIGGER AUSTRALIA

Vol. 1. No. 6.   JULY, 1922.

NEW STATERS' MAP

NORTHERN AUSTRALIA

FEDERAL TERRITORY

NEW STATE

NEW STATE

FEDERAL TERRITORY

NEW STATE

QUEENSLAND

Brisbane

SOUTH AUSTRALIA

FEDERAL TERRITORY

NEW SOUTH WALES

NEW STATE

Sydney

WESTERN AUSTRALIA

Perth

NEW STATE

NEW STATE

VICTORIA

Melbourne

The above map shows the New Staters' idea of a new Australia, divided into 13 States and Territories.

CONTENTS

Deputation to Mr. Hughes
New Staters in Martin
Place.

(Two Pictures).

UNIFICATION.

from the New Staters' Viewpoint.

Private Enterprise Rail-
way System in Argentine

(Map).

Men of the Movement.

Cartoons.

General Features.

Source: Thompson (1922)

29

References

ABS 2006, *Australian Standard Geographical Classification (ASGC)*, Canberra, Australian Bureau of Statistics Release 1216.0 - 2006, July 2006.

Beer, S. H. 1993, *To Make A Nation: The Rediscovery of American Federalism.* Harvard University Press.

Bellamy, J., T. Meppem, et al. 2003, 'The changing face of regional governance for economic development: implications for local government' *Sustaining Regions* 2(3): 7-17.

Brown, A. J. 2002, 'Subsidiarity or subterfuge? Resolving the future of local government in the Australian federal system' *Australian Journal of Public Administration* 61(4): 24-42.

——— 2003, *The Frozen Continent: the Fall and Rise of Territory in Australian Constitutional Thought 1815-2003*, PhD Thesis, Griffith University.

——— 2004a, 'One Continent, Two Federalisms: Rediscovering the Original Meanings of Australian Federal Political Ideas', *Australian Journal of Political Science* 39(4): 485-504.

——— 2004b, 'Constitutional Schizophrenia Then and Now: Exploring federalist, regionalist and unitary strands in the Australian political tradition', in K. Walsh (ed.), *The Distinctive Foundations of Australian Democracy: Lectures in the Senate Occasional Lecture Series 2003-2004* Papers on Parliament No. 42, Department of the Senate, Parliament House, Canberra.

——— 2005, 'Regional Governance and Regionalism in Australia' in Eversole, R. and Martin, J. (eds), *Participation and Governance in Regional Development: Global Trends in an Australian Context*, Ashgate, Aldershot UK.

——— 2006, 'The Constitution We Were Meant to Have: Re-examining the strength and origins of Australia's unitary political traditions', in K. Walsh (ed.) *Democratic Experiments: Lectures in the Senate Occasional Lecture Series*, Department of the Senate, Canberra.

Brown, A. J. and M. Drummond, 2001, 'Did Federation give us too many politicians?', *The Courier-Mail*, Brisbane, 31 March 2001: 30.

Brunckhorst, D. J. and I. Reeve, 2006, 'Lines on Maps: Defining Resource Governance Regions from the 'Bottom-Up'', Refereed paper to *Australasian Political Studies Association Conference*, University of Newcastle, 25 September 2006.

Business Council of Australia 2006, *Reshaping Australia's Federation: A New Contract for Federal-State Relations*, Melbourne.

Craven, G. 2005, 'The New Centralism and the Collapse of the Conservative Constitution', Senate Occasional Lecture, Department of the Senate, Canberra, 14 October 2005.

——— 2006, 'Are We All Centralists Now?', Address to Gilbert and Tobin Centre Constitutional Law Conference, Sydney, 24 February 2006.

DEH 2000, *Interim Biogeographic Regionalisation of Australia*, Version 5.1, Canberra, Commonwealth Department of Environment and Heritage.

DEH 2004, *Natural Resource Management Regions*. Canberra, Commonwealth Department of the Environment and Heritage, June 2004.

DOTARS 2005, *National Network of Area Consultative Committees' Report to the Community 2004–05*. Canberra, Commonweath Department of Transport and Regional Services.

DOTARS 2007, *Area Consultative Committees (ACC) Boundary Review*. Canberra, Commonweath Department of Transport and Regional Services. Accessible at http://www.acc.gov.au/boundary.aspx.

Ford, R. T. 2001, 'Law's Territory (A History of Jurisdiction)', in N. Blomley, D. Delaney and R. T. Ford (eds), *The Legal Geographies Reader: Law, Power and Space*, Blackwell, Oxford, pp.200-217.

Galligan, B. (ed.) 1986, *Australian State Politics*, Longman Cheshire, Melbourne.

——— 1995, *A federal republic: Australia's constitutional system of government*. Cambridge University Press.

Gillespie, J. 1994, 'New federalisms' in J. Brett, J. Gillespie and M. Goot (eds) *Developments in Australian Politics*, MacMillan Education Australia, Melbourne, Victoria, pp.60-87.

Gray, I. 2004, 'What is Regionalism?', in W. Hudson and A. J. Brown (eds), *Restructuring Australia: Regionalism, Republicanism and Reform of the Nation-State*, Federation Press, Sydney.

Ha 1997, High Court of Australia, 'Ha and Anor v New South Wales', *Commonwealth Law Reports* Volume 189, p.465.

Hollander, R. and H. Patapan, 2007, 'Pragmatic Federalism: Australian Federalism from Hawke to Howard', *Australian Journal of Political Science* 42(2), forthcoming.

Holmes, J. and C. Sharman 1977, *The Australian Federal System*, Allen & Unwin, Sydney.

McMullan, B. 2007, 'Reforming the Federation: A Once-in-a-Lifetime Opportunity', Speech to Institute of Public Administration Australia (IPAA) Roundtable on Federalism, Canberra, 18 May 2007.

Parkes, H. 1890, *The Federal Government of Australasia: Speeches*. Turner and Henderson, Sydney.

———— 1892, *Fifty Years in the Making of Australian History*. Longmans Green and Company, London.

Parkin, A. and G. Anderson, 2007, 'The Howard Government, Regulatory Federalism and the Transformation of Commonwealth-State Relations', *Australian Journal of Political Science* 42(2), forthcoming.

Saunders, C. 2000, *Parliament as Partner: A Century of Constitutional Review*. Commonwealth Department of the Parliamentary Library.

———— 2001, 'Dividing Power in a Federation in an Age of Globalisation', in C. Sampford and T. Round (eds), *Beyond the Republic: Meeting the Global Challenges to Constitutionalism*. Federation Press, Sydney, pp.129-145.

Sawer, G. 1967. *Australian Federalism in the Courts*. Carlton: Melbourne University Press.

Thompson, V. (ed.) (1922), *New State Magazine*, vol. 1, no. 6. Mitchell Library, Sydney.

Twomey, A. and G. Withers, 2007, *Australia's Federal Future: Delivering Growth and Prosperity,* Federalist Paper 1, Council for the Australian Federation.

Walker, E. R. 1947, *The Australian Economy in War and Reconstruction*, Oxford University Press, New York.

Weller, P. 2000, 'Introduction: in search of governance', in G. Davis and M. Keating (eds), *The Future of Governance: Policy Choices*, Allen & Unwin, Sydney.

Wilkins, R. 1995, 'Federalism and Regulatory Reform', in P. Carroll and M. Painter (eds), *Microeconomic Reform and Federalism*, Federalism Research Centre, The Australian National University, Canberra, pp.216-222.

WorkChoices 2006, High Court of Australia, 'NSW v Commonwealth' *Australian Law Reports* Volume 231, p.1.

Chapter 3: The Political Viability of Federal Reform: Interpreting Public Attitudes

Ian Gray and A. J. Brown

Introduction

Does 'regionalism' have a popular basis in Australian political culture? When mapping possibilities for the future of Australian federalism, what is the contemporary 'realm of the possible' in terms of political support for reform to address long term deficits in regional governance? These questions are fundamental to understanding where current tensions and trends are leading the federal system. As outlined in the preceding chapters, and shown by many that follow, Australian federalism is not static – in response to diverse pressures, it is shifting and facing new institutional developments. But which options are recognisable by the larger community, which have their support, and which are sustainable? When it comes to institutional strategies for making and delivering better public policy at a community level, which might have greater success or durability if they *did* resonate more strongly with citizen preferences? How much support exists for institutional restructuring, and where in our community is it based?

Understanding public opinions about Australian federalism is important, not only for answers to these practical questions, but because many political leaders and commentators presume that if it exists at all, public awareness of federalism is unsophisticated. A leading analyst, Brian Galligan, suggests we should resign ourselves to a permanent state of popular disaffection with the federal system, predicting there will probably always be 'critics calling for its abolition' even though 'abolitionist scenarios are for idle speculators' (Galligan 1995: 61, 253). These observations recognise the regularity with which public debate returns to the question of whether federalism needs major restructuring, if not through the creation of new states as once envisaged under the Constitution, then through the replacement of all states with alternative regional governments. Even Australia's second longest serving Prime Minister can be found among the 'speculators', having said that 'if you were starting Australia all over again you would have a national government and 20 regional governments' (Howard 1991); 'if we had our time again, we might have organised ourselves differently' (Howard 2005). Nevertheless, John Howard, like Brian Galligan, agrees we do not have this luxury, and retreats to the view this would now be an 'empty theoretical exercise' (Howard 2002) or 'pure theorising' (Howard 2005). But meanwhile, the debate refuses to go away, public criticism of federalism continues, and policy pressures continue to mount. As recently as March 2007, the *Sydney Morning Herald* recorded the following results to a snap on-line poll:

Our six states, who needs 'em? More than a century after federation, does Australia still need the States?	
Absolutely. Without the States local issues would be swamped by Canberra.	36%
Abolish them. They are a waste of taxpayers money.	64%
Total Votes: 1789 (SMH 12 March 2007)	

Do such calls for change amount to more than mere speculation, and by more closely examining them, can we now help inform a more coherent approach? This chapter seeks to make better sense of public opinion about the federal system using evidence from pilot surveys of random samples of Australian adults undertaken in Queensland in 2001 and, more recently, in New South Wales (NSW) in 2005. To better establish whether popular pressure for reform really only consists of idle speculation, these surveys have begun to explore the breadth of support for and change in the federal institutions, so as to better inform discussions about the institutional options that might be worth considering. The first survey, in September 2001, asked 301 Queensland adults about their attitudes to existing institutions and their expectations of, and preferences for, change or maintenance of the status quo (Brown 2002a, 2002b). In late 2005, these questions were repeated in a survey of 502 adults in of New South Wales, supplemented by more detailed questions on satisfaction with government and demographic data. This second study provides the bulk of analysis that follows, and was conducted by Griffith University's Federalism Project and Charles Sturt University's Centre for Rural Social Research with funding from a Griffith University Research Encouragement Grant, Charles Sturt University School of Humanities and Social Sciences and NSW Farmers' Association (see Brown, Gray and Giorgas 2006).[1] These surveys have helped form the background to national attitudinal research, now in progress.

Both surveys were conducted by telephone with respondents selected at random from telephone listings, being the person aged over 18 years whose birthday came next in each household contacted. In both studies, to facilitate regional comparisons, rural regions were oversampled. In Queensland, this enabled comparative analysis of attitudes in Greater Brisbane and the Gold and Sunshine Coasts, against those of Southern Queensland, Central Queensland, and North Queensland (Brown 2002b). In the NSW survey, this enabled comparison between Greater Sydney, Hunter and New England, Illawarra and South East NSW, Western NSW, and the Riverina (Brown et al 2006: 294-7). In each case the results were also then re-weighted by area and age to give statistically accurate statewide results (indicated as (w) in the relevant tables below). In both studies, urban and metropolitan results proved just as interesting as rural ones, and are clearly of great political significance since it is these regions that contain the bulk of the voting population.

This chapter extends and reinforces some earlier findings from these studies, with particular reference to understanding the relationship between federalism and regionalism. The first part of the chapter examines the breadth of popular sympathy for change, and also its geographic distribution. These results confirm that Australians' appetite for some reform of federalism is not restricted to idle speculators and that for many – indeed for a majority of citizens – it appears to extend significantly beyond the realms of 'empty' political theorising. To better understand who holds the strongest views in support of change, the second part of the chapter compares those most and least satisfied with existing institutions and those favouring more radical preferences for the future, against all other respondents, in a bid to locate any major demographic or sociological differences. The results show that critical attitudes of federalism and more radical preferences for change – which are not necessarily directly related – are widespread features of Australian society and not readily confined to particular regions or social groups. Instead, more radical preferences for change prove most popular among those citizens most directly engaged in the economy (by way of employment), especially by way of government employment, as well as those most directly engaged in governance more generally through community organisations or committees. It seems not only that many more Australians are interested in reform than previously understood, but that many also expect it. Given the dynamic state of developments in governance, what does this suggest about the realms of 'the possible' for institutional reform?

Idle speculation or a more general query? Federalism and public opinion in Queensland and NSW

Ideally, Australians should not have a low opinion of their political system, or show themselves resigned to living with one they do not accept. Institutional systems are important to people's life chances, well-being and democratic participation. The responsiveness of the political system to globalisation and uneven development, particularly with respect to the prospects for different regions, is a current theme in international and Australian debate. Federal, state and local governments alike show their own attempts at being more regionally-responsive, and have always done so in different ways, at different times, to widely varying degrees. Debate about these processes is usually restricted to temporary changes in administrative rather than political arrangements. Does Australian public opinion show an appetite for a more lasting, structural solution to pressure for a more responsive system?

The first major finding from the surveys is that citizens of Queensland and NSW are not overly depressed about the state of Australian democracy overall – but do currently hold a more critical opinion of federalism as an element of the political system, than they do of the system in general. Table 3.1 sets out how the respondents to each survey answered a general question about 'the way democracy works in Australia', with 78% and 63% of Queensland and NSW respondents respectively indicating themselves to be fairly or very satisfied. Notwithstanding the difference between the state results, this overall satisfaction is consistent with the results of major national surveys such as the Australian Survey of Social Attitudes, showing a stable 77.6% and 75.7% of respondents to be satisfied with the way democracy works in 2003 and 2005 respectively.

Against this broad satisfaction with democracy, how do we identify specific views about the federal system? Table 3.2 shows that this depends on the question asked. In Queensland, when asked about 'the way the federation currently works', an even higher number of respondents indicated they were satisfied – but this was a general way of asking the question, at the height of the 2001 Centenary of Federation. By contrast, NSW respondents were asked about their satisfaction with federalism as a 'system of government', defined as 'a three-tiered system of government, with federal, state and local governments.' For these respondents, satisfaction dropped from 63.1% (with democracy) to 50.3% (with the federal system), while dissatisfaction rose from 34.7% (with democracy) to 48.1% (with the federal system).

These results may indicate that NSW citizens have a more critical view of both democracy (and presumably also federalism) than citizens elsewhere. Regardless, the key result is the size and direction of the change in reported satisfaction among NSW respondents, when asked about the federal system as against democracy in general. These data confirm that the three-tiered system is sometimes viewed differently to the democratic system as a whole. What leads to this more critical view of the structures of federalism? While more qualitative and quantitative research is needed to answer this definitively, the present surveys go some way towards the answer by providing data both on: (1) the different relative levels of satisfaction that citizens feel in respect of each of the current tiers of government – federal, state and local; and (2) whether and how citizens would prefer the institutions of federalism to evolve.

Table 3.1. Satisfaction with democracy (Australia, Queensland, NSW)

	Australia %		Queensland %	NSW % (w)
	'How proud are you of Australia in ... the way democracy works?'	'On the whole, ... how well does democracy work in Australia today?' [adapted from 0-10 scale]	'On the whole, how satisfied or dissatisfied are you with the way democracy works in Australia?'	'Overall, how satisfied are you with the way democracy currently works in Australia?'
Very	24.5	37.2	10.0	12.3
Fairly	53.1	38.5	68.0	50.8
Satisfied	77.6	75.7	78.0	63.1
Not very	13.0	13.7	13.0	24.8
Not at all	2.7	4.7	7.0	9.9
Not satisfied	15.7	18.4	20.0	34.7
No opinion	6.8	6.0	2.0	2.1
Total	100.0	100.0	100.0	100.0
Source:	Australian Survey of Social Attitudes 2003 (n = 2130)	Australian Survey of Social Attitudes 2005 (n = 1889)	Qld survey 2001 (n = 301)	NSW survey 2005 (n = 502)

Table 3.2. Satisfaction with federalism (Queensland, NSW)

	Queensland %		NSW % (w)	
	'On the whole, how satisfied or dissatisfied are you with the way ...		'Overall, how satisfied are you with the way democracy currently works in Australia?'	'Australia has a **three-tiered system of government, with federal, state and local governments.** Overall, how satisfied are you with the way this system of government currently works in Australia?'
	... **democracy** works in Australia?'	... **the federation** currently works in Australia?'		
Very	10.0	14.0	12.3	5.2
Fairly	68.0	68.0	50.8	45.1
Satisfied	78.0	82.0	63.1	50.3
Not very	13.0	8.0	24.8	37.4
Not at all	7.0	8.0	9.9	10.7
Not satisfied	20.0	16.0	34.7	48.1
No opinion	2.0	2.0	2.1	1.5
Total	100.0	100.0	100.0	100.0
Source:	Qld survey 2001 (n = 301)		NSW survey 2005 (n = 502)	

To establish the level of satisfaction with each existing tier of government, the NSW survey asked respondents in which of the three different governments they had most faith and confidence (Table 3.3) and how they would rate the performance of each of the different levels of government (Table 3.4). If the main basis of many respondents' dissatisfaction with current federalism was a feeling that the federal government was becoming too centralised, overpowerful or operating in areas beyond its competence, we would expect the federal government to rate poorly in response to both questions. Conversely, if the main basis of dissatisfaction was corruption, incompetence or under-capacity in Australia's comparatively weak system of local government, then that too should be discernable. However as the data show, the least faith and confidence, and poorest assessment of performance emerged in respect of the state level. Only 12.8% of respondents were prepared to rate the performance of the state level as 'good' or 'very good' – less than half the number prepared to rate either federal or local government in this way – with many more respondents convinced that the performance of state government was positively 'poor' compared to the other tiers. As set out in Table 3.5, the notion that it is the place and role of state governments that represents the weakest link in the present federal system, is confirmed by the strong correlation between those expressing the least satisfaction with the system overall, and those most critical of state governments.

Table 3.3. Most faith and confidence in a level of government (NSW)

'We find that people have different degrees of faith and confidence in the different governments that affect them directly. In your case, which do you have most faith and confidence in?'

	No. of respondents	% of respondents
The Federal Government	205	40.9 %
Your State Government	125	24.9 %
Your Local Government	172	34.2 %
Total	502	100.0 %

Table 3.4. Performance of different levels of government (NSW)

'On a scale of 1 to 5, how would you rate the performance of the different levels of government in Australia? 1 is very poor, 5 is very good.'

	% of respondents				
	Very poor / poor (1/2)	(3)	Good / very good (4/5)	No opinion	
The federal government	34.3	36.2	28.1	1.4	100.0
State governments	51.0	34.0	12.8	2.2	100.0
Local government	38.1	34.7	26.0	1.2	100.0

Table 3.5. Performance of state government, by extremes of satisfaction with the federal system (NSW)

'On a scale of 1 to 5, how would you rate the performance of the different levels of government in Australia? 1 is very poor, 5 is very good.'

	% of respondents				
	Very poor / poor (1/2)	(3)	Good / very good (4/5)	No opinion	
State government (as rated by all respondents)	51.0	34.0	12.8	2.2	100.0
State government (respondents 'very satisfied' with the current system of government)	26.9 (7)	23.1 (6)	50.0 (13)	0.0 (0)	100.0 (26)
State government (respondents 'not at all satisfied' with the current system of government)	75.9 (41)	11.1 (6)	5.6 (3)	7.4 (4)	100.0 (54)

In some circumstances, this significantly greater disapproval of state government could simply reflect short-term unpopularity or falling legitimacy on the part of a particular elected government. However there is good reason to believe that no such simple explanation applies here. At the next NSW State Election, in March 2007, there was no change of government. More importantly, the survey asked respondents whether their views about faith and confidence in different levels of government would change 'if there was an election and the government changed, i.e. other politicians were in power'. Of those respondents indicating they had least faith in the federal government, 62.1% said that if the government changed, they would then hold either a 'somewhat different' or 'completely different' view. By contrast, this was true of only 48.3% of those respondents indicating they had least faith in the state government. In any event, even if the expressed disaffection with state government was partly party-political – as it no doubt was – this does not mean it could not also be partly 'constitutional' in nature, nor that at least some root causes of the expressed disaffection might not relate to institutional or structural problems even if the government of the day was inevitably to be blamed.

For these reasons, the questions in the survey dealing with expected and preferred constitutional outlook become important. In NSW, half the respondents (50.3%) still indicated they were satisfied with the current three-tiered federal system. Accordingly, even if this confirms a high level of disaffection with current federal structures, the disaffection is clearly not total. If there are options for institutional restructuring that would improve the system, as canvassed through many of the chapters of this book, then their feasibility and acceptability will be determined as much by those who are currently reasonably satisfied with the system, not simply those who are not. Moreover, even citizens who are reasonably satisfied may also hold relevant views on these subjects, because they may also expect or desire change for the better, and may see new ways of doing business, without necessarily feeling positively disaffected with the current system.

To establish how citizens expect and would prefer the basic institutions of federalism to evolve, both surveys asked respondents to choose which of four scenarios best described how they expected the federal system to look in another 50 to 100 years. A further question then asked respondents to choose which of the same four scenarios best described their preference for how the federal system *should* look in another 50 to 100 years. As explained elsewhere, these scenarios were not randomly generated but calculated to reflect some of the major alternatives suggested in the 'real world' of Australian political debate mentioned earlier (Brown 2001; 2002a; Brown at al 2006: 286-287; see also Brown this volume). The four scenarios, in order of presentation in the interviews, were:

a.   retention of the status quo ('the same system as today');
b.   the creation of new state governments on the existing three-tiered model;
c.   a more general constitutional restructure replacing existing state and local governments with a new regional government framework;
d.   the growth of a 'fourth tier' of regional institutions in addition to existing state and local governments.

Table 3.6 shows the results for both questions, for Queensland (2001) and NSW (2005). There are some differences because in the NSW survey, greater effort was made to elicit and separate responses 'other' than the offered scenarios, in addition to recording those who indicated 'no opinion' or 'don't know'. However there are similarities in the predictions made by respondents about how the federal system will look. Despite at least half the NSW respondents being satisfied with the current system, only 23.5% predicted that it would remain the same; along with 27% of respondents in Queensland. In both States, a clear majority – 63% of Queensland respondents and 64% of NSW respondents – showed a positive expectation of structural change in the federal system by choosing one of the nominated scenarios other than 'the same system as today' (i.e. not including 'others' and 'don't knows').

Table 3.6 and Figure 3.7 also show the Queensland and NSW results as to whether citizens would welcome such change. In Queensland, about the same number of respondents as expected the system to remain static, also preferred this outcome (although they were often not the same: see Brown 2002a). In NSW, the number who wished the system to remain the same fell to a lowly 12.5%. In both States, a majority – 62% in Queensland, and 74.2% in NSW – indicated they not only expect, but would prefer structural change. In each case, we can also see the total number of respondents who expect change whether or not they prefer it, or prefer it irrespective of whether they expect it to happen. In Queensland, this totalled at least 74% of all respondents; and in NSW, at least 79.9% of respondents.

Table 3.6. Expected and preferred federal systems (Queensland 2001 and New South Wales 2005)

		'Think forward, and tell me which of the following four scenarios best reflects how you think our system *will probably look* [50 to] 100 years from now.'		'Now I'd like to know how you think our system *should look*, in another [50 to] 100 years from now. I'll give you the same four scenarios, if you can tell me which best reflects how you think it should look.'	
		Qld 2001, n = 301 (w) %	NSW 2005, n = 502 (w) %	Qld 2001, n = 301 (w) %	NSW 2005, n = 502 (w) %
A	The same system as today.	27.0	23.5	29.0	12.5
B	The same three tiers, but with Australia divided into more States.	12.0	6.1	15.0	4.8
C	A two-tiered system, with a national government, and new regional governments replacing the current state governments.	36.0	38.8	31.0	47.4
D	A four-tiered system, with new regional governments as well as national, state and local government.	15.0	13.7	16.0	9.6
E	Other	10.0	4.4	9.0	10.6
F	Don't know		12.6		15.1
		100.0	100.0	100.0	100.0

Figure 3.7, Preferred federal systems (Queensland and New South Wales)

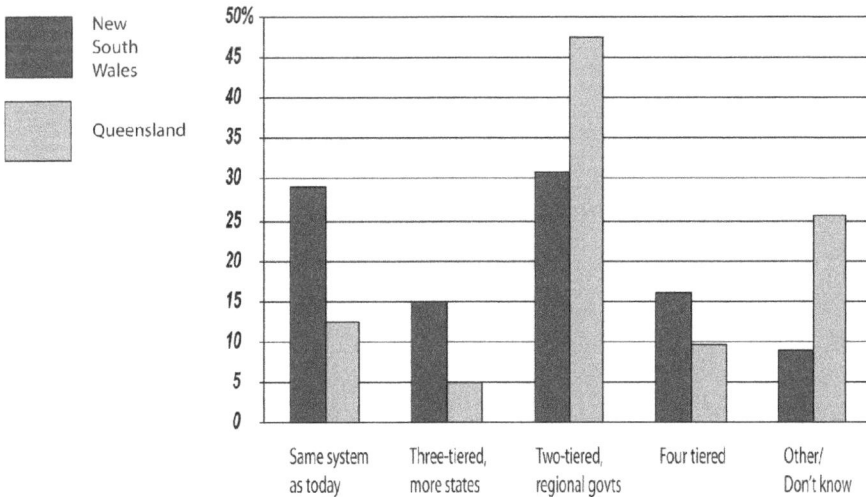

41

The relatively low proportion of 'don't know' responses is one indicator that citizens do have some grasp of the issues and hold at least some kind of view on these issues. However, research is ongoing in order to better establish how respondents interpret these scenarios, and whether they fairly represent citizens' expectations and preferences. For example, NSW respondents were also asked whether their concept of a 'two-tiered system' was one based on the amalgamation of local and current state administrations into new regional governments (52.6% of respondents indicated this to be their preference), or one based on simple abolition of state governments leaving current local government as the second tier (36.3% of respondents indicated this). Extrapolating from this, a further notional breakdown of future options is possible, as suggested in Figure 3.9 later in the chapter.

Nevertheless, an important result is the fact that many among the majority of respondents who envisage or desire change in the structure of federalism, did not express themselves to be positively dissatisfied with current arrangements. Table 3.8 confirms this, showing some more about the views of the 57% of NSW respondents who preferred the more radical scenarios, which involved new 'regional' governments instead of (scenario C) or in addition to (scenario D) the current States. These respondents were spread across the continuum in their satisfaction with the existing system, and were only slightly more likely than the remainder to criticise the current performance of state governments. The data, therefore, suggest not only that citizens are roughly evenly divided on the adequacy of the current system, but that even many of those who regard the current system as adequate, also envisage change and improvement. Indeed, the data suggest that many of these respondents, even if utopian, are not 'rosy eyed' about the prospects of change – although only 12.5% of respondents believed the status quo should remain, almost twice as many predict the status quo as the inevitable outcome.

Table 3.8. Performance of state government, by preferred scenario (NSW)

'On a scale of 1 to 5, how would you rate the performance of the different levels of government in Australia? 1 is very poor, 5 is very good.'

	% of respondents				
	Very poor / poor (1/2)	(3)	Good / very good (4/5)	No opinion	
State government (as rated by all respondents)	51.0	34.0	12.8	2.2	100.0
State government (respondents preferring 'regional' scenarios C or D)	54.8	33.7	10.4	1.0	100.0
State government (all other respondents)	47.8	35.1	14.1	2.9	100.0

Looking for differences: what determines citizens' interest in change?

Even if popular interest in the evolution of Australian federalism appears to be confirmed as a broad phenomenon rather than a maverick or fringe one, we need to know what sustains this interest, and what differentiates those convinced that change is desirable, from those content with the status quo. Are there particular features of these groups that would indicate their concerns might be addressed in other ways, not involving change to the federal system? Alternatively, even if institutional change provides a relevant part of the answer, are arguments for and against change deadlocked in a way that renders productive debate unlikely?

One of the most important questions is whether opinions differ significantly between rural and urban respondents. In NSW, as in Queensland, the history of regional agitation for political autonomy in the form of new states suggests that any interest in change should be concentrated in rural areas, remote from the State capitals. If there is rural interest in change, history also suggests this should take the relatively conservative form of a preference for more states, within the existing federal tradition. However as already discussed elsewhere, and demonstrated in Figure 3.9, the data show little difference between the major urban and rural regions in terms of preferred scenarios, as well as on other indicators (see Brown et al 2006: 292-7). This picture defies most previous political stereotypes. Interest in change is spread across urban and rural situations, and rural respondents were strongly in favour of a constitutional overhaul in which state governments were entirely replaced by new regional governments. As shown when the strong preference for a 'two-tiered' system is split between the two options mentioned earlier, rural respondents do appear to place a slightly higher value on existing local government, and on the option of retaining it as the basis of regional government. Again, however, the differences are marginal. Expectations and preferences for reform clearly span any urban-rural divide.

To look further for what distinguishes citizens' views, it is worth more closely examining the people who appear to have made up their minds, as indicated by those holding the apparently strongest views. In the New South Wales data, this is best indicated by looking at the 26 respondents (5.2%) who indicated they were 'very satisfied' with the existing system, as against the 54 respondents (10.7%) who indicated they were 'not at all' satisfied (Table 3.2 above). While the numbers in each group are small, they do help to identify a pattern. These groups were compared in Table 3.5, in respect of their rating of the performance of state governments. By further comparing two groups across a range of variables, we can look for or exclude various explanations of conservatism and radicalism with respect to federalism.

Figure 3.9. Preferred federal systems, by major regions (NSW)

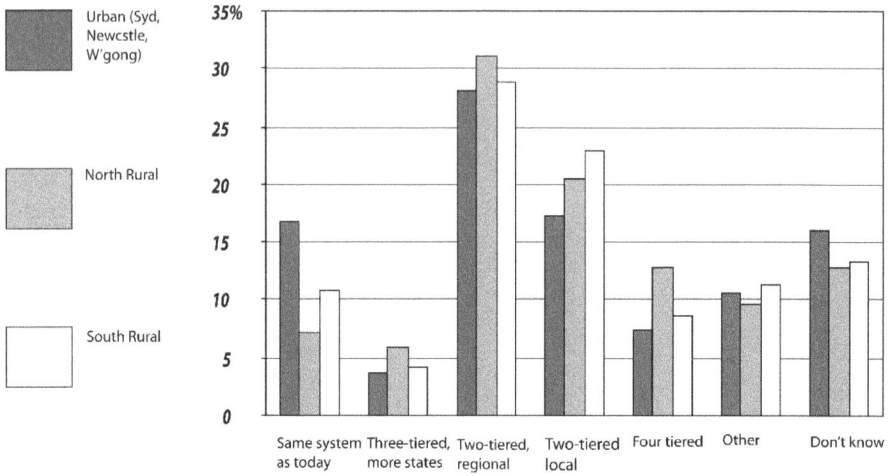

Firstly, strength of view does not appear to be related to gender (Table 3.10). The 26 most satisfied and the 54 least satisfied are equally divided among males and females. Tables 3.11 and 3.12 similarly indicate that period of current residence and level of education are unrelated to attitudes to federalism at their extremes. The only potentially significant indicators appear to be location, and age (Tables 3.13 and 3.14). As noted above, city-dwellers appear slightly more likely to prefer the status quo rather than scenarios involving change, and Table 3.13 shows that even though those expressing least satisfaction with the current system are divided equally between urban and rural locations, most of the 'very satisfied' are urban residents. Even more clearly, age appears to be a strong predictor. It is notable that a radical attitude appears to come with advancing age, rather than the more common notion that younger people are more radical and older people more conservative. This begs the question, whether there are particular aspects of life experience that lead to increased dissatisfaction with the federal system. From a demographic perspective, it is significant that as older age groups increase as a proportion of the Australian population, the proportion of citizens interested in supporting change to the system can also be presumed to increase.

Table 3.10. Attitudes to three-tier system by gender (NSW) (number of respondents)

	Very satisfied	Not at all satisfied
Male	13	28
Female	13	26
	26	54

Table 3.11: Attitudes to three-tier system by period of residence at current place of living (NSW) (% and number of respondents)

	Very satisfied	Not at all satisfied
Less than 10 yrs	13 (50%)	21 (40%)
10 – 25 years	7 (27%)	20 (38%)
More than 25	6 (23%)	12 (22%)
	26 (100%)	53 (100%)

Table 3.12: Attitudes to three-tier system by level of completed education (NSW) (number of respondents)

	Very satisfied	Not at all satisfied
School only	12	27
Post-school	15	27
	27	54

Table 3.13: Attitudes to three-tier system by rural/urban place of residence (NSW) (number of respondents)

	Very satisfied	Not at all satisfied
Urban	18	26
Rural	8	28
	26	54

Table 3.14: Attitudes to three-tier system by age (NSW) (number of respondents)

Age (years)	Very satisfied	Not at all satisfied
18-19	2	0
20-29	4	8
30-39	4	7
40-49	4	6
50-59	5	16
60 +	8	17
	27	54

Given the insignificance of most of these differences, however, another means of exploring the demographic basis of citizens' views is to compare those respondents who support the more radical scenarios for the future, against the remainder of the sample. In this case, we can compare the 57% of NSW respondents who preferred the scenarios involving new 'regional' governments, either instead of (scenario C) or in addition to (scenario D) the current states, with all other respondents. In particular, we can look to these respondents as favouring institutional options that explicitly reflect an alternative concept of 'regionalism', by strengthening public institutions of governance at this regional level – however defined, and irrespective of other implications for the political system.

Nevertheless when it comes to location, gender, and education, similar results prevail. As already noted, there is little geographic variation in preferences, with rural respondents only slightly more likely than urban ones to prefer the 'regionalist' options. The 'regionalists' were also only slightly more likely to take a poor view of state governments than the remainder. Table 3.15 suggests that those choosing a regional option are slightly more likely to be male than female. Table 3.16 shows that the 'regionalists' appear slightly better educated, being equally divided in education levels whereas a majority of the remainder have only school education – but the difference is slight. On the question of age, unlike satisfaction with the federal system, there is no significant difference between these groups (Table 3.17). This again tends to reinforce the assumption that that the capacity to envisage or support change is not dependent on active dissatisfaction.

Table 3.15: Support for 'regional' options by gender (NSW) (per cent of respondents)

	Respondents preferring options C or D	Other respondents
Male	50.5	45.9
Female	49.5	54.1
	100.0 (n = 297)	100.0 (n = 205)

Table 3.16: Support for 'regional' options by level of education (NSW) (per cent of respondents)

	Respondents preferring options C or D	Other respondents
School only	51.5	56.4
Post-school	48.5	43.6
	100.0 (n = 297)	100.0 (n = 202)

Table 3.17: Support for 'regional' options by age (NSW) (per cent of respondents)

	Respondents preferring options C or D	Other respondents
18-19	1.0	0.5
20-29	8.4	10.2
30-39	16.5	17.1
40-49	27.3	23.4
50-59	21.5	17.1
60+	25.3	31.2
	100.0 (n = 297)	100.0 (n = 205)

With views of the federal system and different constitutional preferences so evenly spread throughout the population, it is necessary to drill even further into the demographic data in order to identify clearer potential determinants of which citizens are likely to hold particular preferences. Other data collected included the nature of respondents' employment, and their level of civic engagement either through some form of government-related committee or certain types of community organisations. One clue that these data might finally reveal more information is contained in the findings above, that dissatisfaction with the current federal system appears to increase with age; and that preferences for 'regionalist' options might increase with level of education. If it is true that citizens' views of the federal system are determined by particular aspects of their life experience, some indication of this should also emerge from the data on employment and civic engagement.

Table 3.18 compares support for the 'regionalist' options and the remainder, according to the nature of respondents' employment. Immediately differences emerge. The two sets of options are equally likely to be supported by private employers and the self-employed, and by those in private sector employment. However, the 'regionalist' options are significantly more likely to be supported by the 112 respondents employed in government; and significantly less likely to be supported by those not in any employment at all. These data also reveal an even more specific and surprising result – the government employees most likely of all to prefer the 'regionalist' options were state government employees.

Table 3.18: Support for 'regional' options by employment (NSW) (per cent and number of respondents)

	Respondents preferring option C1	Respondents preferring option D	Respondents preferring options C or D	All other respondents
	% (n)	% (n)	% (n)	% (n)
Employees				
Government – Federal	2.8	4.7	3.0	1.5
State	20.1	16.7	19.5	8.8
Local	2.4	6.3	3.0	3.4
Other	2.4	4.7	2.7	0.5
Subtotal	27.7	31.3	28.3	13.7
Non-government	23.7	39.6	26.3	28.3
All employees	51.4 (128)	70.8 (34)	54.5 (162)	41.9 (86)
Employer / self-employed	14.5 (36)	12.5 (6)	14.1 (42)	13.7 (28)
Unemployed and seeking work	2.4 (6)	0.0 (0)	2.0 (6)	4.4 (9)
Not employed and not seeking work (incl. retired, home duties)	31.7 (79)	16.7 (8)	29.3 (87)	40.0 (82)
	100.0 (249)	100.0 (48)	100.0 (297)	100.0 (205)

This is further demonstrated by Figure 3.19, showing the spread of support for all options according to employment type. Overall, the 112 government employees captured by our sample are the most likely to have a view (with the lowest rate of 'don't knows'), but the least likely to believe that the federal system should remain the same. Directly contrary to the expectation that employment by state government would be associated with an opposition to change, and especially to change to the role of state governments themselves, 50 of the 75 state government employees in our sample (i.e. 66.7%) preferred the option most consistent with total abolition of their own employer – the single highest identifiable source of support for this option. The capture of a sizeable group of state government employees in the sample was somewhat accidental, since this was not a determining feature of the way the sample was drawn. It is clearly not a representative group – only 22 of these 75 respondents were from the urban zone, and their support for the 'two-tiered' option was lower (56.5%, as against 71.2% support among rural state government employees). However, even the result from urban state employees was well above the state mean. The views of state employees overall seemed less likely to have been determined by temporary party-political factors, with 53.3% of these respondents indicating they would retain 'exactly the same' or 'much the same view' of the relative performance of different levels of governments in the event of electoral change (as against 46.4% of all respondents), and only 10.7% indicating they would have a 'completely different view' (as against 15.1% of all respondents).

Figure 3.19. Preferred federal systems by employment (NSW)

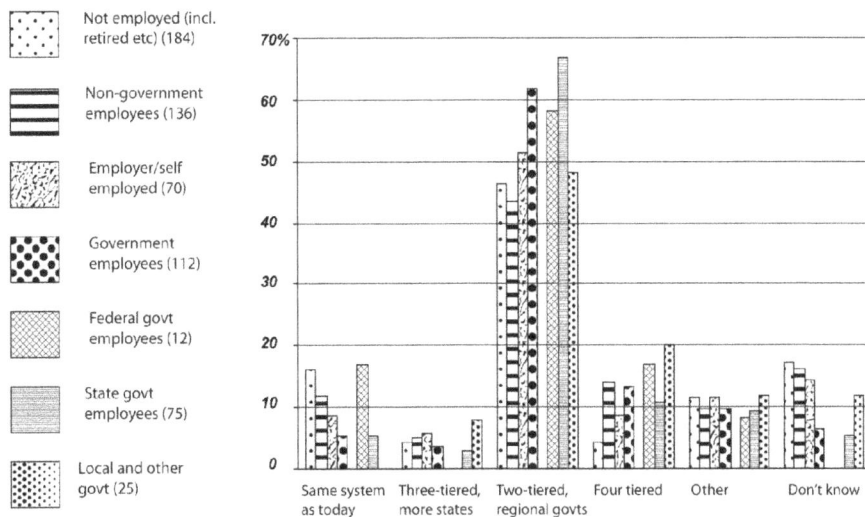

Table 3.20 and Figure 3.21 set out the equivalent results for the 57 respondents who indicated they were 'an active member of any organisation involved with regional development or resource management', and the 29 respondents who indicated they were an 'active member of any official government committee or advisory group'. Examples given of the former were Landcare and other local environment groups, and Chambers of Commerce and economic development groups. The latter included federal, state or local committees, or a committee involving a combination of governments. There is almost certainly overlap between these groups, as well as overlap between the second group and the government employees noted earlier; but as shown, the results do differ. Members of organisations and committees are typically around twice as likely as non-members to favour one of the 'regionalist' options, notably the option of a 'two-tiered' restructure. Like government employees, members of organisations and committees are also more likely to have a view, with very low rates of 'don't know' responses.

Table 3.20: Support for 'regional' options by civic engagement (NSW) (per cent and number of respondents)

3.20a	Respondents preferring option C	Respondents preferring option D	Respondents preferring options C or D	All other respondents
	%	%	% (n)	% (n)
Organisation members	14.1	12.5	13.8 (41)	7.8 (16)
Non-members	85.9	87.5	86.2 (256)	92.2 (189)
	100.0	100.0	100.0 (297)	100.0 (205)
3.20b				
Committee members	7.2	8.3	7.4 (22)	3.4 (7)
Non-members	92.8	91.7	92.6 (275)	96.6 (198)
	100.0	100.0	100.0 (297)	100.0 (205)

Figure 3.21. Preferred federal systems by civic engagement (NSW)

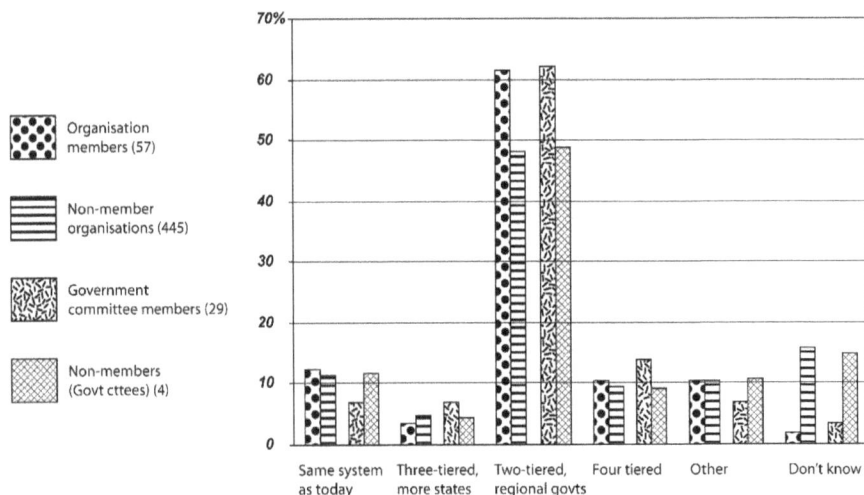

These differences tend to confirm that while support for change and adaptation of the federal system is widespread, it is particularly associated with life experiences, including not simply age but different types of employment and levels of civic engagement. The logical question to ask, highlighted by the surprising response from the majority of state government employees, was whether particular types of employment and civic engagement would be more or less likely to lead citizens to favour institutional change. In particular, returning to the overall question of whether change based on a greater recognition of regionalism has a basis in Australian political culture, it is sensible to ask whether those citizens who say they would prefer such change are speaking from a position of naivety or relative ignorance about the existing federal system. The results based on age and education, explored further above, tended to suggest otherwise (Brown et al 2006: 297-298). So did results from the earlier Queensland survey, which revealed that at least some groups of citizens with heightened direct experience of the workings of government – officials and employees of local government – were more rather than less likely to support reform than the average, less involved citizen (Brown 2002b: 29).

These results confirm that, whether or not related to active dissatisfaction with the federal system, preferences for change that are consistent with some of Australia's longest-running federal political debates form the views neither of a small fringe minority, nor of citizens with any particularly uninformed or simplistic basis for their opinions. As well as being held very broadly across the community, these convictions about the desirability of reform are strongest among those we would expect to know most about the practical realities of how federalism works, even when reform (if it happened to them) would require upheaval of their own professional world.

In conclusion: a new window on the feasibility of reform

Based on surveys of public opinion in Queensland and, more recently, in NSW, this chapter has shown that both critical attitudes of federalism and more radical preferences for change – two things that are not necessarily directly related – are widespread features of Australian society and not readily confined to particular types of regions or social groups. In fact, where the more radical preferences for change are strongest, is among those citizens who are most directly engaged in the economy (by way of employment), and particularly directly involved in government employment, as well as those most directly engaged in governance more generally through community organisations or committees. These respondents also confirm that opinions about the future development of the federal system are not necessarily as speculative or unsophisticated as might otherwise be assumed, not only through their greater knowledge but the greater certainty of their responses. Furthermore, it seems not only that many more Australians are interested in reform than previously understood, but that many also accept it as inevitable.

Given the dynamic state of developments in governance, what does this suggest about the realms of 'the possible' for institutional reform? The most important results are that in both Queensland and NSW, the public appetite for reform appears to be alive and well and widespread throughout the community. In both these states, the concept of 'the region' as an alternative scale of governance also has considerable popular currency, including in urban regions; and there is a widespread appetite for political and constitutional strengthening of governance at this level. The absence of major locational, demographic and sociological differences in the attachment to the specific options for achieving this, also indicate that debate about the specific institutional path is relatively wide open. Neither political analysts, nor political leaders, have any reason to assume that citizens are incapable of or disinterested in participating in a debate about an improved system. On the contrary, there is every sign that most Australians harbour an abiding conviction that a better system can and should evolve in response to current pressures and do so in a way which delivers a more truly federal, politically-regionalised approach to governance. Perhaps most importantly, in these states there is little sign of public interest in a debate about half-measures, or options which represent artificial compromises between the historical theory of federalism as played out in Australia (for example, based on the idea that regions can be better served by the creation of new states) and more practical ideas about how government should work. Citizens appear more interested in options that most past political leaders and commentators would define as quite radical. This provides a rare opportunity for policy-makers with any temptation to be visionary.

In terms of institutional options, the answers do not necessarily lie in the particular scenarios offered in these surveys. For any number of reasons, including some outlined above, Australia is no more likely to ever move to a totally 'two-tiered' version of federalism – the scenario preferred by many respondents – than it is to stay exactly the same. In practical terms, despite the low level of public support for the creation of new states (as presently understood), constitutional reality may dictate that this is the easiest –and possibly the only – way to create any kind of permanent new regional governments, if these are to be formally entrenched. Similarly, for state governments to join with other tiers in the development of an agreed framework of regionalised governance is immediately more viable than other options, because this could be done without any constitutional change. As a result the most accurate predictions are perhaps those made by the 15% of Queensland respondents, and 13.7% of NSW respondents (weighted), that Australia is destined to continue to develop its fourth tier of regional institutions into a recognisable level of government in its own right, before any thoroughly reformed federal system is likely to emerge. Interestingly, in the NSW survey this prediction was backed by 15.2% of all government employees, and 20.7% of all members of government-related committees, irrespective of whether they actually see this as a desired outcome. In this respect, even when seen through the eyes of public opinion, the options for developing a federal system are not simplistic but complex.

Is change to the federal system politically viable? The full answer depends on national research of a similar kind, now in progress. However the findings above suggest that with suitable leadership and an appropriate process, public opinion is an asset to be tapped rather than necessarily a barrier to change. As with federation itself, it may be public opinion that leads the way, if in the eyes of the broader community the responsiveness of political elites is left wanting.

References

ASSA (2003). *Australian Survey of Social Attitudes Dataset 2003*. Source: Australian Social Science Data Archive, Research School of Social Sciences, The Australian National University. <http:\\assda.anu.edu.au>

———— (2005). *Australian Survey of Social Attitudes Dataset 2005*. Source: Australian Social Science Data Archive, Research School of Social Sciences, The Australian National University. <http:\\assda.anu.edu.au>

Brown, A. J. (2002a). 'After the party: public attitudes to Australian federalism, regionalism and reform in the 21st century' *Public Law Review* 13(3): 171-190.

———— (2002b). 'Subsidiarity or subterfuge? Resolving the future of local government in the Australian federal system.' *Australian Journal of Public Administration* 61(4): 24-42.

Brown, A. J., I. Gray and D. Giorgas (2006), 'Towards a more regional federalism: rural and urban attitudes to institutions, governance and reform in Australia', *Rural Society* 16(3): 283-302.

Galligan, B. (1995). *A federal republic: Australia's constitutional system of government*. Cambridge University Press.

Howard, J. (1991). As quoted in *The Australian*, 9 November 1991; see L. Tanner (1999), *Open Australia*, Pluto Press, Sydney, pp.207-208.

———— (2002). 'Address to the National Assembly of Local Government', Alice Springs, as quoted by J.Hassan, 'Two tiers out of three ain't bad: Howard', *Government News*, December 2001 / January 2002.

———— (2005). 'Reflections on Australian Federalism', Speech to the Menzies Research Centre, Melbourne, 11 April 2005.

ENDNOTES

[1] The full text of the questionnaire and further information on the project is available at *www.griffith.edu.au/federalism*.

Part 2. Drivers for Change: New Approaches to Federalism and Regionalism

Chapter 4: Towards a Wider Debate on Federal and Regional Governance: The Rural Dimension

Mal Peters

Introduction

Sir Henry Parkes, the father of federation, put forward the proposal in his 1889 Tenterfield oration that a 'Convention of leading men of all the colonies should meet to devise the constitution which would be necessary for bringing into existence a federal government with a federal parliament'. His ambition to have a federal convention was realised and in 1891 a draft Australian constitution was presented to the Colonial Parliaments. Following the Federal Conventions of 1897-1898 and further work, a Constitution was formed that binds together the Commonwealth of Australia today.

Sir Henry and other federal founders were visionary – they envisaged a constitution that would adapt, if necessary, to meet future challenges. We need to stop and ask ourselves what they would do if they were undertaking the task again today because not even Sir Henry Parkes could have imagined the problems that would become apparent in Australia in the 21st century. The Australian public have to a large extent become very cynical about all levels of government. In the recent survey by Griffith University (Gray and Brown, this volume), 74% of NSW respondents expressed clearly that they want a change to the structures of Australia's governments in the long-term. That cynicism and distrust has increased in recent years because of government actions in a number of areas. People feel disempowered; the vast majority of people expressed a clear opposition to the sale of national icons, such as Telstra, but were ignored.

The current Australian Government has embarked on a centralising program like no other, controlling more and more from Canberra. In the High Court of Australia, we recently saw the spectacle of 35 very expensive lawyers challenging the Australian Government on industrial relations reform, at the behest of State governments, all at massive taxpayer cost (WorkChoices 2006). But they lost.

State governments appear unable to enact any strategy beyond the next election timeframe. We have areas of coastal Australia experiencing massive growth – upward of 7% in some areas of Queensland – with a huge lag in infrastructure to support that growth. The health system in NSW has virtually collapsed with some 2,000 people not seen within the recommended 10 minutes at hospitals when faced with life threatening conditions.

Local government fares no better. Traditionally, local governments tended to focus on, and were mostly responsible for, decisions relating to land use zoning and associated infrastructure requirements. However, over the past decade or more there has been increased engagement by local government, through the Australian Local Government Association (ALGA), in the development of national regional development policy. There is also evidence of a steady devolution of responsibility to local government alongside a growing expectation by State and Federal Governments that local shires adopt a more strategic approach to their activities. Despite this, an independent inquiry by Percy Allen, a former head of NSW Treasury, has found that a quarter of the 152 local councils in NSW are like councils in third world countries – starved of funds and unable to perform efficiently.

Many experts and commentators see the current system of government as being in a crisis. I contend it *is* a crisis. However, with goodwill and commitment we can put the building blocks in place to better inform change where it is underway, and drive new change where it is needed. There are solutions; we just have to find them.

Rural Australia and the need for reform

Unless a better way of governing this country is found, I believe that rural and regional Australia will continue to suffer badly. I will speak largely about rural Australia, obviously because it is what I know, and who I have been fortunate to represent in recent years in my former role as President of the NSW Farmers' Association.

There is a significant population imbalance in Australia. We are just about the most urbanised country in the world. Only 28% of Australians live in inland Australia in small rural centres and regional cities. Approximately 82% of the Australian population lives in major metropolitan regions and within 50 kilometres of the coast. The 2001 Census of Population and Housing showed that of the 6,371,745 people in New South Wales, 68.1% of the population lived in just six urban centres: the four with populations above 100,000 (Sydney 3,502,301; Newcastle 279,975; Central Coast 255,429; Wollongong 228,846) together with the Tweed Heads part of Gold Coast-Tweed Heads (45,024) and the Queanbeyan part of Canberra-Queanbeyan (29,928). This is notwithstanding that in all, there were 244 urban centres and 270 localities in NSW in 2001.

Rural Australia is in slow decline and is increasingly being omitted from key policy considerations. There is evidence that over 40% of towns in NSW are in decline. The towns most likely to be in decline are in the more remote areas. Meanwhile the 60% of towns that are growing are largely in coastal, semi-urban or mining areas. Growing or declining population can be an important indicator of the economic health of a regional community. A number of studies by the

Australian Bureau of Statistics (ABS) and the Australian Bankers Association (ABA) have analysed demographic trends and their impacts on regional communities and in particular their impacts on smaller regional centres. While population loss or stagnation is only one among a number of potential indicators of decline, it is an important one and is the focus of much regional development discussion.

The ABS (1998) has made a number of points about the decline of small towns that place the problem in perspective. In 1986 there were 578 towns in Australia with a population between 1,000 and 19,999; in 1996 there were 678, or 100 more such towns. They contained 2.5 million people, or 324,000 more than in 1986. Of the 578 towns in 1986, 47% had grown by at least 10%. Most towns experiencing substantial population growth were coastal, peri-metropolitan or associated with particular growth industries such as tourism or wine growing. However 31% of these towns had lost population, with 10% declining by at least 10%.[1] Towns in decline were usually inland, in wheat-sheep belts, dry land grazing regions or mining regions. The proportion of people living in towns under 1,000 and on farms (defined as rural) also fell.

Another study, commissioned by the ABA (1998), examined trends in the position of local government areas from 1976 to 1996. Of the 700 local government areas (LGAs) across Australia, the study examined the 456, which it defined as 'rural', containing fewer than 17,500 people in 1996. Of these 456 LGAs, 215 had been subject to 'a process of sustained population loss since 1976':

> The result is a process of demographic erosion that has reduced the number of people in 215 rural municipalities from 883,747 in 1976 to 778,452 in 1996 which is a decrease of 12% (ABA 1998: 2).

According to Nugent (1998), NSW population movements between 1991 and 1996 reveal complex intrastate demographic trends: the continuing domination by Sydney of the State's population, a pattern of inland migration to the coast and interstate, and very low growth or decline among inland regions. On one hand, 88% of coastal centres experienced population increase, with coastal towns having an average growth rate over the period of 16% compared to 5.7% for all rural centres. On the other, inland regions' average annual growth between 1991 and 1996 was a low 0.03% (0.63% from 1986-1991), and the population of most inland areas fell. Non-coastal centres grew at a significantly lower rate than the rest of the State. While towns with populations of 10,000 to 20,000 grew strongly, as did towns with 500 to 2,000 people, towns of 3,000 to 10,000 people recorded the lowest growth and lost population.

From this analysis there are a number of conclusions that can be drawn about demographic trends in relation to smaller regional centres in New South Wales. A majority of the small regional centres are losing population, and not all larger regional centres are growing strongly. Regions are not simply losing population to Sydney but to other states and territories. Inland regions are generally faring poorly in terms of population growth. It is important to note that the decline of many small towns and the forces driving this decline are not confined to New South Wales but are also occurring in other States and Territories.

Population growth or loss is not the only barometer of community economic health. It is also important to look behind the demographic trends to examine the underlying strength of regional economies. However as the population distribution continues to change, so, naturally, does the level of attention and understanding that governments have of rural issues. It is here that it becomes clear that Australia's system of government has not adjusted to accommodate these changes.

In my former role as President of the NSW Farmers' Association, I was continually frustrated in my approaches to government with their lack of understanding about rural issues. With only 11 rural-regional seats in the NSW Legislative Assembly of 99, it is little wonder that politicians place their focus on metropolitan and coastal issues.

A particular example of this lack of understanding came when the Federal Treasurer, Peter Costello, was reported as saying that a fall in agricultural production and rural exports due to drought was not enough to derail the strong growth of the entire economy. This 'city-centric' remarked showed little understanding of the way a drought cuts jobs, bankrupts business and destroys farming communities. It is not so much the fact that agriculture contributes 4% to the country's GDP; it is the fact that in many communities the income that flows from our exports forms the basis of local economic activity. Work by the Australian Farm Institute (2005), has shown that the Farm Dependent Economy, which takes into account all the flow-on economic activity of agriculture, is about 12% of GDP, equating to $72 billion. The Treasurer's comments ignored the social impact of drought, and the multiplier effect it has in regional communities. Little did he realise that a fall in the gross value of agricultural production of 19% (around $32 billion) as a result of the drought would lead to a decline in Australian GDP of around 1% and a loss of 44,800 jobs (11% of employment in the sector) in the five years to February 2004.

From the perspective of rural communities and agricultural industries, there are two major reasons why we need to look to reform of our system of government, to overcome and compensate for this institutionalised lack of understanding. One is the hidden costs to the entire Australian community of poor decision-making in relation to rural issues. The second is the human and social impacts of change affecting rural areas, which are not being effectively addressed by the current system. I will outline these briefly in turn.

Investing in rural sustainability

'City-centric' policymaking is not just a problem of the political process. It is also supported by views held by city media and some parts of corporate Australia, especially in relation to farming and the environment. Notwithstanding the decline in political significance of rural towns, the sustainability of rural industries is a national issue.

When it comes to quality decision-making by government, some of the clearest challenges can be seen in issues of infrastructure. If the agricultural sector and regional Australia is to grow and compete in the global environment, regional economies must be connected with the rest of the country and the world. This requires infrastructure to connect roads to railways to ports, telecommunications, energy and water. Much publicly funded rural infrastructure is in decline and needs urgent upgrading. In many metropolitan areas, this is being addressed through the emergence of public-private partnerships. However public-private partnerships are not viable for many projects in rural areas for a number of reasons, including apparent lack of political will, regulatory impediments, and difficulties in collecting tolls.

The freight task for Australia is estimated to double by 2020. Transport infrastructure must be improved, or triple the current number of truck movements will be occurring on our roads. In NSW, four rail lines have ceased operating in recent months. This alone means an additional 79,000 B-double truck movements on country roads in order to transport grain. But, according to the Shires Association of NSW, there is already a $156 million shortfall in funding for local government roads. Closing rail lines therefore only adds financial pressures on local governments, exacerbating what Percy Allen recently said about third world councils. The state of major highways is not simply an economic issue for the nation, but a safety issue. More than 15 years ago, the investigation into the deaths of 55 people in two bus crashes recommended that the Pacific Highway should be made dual carriageway along its entire length. Only 30% has been completed.

An efficient telecommunications system is critical to agricultural production. From a social perspective, telecommunications are also a lifeline for rural people, keeping them in touch with each other and the world. A sub-standard telecommunications system means isolated people, and is a life and death matter in emergency situations. As governments retreat from direct investment in this infrastructure, and increasingly leave telecommunications to the market, there is an abiding lack of political understanding of the relative impacts in rural areas. However if regional communities themselves wish to reinvest in infrastructure, they do not currently have the political autonomy, financial resources or regulatory authority to do it.

A major issue that maintains a sense of regional divide in Australia – or more particularly, city-country divide – is debate over the management of natural resources. One of the main (and obvious) differences between urban and rural areas is the landscape. Our whole society values the environmental qualities of rural landscapes, their biodiversity, what they provide in water quality, and the opportunities they provide for recreation and leisure. The challenge is to find ways to ensure that government funding maximises the wider benefits of the countryside and ensures that that they are shared as equitably as possible. But it is an open question whether investment in sustainable natural resource management, under current structures of government, have any real chance of being effective (see Bellamy this volume).

The issue of equity becomes even larger when it comes to the challenges of social sustainability in rural areas. Throughout rural areas there are vulnerable groups who are at particular risk of exclusion. Children and young people, lone parent families, those with disabilities and older people are obvious examples. Their needs are often harder to identify and it can cost more to deliver the services they need. Government has a responsibility to ensure equitable access to quality public services and to ensure that everyone (especially the vulnerable) can access them.

Two recent studies highlight the social problems confronting rural Australia. The first by Mission Australia was titled *Rural and Regional Australia: Change, Challenge and Capacity*. The study revealed a 'diverse story of disadvantage' for the 36% of Australians living outside metropolitan regions. It showed that that country young people are less likely to finish school and 1.7 times more likely to suffer an alcohol-related death than those living in metropolitan areas. Inequalities in health, job opportunities and quality of life for rural Australians can be seen in income levels in non-metropolitan areas, which tend to be lower, with almost 17% of non-metropolitan households living on a weekly income of $300 or less compared with 12.8% of city dwellers.

The NSW Farmers' Association's 'Building Rural Community' survey, carried out in mid-2005, revealed major concerns about the availability and quality of services in health, education (highly variable), transport, banking, police, child care, and aged care. We know from our work with the Rural Mental Health Alliance that the rural suicide rate is roughly twice that of urban areas. Rural communities rely on a high level of 'volunteerism', but this is not necessarily sustainable, with burn-out a significant problem which affects cultural, sporting and recreational activities.

Employment is also a major concern in rural areas. At least until the drought began to have its impact, employment in the farm sector itself was strong. Using ABS data, Herreria et al (2004) provided a review of the social profile of people employed in agriculture, forestry and fishing industries between 1996 and 2001. The data was classified according to whether the employees were located in 'metropolitan', 'regional', 'coastal', 'inland' or 'remote' regions.[2] Employment in the farm sector increased in all regions of Australia, with the exception of coastal regions, which experienced a 0.5% decline (most prominent for females with a 1.8% decline in employees in coastal regions). The number of indigenous people working in the sector also increased in all areas (this ranged from a nearly 60% increase in metro areas down to a 2.8% increase in regional areas), with indigenous people now accounting for 1.3% of people employed in the farm sector in Australia. Reinforcing the social issues, over 9% of farm sector employees now live alone – an increase of 18% in inland areas and approximately 20% in remote areas.

However the employment picture in rural areas is now not so optimistic. On one hand, rural areas continue to suffer major shortages of professionals and skilled labour. On the other, they now also exhibit relatively high levels of unemployment. The reasons are not just the drought, but other structural shifts in the economy. The age and qualification profiles of workers in rural NSW suggest substantial skill gaps, making many unemployable. Training has not kept pace with the transformation of agriculture in the last two decades, and a large proportion of the rural population do not have the necessary skills to perform the job. According to Herraria et al (2004), 23% of farm sector employees across Australia had less than 10 years of schooling, and only a little over 6% had a bachelor degree or higher qualification. The lower figures came from inland (5.5%), coastal (5.1%) and remote (4.5%) areas. The greatest change in the number of employees with bachelor degrees or higher education was among women, where the number increased by almost 50% over the five years to 2001.

Other well-known reasons for the decline include companies relocating from smaller towns due to worsening infrastructure, and rationalisation by government departments, banks and other large companies including closure of smaller branches and offices. Table 4.1 shows the overall picture, based on the number of unemployed and unemployment rates in NSW for the March quarter 2004 and March quarter 2005. While unemployment overall is at historically low levels, it is clearly not so low in rural Australia. In March 2005, a staggering 43% of all of the unemployed people in NSW were in non-metropolitan NSW. The unemployed in country NSW made up 14% of the entirety of unemployed people in Australia.

Table 4.1. Unemployment Rates

Regions	Unemployment No.		Unemployment Rate (%)		Labour Force
	Mar 04	Mar 05	Mar 04	Mar 05	Mar 05
Australia	599,300	554,400	5.9	5.4	10,312,100
New South Wales	190,700	180,500	5.7	5.3	3,376,500
Sydney	113,800	103,000	5.2	4.6	2,214,600
Non-Sydney	76,900	77,500	6.5	6.7	1,161,900

Source: NSW Farmers Association 2005

Solving these employment problems, and larger social issues that surround them, is not simply an economic challenge. It is a more general challenge of governance, because much of the key to attracting and retaining skilled workers in rural industries hinges on a broad understanding of regional development, including developing more attractive and sustainable living environments.

With no other level of government properly placed to lead the charge, many local governments have tried to use strategies to retain and attract skilled workers. These strategies, aimed at offering the best possible quality of life and environment for all local citizens, based on principles of social justice and equity, as well as best practice in planning for land use, infrastructure and services. This includes providing appropriate protection and enhancement of heritage character and cultural identity; designing and implementing programs that are ecologically sustainable and provide for the retention of important features of the natural environment; providing the choice of housing sought by communities; and offering varied and accessible employment opportunities. Some of the broad programs and projects undertaken by local governments include:

- pursuing greater efficiency, community orientation and quality outcomes in procedures for development control and other forms of regulation associated with the planning and management of urban areas;
- implementing planning programs that address the need for better environmental design within both housing stock and public buildings, with particular emphasis on solar access, latitude design modifications, alternative wastewater use, land subdivision, use of communications technology, shared facilities and economy of scale; and
- promoting and funding better urban design outcomes; supporting rural and regional infrastructure projects; and participation in integrated planning and service delivery projects.

The problem is that local government, as it currently exists, still cannot do enough. Despite the effort to attract and retain suitably skilled labour, these strategies and programs do not seem to be working, and people continue to leave rural areas for metropolitan areas. The reasons were highlighted by the NSW State Chamber of Commerce or SCC (2000) in its submission to the Commonwealth Government's Regional Business Development Analysis. According to the SCC, the difficulties in attracting and retaining skilled labour in rural areas also relate to:

- lack of recreational and cultural facilities;
- lack of quality educational facilities – particularly nearby private schools;
- the inability of regional business to pay metropolitan wage rates;
- limited employment opportunities and job prospects; and
- reduced access to medical facilities and doctors.

According to the SCC, regional businesses identify lifestyle as the most important factor in attracting skilled workers to regional areas. The fact that regional areas afford more relaxed, slower pace of life in country surrounds, can be synonymous with an improved quality of life. However people are not prepared to sacrifice everything for these particular qualities. One Chamber member commented as follows:

> Some people want to relocate out of Sydney for the quiet life. Most don't. They want the coastal or rural life, but they still want good coffee, they want kids' schooling, want access to libraries, restaurants, city type activities. People naturally enough would like the best of both worlds. That is why the idea of stimulating the growth of regional centres is essential.

Local government simply does not have the capacity, legal power or financial resources to influence the more structural conditions for this kind of development, even when it has the vision. However, neither can the state and federal governments do it, because they are not fundamentally rooted in the region, and are inevitably dominated by metropolitan concerns. As a result, they simply do not have the commitment to the type of medium and long-term changes needed, even where they have the knowledge or understanding. In NSW, government policies to address the problems faced by rural areas are not working because government has failed to understand the dynamics of the social profile of the farming sector and the rural community in particular. While the problems experienced by people living and working in rural areas are often the same as those in urban areas, the solutions often have to be tailored to take into account issues such as remoteness and higher costs of travel (in both time and money). In addition, the diversity of rural areas means that different delivery solutions and priorities may be needed in different areas.

After many decades of trying, it is clear that the broader approach to regional development needed to make rural communities sustainable, is not achievable under our current system of government.

Towards a wider debate on regional governance

It is time to move forward in recognising that our institutions of government can and should be better organised to give all regions a fair go. In particular, it is time to escape the 'city-country' divide that currently holds us back. The public attitude survey of NSW residents, supported by the NSW Farmers' Association (Gray and Brown, this volume) provides a new reason for this, because it suggests city people are actually no happier about the current system, and just as interested as country people in long-term change. Urban regions have their own unique problems which are apparently being no better served by the current federal system, particularly by state governments, than rural ones.

There are other things in common. In November 2002, the NSW Farmers' Association undertook a Parliamentary Audit of laws and regulations, which revealed that farmers are being regulated out of business by a mountain of bureaucratic red tape. Farmers' in NSW must comply with at least 56 different agricultural and environmental laws and regulations that have been introduced over the years. In 2003, of the 1,800 Commonwealth Acts of Parliament in place, 170 had been passed in the previous year. In four years from 2000 to 2003, the Commonwealth Parliament passed the same amount of legislation as it passed in the 69 years to 1969 at an administrative cost to Australian taxpayers of $4.5 billion in 2001-2002 alone. Similarly, in 2005, there were 1,300 NSW Acts of Parliament in place, 115 of which had been passed in the previous year. During 2000-2003, the NSW Parliament passed 300 pages of Acts, Rules, regulations and by-laws each sitting week.

The OECD estimates that the compliance cost of regulation for small and medium-sized Australian businesses in 1998 was more than $17 billion. Urban and rural businesses alike have an interest in reducing this burden of red tape, and the overall cost of government, if the path to a more efficient federal system can be found.

Given these facts, it is fast looking like there is every political reason for governments to look at long-term reform of the federal system, and few reasons left for them not to. Reforming basic institutions may not solve all the problems outlined in this chapter, at least not overnight, but we have to seriously consider the options. It was for this reason that the NSW Farmers' Association took a lead in research and debate about options for a better system of government, through a taskforce established in 2004. Together with Griffith University and allied research bodies, we are now supporting the development of a new framework for evaluating trends and possibilities for our system of government. Key elements of that framework are set out in an Association discussion paper (see Appendix this volume).

While the NSW Farmers' Association Taskforce has particular options it favours for reform, we recognise that a range of options need to be discussed. The common element of these options is a recognition that our federal system needs to provide regional communities – rural and urban – with greater capacity for developing and sticking with their own solutions to their own problems, by allowing stronger forms of government to evolve at the regional level. Local government is trying, but can't do it alone. State governments have had the chance, and both can't and won't. The federal government is a growing force in the lives of rural regions, and increasingly provides the national standards that determine how business runs and how the environment is managed, but it is too remote from local communities to run all their affairs.

An agreed model for evaluating options for new states or regional governments in Australia is vital. A problem of past debates has obviously been disagreement over the criteria that should be used to assess the potential benefits of reform, leaving uncertainty about its likely overall effects, and helping preserve a status quo widely regarded as less than optimum. There is a clear need for further research to assess the potential benefits, costs, and options for reform. It is for this reason the Association has given funding to help trigger more detailed analysis of the costs, benefits and economic feasibility of reform options in the area of federal restructuring.

The Association has also discussed a new alliance of interest groups to take this issue forward. We need a collaborative effort, including a broad range of Australian business, community and non-government organisations in a larger debate about how structural reform of the federal system might better serve the people of Australia – urban and rural alike. There is great need for more informed debate about the evolution of our institutions, which is above party politics. There is currently a big gap in this debate, after the conclusion of the Constitutional Centenary Foundation (1991-2000), and the winding-up of think-tanks like the ANU Federalism Research Centre. Many organisations are interested in this debate, as shown by the Business Council of Australia's *Aspire Australia 2025* report (2004) and recent *Reshaping Australia's Federation* action plan (2006). Business and non-government groups need to work together to improve our fundamental structures of democracy and governance.

New ideas and new solutions need to be put before Australia's people and governments. We need new methods for analysing the potential for structural reform that can better equip the nation for present times and future challenges. There is a clear case for structural reform of the Australian federal system to deliver:

- a more effective political system that is inclusive of all and does not discriminate against certain regions;
- more efficient and responsive public administration;

- greater social, economic and environmental sustainability in rural and regional Australia; and
- greater cooperation between governments.

As set out in the discussion paper, reform should be aimed at providing a more efficient, durable apportionment of policy responsibilities between national and regional levels of governance; enhancing the governance capacities of urban and rural communities at the local and regional levels; increasing the responsiveness of state or regional government to the pressing needs of Australia's regions; streamlining and reducing the net cost of government where possible; and providing an enhanced environment for sustainable economic innovation.

We are desperately in need of leaders who can see past the next election, with a vision similar to Sir Henry Parkes. As is always the case with politics, if necessary, the community needs to demand such vision from its political leaders, and researchers and advisors need to provide the new and better information they will then require. We are indeed fortunate to live in this great nation. We need to embark on this important journey to reform our governance system to make it even greater. Our collective vision will be required to commence this process. It has been over 100 years since Henry Parkes gave us his. It's time for action. Australia needs it.

References

ABA 1998, *Demographic Trends and Services Provision in Australia*, Report prepared for Australian Bankers' Association by KPMG Management Consulting.

ABS 1998, *Australian Demographic Statistics*. Australian Bureau of Statistics, Canberra.

AFI 2005, *Australia's Farm Dependant Economy Report*, Australian Farm Institute Sydney.

Business Council of Australia 2004, *Aspire Australia 2025*. Melbourne.

———— 2006, *Reshaping Australia's Federation: A New Contract for Federal-State Relations*, Melbourne, October.

Herreria, E., A. Woodhead, R. Tottenham and C. Magpantay 2004, *Social Profile of People Employed in the Agriculture, Forestry and Fishing Industries*, Rural Industries Research and Development Corporation Publication No 04/122, Canberra.

Mission Australia 2006, *Rural and Regional Australia: Change, Challenge and Capacity*. Sydney.

NSWFA 2005, *Building Rural Communities Project: Discussion on the Way Forward*, A survey conducted by NSW Farmers' Association, Sydney.

Nugent, S. 1998, 'Why Sydney Keeps Growing – Trends in Population Distribution in New South Wales 1991-1996', *People and Place*, Volume 6, No.4.

SCC 2000, *Regional Business Development Analysis,* Submission by State Chamber of Commerce to the Federal Government's Regional Business Development Analysis Panel.

WorkChoices 2006, High Court of Australia, 'NSW v Commonwealth' *Australian Law Reports* Volume 231, p.1.

ENDNOTES

[1] Towns in New South Wales having lost 10% of population or more between 1986 and 1996 were Werris Creek (-18.4%); Barraba (-15.4%); Dorrigo (-13.2%); Wee Waa (-11.7%); Narrabri (-11.4%); Murrumburrah-Harden (-16.9%); Batlow (-12.9%); Scone (-18.8%); Nyngan (-10.5%); and Wilcannia (-34.4%). A number of further towns had large absolute declines of less than 10% - Moree (-945); Lithgow (-928); Gunnedah (-829); and Kempsey (-705).

[2] Metropolitan refers to capital cities. Areas outside of metropolitan areas are classified as non-metropolitan. Non-metropolitan is sub-categorised into:

- Regional – includes all Statistical Local Areas (SLA) that contain the whole or part of an urban centre with a population exceeding 100,000;
- Coastal – includes SLAs in the more densely populated areas of Australia, generally within 80 km of the coast;
- Inland – includes areas inland of the coast but excluding remote areas of Australia;
- Remote – sparsely populated SLAs as classified by the Accessibility/remoteness index of Australia.

Chapter 5: Rescuing Urban Regions: The Federal Agenda[1]

Brendan Gleeson

An urban nation in denial

Australia has long been, and remains, an essentially urban nation. Presently, nearly two out of every three Australians resides in one of the large urban regions that centre on our state capitals, and there is no sign that this proportion is diminishing. Most Australians prefer to live in the major metropolitan regions, which continue to offer the greatest opportunities for economic, social and cultural satisfaction.

'Seachange' and 'treechange' migrations are of great national significance because they are occurring in areas that appear ill equipped, in a variety of ways, to accommodate major population increases (Burnley and Murphy 2003). They are also raising demands for social and physical infrastructure which may not be viable or sensible to provide in these areas for a variety of reasons. These reasons include the difficulty of providing major new infrastructure networks in environmentally sensitive regions.

Ex-urban migration also partly signals that not all is well in our cities, or at least some of them, and that growth pressures in combination with urban mismanagement are literally driving some households away. Nonetheless, cities and large settlements still occupy the centre fields of Australian life.

The Australian geographer, Clive Forster, reminds us:

> It is in city environments that most of us make our homes, seek employment, enjoy recreation, interact with neighbours and friends, and get education, health care and other services. Our cities determine how we live (2004:xvi).

For much of our European history, however, the material significance of Australia's cities has tended to be ignored or understated in public discussions. Public denial of our continuing deep commitment to city living is nothing new. Anti-centricurbanism is a heart murmur that the nation was born with. In 1897, the NSW Government Statistician, T.A. Coghlan, lamented 'the abnormal aggregation of the population into their capital cities', viewing this as 'most unfortunate element in the progress of the colonies'.[2]

The refusal to recognise our seemingly innate urbanity, and the pleasure and productivity that we have derived from our cities, is one national trait worth abandoning. It weakens us because it keeps us in constant denial about the true state of our settlement patterns. Disavowal of Australia's deeply urban character reduces our willingness and capacity to understand the shifts that are always transforming our cities. It doubtless helps to explain why the 'seachange' phenomenon has been rhetorically overplayed in political and social discussion, without much reference to the continuing overwhelming demographic significance of the cities.

The long term working of our federal system has also tended to overlook the political and policy significance of cities and urban regions. There has been very little, and only episodic, explicit attention given to the cities by Commonwealth Governments (Orchard 1995; Parkin 1982). This record of neglect has been justified and reinforced by political leaders, scholars and jurists who have asserted that the national government has no authority and no power to intervene in urban affairs (Troy 1978).

There has not tended to be an equally theoretical counter-position which has asserted that the Commonwealth does, in fact, have the power and/or the duty to act on urban matters. Even the supporters of a national urban policy agenda have tended to acknowledge, if implicitly, that the authors of the constitution did not appear to anticipate a Commonwealth interest in the cities (Troy 1985: 265).

There have, however, been several important instances where political advances have simply gone around the Maginot Line of constitutional objection to claim urban policy for the Commonwealth. The most notable of these were the urban and housing development initiatives of the Whitlam Government (1972-5)[3] and the Hawke-Keating Governments' Building Better Cities program (1991-6).

Nearly two decades ago, the urban scholar Patrick Troy (1978) made the distinction between theoretical and practical federalist positions when examining the history of Commonwealth intervention in the cities. The pragmatic position is that the Commonwealth can do what it likes in the field of urban policy if it is prepared to mobilise the many fiscal and policy levers at its disposal. The theoretical federalist imagines a constitutional impediment to national urban policy. Troy noted that:

> ... the argument that the commonwealth lacks the constitutional power to become involved in urban and regional development, while legally correct, is an argument which has only been used when it has been politically convenient. The 'constitution' has been the last refuge of the rationalist (1978:7).

Two conclusions about the Commonwealth's urban interests

There are two possible conclusions to be drawn from the Australian Government's intermittent record of involvement in urban affairs. First, whilst the Commonwealth may not be obliged and directly empowered to intervene in the cities, there are no practical barriers to it doing so. Episodic federal intervention has mobilised a range of direct and indirect levers to influence urban development, often successfully. The Whitlam Government's urban and regional development program, for example, produced many material improvements to urban infrastructure and amenity that would not otherwise have occurred. Consider one possible list of federal direct and indirect interventions in urban regions since the World War Two (Table 5.1):[4]

Table 5.1. Federal Involvement in the Cities since World War Two – A Select Summary

1	Federal investment in state and territory urban road systems	1920s-30s
2	Creation of Commonwealth Housing Commission	1943
3	Commonwealth-State Housing Agreements	1945-
4	Commonwealth pressure on States to sell public housing to sitting tenants	1950s-
5	Creation of Commonwealth Department of Works and Housing	1945
6	First home owners scheme	1960s-
7	Major commitment to building Canberra and establishment of National Capital Development Commission (1958)	1954-
8	Similar commitment to building Darwin reflecting Commonwealth responsibility for territories, including the Australian Capital Territory and the Northern Territory	1970s-
9	Creation of Commonwealth Bureau of Roads to examine urban and rural roads needs	
10	Creation of the National Urban and Regional Development Authority (NURDA) that became the Cities Commission under the subsequent Labor government	1972
11	Creation of the Department of Urban and Regional Development and allied initiatives including the Area Improvement Program, the Australian Assistance Plan, the Sewerage Backlog Program, local traffic calming programs and the creation of Land Commissions	1972
12	Creation of Department of Environment which had urban responsibilities including development of Environmental Impact Statements	1972
13	Expansion of federal assistance to local governments via reconstituted Commonwealth Grants Commission	1973
14	Commonwealth creation of Heritage Commission which had concern for built (i.e. urban) as well as natural heritage	1975
15	Creation by Fraser Government of Department of Environment, Housing and Community Development	1975-83
16	Hawke-Keating Governments' Building Better Cities Program	1991-96
17	The development of national Building Code of Australia	1990
18	National Competition Policy directions that have restructured urban service provision.	1995-

A second insight that emerges from inspection of the historical record is that federal urban policy ambitions are not simply the preserve of the Australian Labor Party. The decision to eschew responsibility for urban affairs is governed by political not constitutional considerations. Both major political blocs have made this decision at different periods.

And yet, both have also produced urban policy initiatives. Labor is remembered for the scale of its national urban policy ambitions; notably during the Whitlam and Hawke-Keating eras. Much less recalled in public and scholarly debate are the urban initiatives of conservative national governments, including the creation of the National Urban and Regional Development Authority by the McMahon Government in 1972. The decision of the current Howard Government (1996-) to eschew urban policy commitments is not a natural or inevitable consequence of the conservative political position.

Political obstacles to federal urban policy occur both within and beyond the national political frame. Opposition also emerges from other points in the federal system, notably from the States, which may, for a variety of reasons, resist Commonwealth urban policy ambitions. This resistance from within the federal system itself has frustrated the pursuit of national urban policy at different historical periods. The Whitlam government's 'new federalism' approach was designed to engender new federal relations that would support its urban and regional development program. Parkin wrote:

> Part of the Whitlam 'new federalism' vision was a sub-state 'regionalisation' of public administration to stand between (and perhaps eventually to replace) state and local government. Regionalisation was seen mainly as a means to bypass the other, allegedly incompetent or uncooperative, levels of government ... (1982:123).

To this end, some 76 new regionalised municipal groupings – Regional Organisations of Councils – were identified 'to pursue co-operative planning and to serve as conduits for Commonwealth funding' (Parkin, ibid.). As Parkin notes, the program, encountered resistance from the States, particularly and predictably those with conservative governments. And yet, there was broader resistance amongst the States to initiatives that were seen to threaten their traditional policy prerogatives, including those that redefined the basic constitution and conduct of local government.

By contrast, the later urban initiatives of the Hawke-Keating administrations were not predicated on a deeper attempt to transform or overhaul the federal system. The Building Better Cities Program, launched in 1991, was marked by 'a more flexible approach to Commonwealth/State relations emphasising a range of processes and outcomes to achieve the objectives of the program rather than rigid Commonwealth control over the States' (Orchard, 1985:72).

The prospects for Commonwealth urban policy

As the preceding discussion showed, there are no constitutional barriers to national urban policy in Australia. Neither has urban policy been completely embraced or completely opposed by either end of the national political spectrum. Federal Labor Governments have undertaken the boldest urban policy interventions but have also demonstrated lapses of commitment to this policy setting. The record of conservative governments is far more modest yet several have produced a range of policy interventions that have shaped urban development directly and indirectly (Table 5.1). All national governments are surely also mindful of the indirect influence they inevitably bring to bear on urban development. As Parkin pointed out, 'No Commonwealth Government, not even one devoutly committed to 'non-interference', can avoid its activities having an urban impact' (1982:117).

What, then, are the prospects for Commonwealth urban policy in the future? Whilst theoretical (i.e., constitutional) opposition to national urban policy lacks credibility, there remains a practical objection that has the capacity to stymie development of any future federal urban agenda. The next barrier might simply be the position that while federal urban policy is possible, it is simply not needed: the States and local governments are readily equipped to handle the task.

There are two classes of rationale, in my opinion, which make urban policy an essential, not optional, feature of the federal agenda. The first is the unyielding need for a nation of cities to have a national urban policy framework. Urban living is a national trait, and therefore must be a preoccupation for any national government. The love of urban life appears thus as a national value and needs to be recognised as such by national governments. Recognition of this national value does not dictate the form of Commonwealth commitment to urban affairs, but underlines the need for federal policies that safeguard the welfare, productivity and sustainability of Australia's cities and urban regions.

Then there are a range of fiscal reasons why the Commonwealth should assume part of the responsibility for safeguarding the health of our urban regions. The national government raises the lion's share of tax and excise revenue, a vast amount of it generated and collected in the cities. The wealth generated by the cities flows from their innate urbanity not from the mere aggregation of economic activity in particular places. This 'productive urbanity' derives from the capacity of urban structures to supply opportunities for social and economic advancement that cannot be offered outside cities. For example, the efficient concentration and connection of high order educational, industrial, commercial and recreational opportunities is a form of productive urbanity possessed by most successful global cities (Property Council of Australia 2002). The chances for economic success are greatly diminished when this productivity is compromised by urban dysfunction – for example, an ineffective transport system.

All governments, including the Commonwealth, therefore, are obliged to spend part of the 'tax take' in ways that protect the uniquely productive qualities of urban areas. A range of commentators (e.g., Forster 2006) and lobbyists have pointed to the recent and continuing failure of state governments to manage Australia's urban regions adequately. Arguably however, the increasingly manifest urban management problems besetting state governments reflect more than simple incompetence. The failings of urban management also highlight the inability of state governments to fund the constant improvements that cities need.

Sydney, for example, is a vastly important national asset. As a second-tier global city it generates a large share of national income and a host of other positive externalities for the nation (Property Council of Australia 2002). Efficient circulation of people and capital is critical in global cities. In the context of environmental pressures, our urban circulation systems also need to be highly ecologically sustainable. It is increasingly evident that Sydney's circulatory systems need dramatic improvement and renewal, to make them more effective and more sustainable (Newman 2006). This essentially is a nation-building task, beyond the capacity of a state government alone. There is a clear case for Commonwealth investment in this great task of urban renovation. As the *Sydney Morning Herald* pointed out in 2005:

> ... the Federal Government's absence from funding the future of Australia's cities has not gone unnoticed. Its return to the table by purposely funding cities, and recognising their importance to the national interest, is critical to fixing the problems facing the Prime Minister's home town.

The failure of the Commonwealth to assume this responsibility perhaps partly explains what the *Sydney Morning Herald* has termed 'The Great Carr Crash' (Davies, 2006). This refers to a decade of controversial and crisis-prone urban governance coinciding with the tenure of the Carr State government (1995-2005). In particular, transport management during this era was characterised, amongst other things, by use of a range of increasingly impulsive governance mechanisms that attempted to overcome a lack of funding for urban improvements. These included the Public Private Partnerships (PPPs) used to build roads projects; many of which proved to be expensive and controversial. These unconventional mechanisms, especially PPPs, are harder to extend to public transport and partly explain why it has fared the worst during an era of general under-investment. Peter Newman, urban scholar and former Sustainability Commissioner for New South Wales, sees federal funding as the key to reducing state government reliance on PPPs in Australian metropolitan management:

> If the Federal Government participated in funding urban infrastructure, then the States could again manage transport infrastructure without the need for private funds and the conditions that inevitably accompany them (Newman 2006).

The second and more contemporary rationale for federal urban policy derives from the external pressures and opportunities that have manifested in the last

30 years. The most important of these are economic and cultural globalisation and global ecological breakdown. The global economic system that has emerged in the past few decades is essentially urban. Cities are the pivots and the engines of the global economy. They have also, to varying extents, decoupled themselves from their national and regional economic contexts and compete directly as discrete economic entities. This urban economic competitiveness occurs both within nation states – think of the tussle between Sydney and Melbourne for urban supremacy – and across national boundaries.

Cities also connect, and not simply compete, in complex ways across national boundaries, outside the normal currents of diplomacy. A key example is the circuitry of global finance, which acts simultaneously to connect cities and set them in contest. It is important therefore from a national perspective that cities are supported and sustained as key engines of economic and cultural opportunity in a challenging global environment (Property Council of Australia 2002).

This idea is well understood by the urban development industry – though it appears not to have been grasped by the present federal government. This position is supported by most leading business lobbies that may have in the past been sceptical of most urban regulation, let alone national urban intervention (see Dennis 2006; Property Council of Australia 2002).

The emergent conventional economic wisdom on federal urban policy sees it as a vital national policy function in the global age. What this perspective does not tend to embrace, however, is the further rationale for national urban policy arising from globalisation – the need to manage the cities in the national interest and ensure that some of the fruit of their new productivity is redistributed to less economically potent regions. There is nothing essentially radical about this idea, which sees a role for urban policy in the maintenance of national cohesion. The tendency of some super city states in the new globalism to see themselves as apart from, and without particular commitment to, their regional and national contexts also needs to be checked. Urban imperia always seem to collapse at some point, and need to be protected from themselves.

Finally, global ecological dysfunction is a new and pressing rationale for national urban policy. Much of this dysfunction is sourced in the growth feast unleashed by globalisation and in its urban pivots. There is simply no prospect of Australia addressing global and regional environmental problems without intervening in and reshaping the course of urban development. Happily, the 2005 federal parliamentary enquiry into sustainable cities demonstrated bipartisan recognition of this issue, at least amongst the political ranks if not hierarchies. The report produced by this inquiry very firmly stated that urban policy was a federal responsibility (House of Representative 2005).

As McManus (2005) argues, Australia's cities urgently need a vast environmental renovation if they are to be made sustainable. This task of ecological renovation can align with many pressing social imperatives in our urban regions. For example, the extensive commutes forced upon many households in Sydney by increasingly disconnected housing and labour sub-markets are a major source of social stress (Flood and Barbato 2005). This stress is doubtless at least partly responsible for the out-migration of professional and key workers from major metropolitan regions, especially Sydney. It is also a profound cause of ecological stress, with lengthy commutes driving up average vehicle journeys and thus greenhouse emissions. This is a complex problem that will need well resourced and decisive intervention across a range of fronts to achieve better jobs-housing balances across urban subregions, by improving housing affordability and public transport services and coverage. It is a task that surely extends beyond the competencies of state governments.

Towards a new urban regionalism?

Finally, it is hardly sensible to simply add a layer of federal-urban intervention without some finer tuning of multi-level governance of the cities. The admittedly limited history of national urban policy in Australia points to the vulnerability of interventions that are linked to a deeper ambition to transform federalism. And yet, the need for new regionally-based approaches to urban management seems evident given the complexity and scale of Australia's principal urban conurbations. The larger metropolitan areas, especially Sydney, Melbourne and Brisbane, are now set within extensive, multi-nucleated urban regions, that include formerly independent regional towns and even cities. Brisbane is part of a larger South East Queensland conurbation that includes Ipswich and the Sunshine and Gold Coasts. Sydney is increasingly seen as part of a larger, connected urban landscape that includes the Hunter and Illawarra regions. Effective management of these extensive urban regions invites some new thinking about regional governance. An expanding international literature has pointed to the heightened significance of metropolitan regions in the globalised economy and to the need for governance structures that can maintain their productivity and sustainability (Dodson and Gleeson 2003).

An opportunity exists to respond to these global imperatives, and to the increasingly manifest sustainability pressures on Australia's cities, through the creation of new structures to manage urban regions. These new regional structures could focus on urban management, without becoming urban governments. They would have some governance qualities, if supervised by elected state and local government representatives, but no direct political authority or responsibilities. The governance of new regional urban management bodies would be strengthened by representation from the Commonwealth, which would also contribute funding. A precedent for this model existed in the cooperative processes that coordinated planning in South East Queensland (SEQ) during the 1990s. Until superseded by a new state based framework in 2005, the *SEQ Regional Framework for Growth Management* was a governance partnership involving the Queensland State Government, the South East Queensland Regional Organisation of Councils and the Commonwealth. Whilst it lacked the directive powers needed for sound urban management, and which now exist in the framework that replaced it, the *SEQ Regional Framework* pointed to the possibilities for cooperative urban regional governance, involving all three tiers of Australian Government. This chapter concludes by briefly considering what a new approach to urban regional governance might look like.

A range of urban commentators and urban advocacy groups believe that responsibility for everyday urban management should be shifted from state governments to new metropolitan planning authorities, preferably with direct representation from local government. Mark Spiller, president of the Planning Institute of Australia, argues that the States are in a better position than they have been in for a long time to undertake large-scale urban interventions (Spiller 2005a). Their fiscal independence and strength has been greatly enhanced by the GST revenue they now receive from the Commonwealth. Leaving aside the inequity of the specific tax in question, the situation demonstrates the opportunities for improved governance generally when the lower levels of government (state and municipal) are guaranteed some measure of fiscal autonomy; minimising the possibilities for blame and cost shifting between political layers. Spiller argues that the States and territories should use their newfound strength to increase their investment in cities and to effect improvements to urban governance.

The Planning Institute of Australia has proposed new metropolitan planning commissions with a clear and well-resourced brief to manage the cities sustainability and in the collective interest (Spiller 2005b). This would contrast very favourably with the present situation, too often marked by weak or under-resourced state planning departments that leave urban management largely to state road agencies and ill-equipped local governments.

In the governance model proposed by the Planning Institute, the States would continue to provide overall policy guidance on urban and regional affairs, whilst the new metropolitan authorities would undertake everyday management, including planning, in a much less politicised context. The authorities would need to be well-resourced and able to undertake the sorts of urban improvements our cities urgently need, especially in the face of mounting sustainability pressures. The Institute envisages a substantial injection of Commonwealth funds to support the projects of urban improvement by new metropolitan authorities.

The Melbourne Metropolitan Board of Works (1891-1991) provides one example (minus the federal support) of the broad urban governance model that the PIA has in mind. During its century-long tenure, this institution arguably provided some of the best periods of urban management witnessed in Australia. The Board was an effective, if imperfect, model of cooperative urban governance, based upon direct representation from the municipal layer over which it presided.[5]

Ultimately, state governments could greatly improve their management of the cities without transforming their governance arrangements in the manner suggested by the Planning Institute. As Parkin observed some time ago:

> … the development of coherent urban policy is not necessarily dependent on largesse of funds. It requires, more importantly, a consciousness of the urban dimension, of the interdependent forces at work within cities, of the distributive impacts of public policy in housing, transportation, public health, welfare, education, urban planning, employment and so on. *It is as much a question of policy orientation, policy priorities and policy organisation as of budgetary capability* (1982:82, emphasis added).

These insightful comments underline how much could be done to improve the governance of Australia's urban regions, if state governments simply gave higher priority to urban policy and approached its objects with imagination and energy. In the decades that have passed since Parkin's observations were recorded, there has been little evidence that state governments are willing to apply his advice consistently. This suggests that the independent metropolitan commission model has substantial practical merit. Further, the cumulative effects of prolonged under-investment in urban infrastructure and services, together with the new challenges arising from globalisation and ecological threat, mean that substantial national investment in the cities is both necessary and urgently required.

There is substantial merit in the Planning Institute's (2005) accompanying proposal for a new national urban investment fund, which the metro-authorities would draw from – perhaps competitively. Importantly, management of the fund would be guided by sustainability principles, not simply by the contemporary obsession with infrastructure enhancement. The political economist, Frank Stilwell (2006), argues that that these funds should come, at least in part, from the enormous pool of superannuation resources that are, arguably, not presently being put to the best use we might make of them.

Overall, this restructuring should work to clarify and make more effective the governance of our cities rather than making that critical task more complex. It is hard to imagine it ever happening without the Commonwealth recommitting itself to a direct interest in the cities and urban regions. As argued earlier, there are no real barriers outside the realms of political preference to the Commonwealth's re-entry into urban affairs. And within the realms of the political, it is perhaps as Parkin observed for the States, only a lack of ambition and imagination that continues to stymie this most vital national endeavour.

References

Burnley, I. and P. Murphy, 2003, *Sea Change: Movement from Metropolitan to Arcadian Australia*, UNSW Press, Sydney.

Davies, A. 2006, 'The Great Carr Crash', *The Sydney Morning Herald*, 9 February.

Dodson, J. and B.J. Gleeson, 2003, 'New planning governance for Sydney: lessons from other contexts', *Australian Planner*, 40(1), 32-39

Flood, M. and C. Barbato, 2005, *Off to Work: Commuting in Australia, Discussion Paper no.78*, The Australia Institute, Canberra.

Forster, C. 2004, *Australian Cities: continuity and change*, 3rd edition, Oxford University Press, Melbourne.

———— 2006, 'The challenge of change: Australian cities and urban planning in the new millennium', *Geographical Research*, 44(2), 173-182.

Gleeson, B. J. 2006, *Australian Heartlands: making space for hope in the suburbs*, Allen & Unwin, Sydney.

House of Representatives 2005, *Sustainable Cities*, Standing Committee on Environment and Heritage, Commonwealth of Australia, Canberra.

McManus, P. 2005, *Vortex Cities to Sustainable Cities: Australia's urban challenge*, UNSW Press, Sydney.

Newman, P. 2006, 'Transport crisis demands a radical new plan', *The Sydney Morning Herald*, 7 March.

Orchard, L. 1985, 'National urban policy in the 1980s' in P. Troy (ed.) *Australian Cities: issues, strategies and policies for urban Australia in the 1990s*, Cambridge, Melbourne, pp.65-86.

Parkin, A. 1982, *Governing the Cities: the Australian Experience*, Macmillan, Melbourne.

Planning Institute of Australia 2005, '10 point plan for Commonwealth engagement in sustainable cities and regions', accessed at www.planning.org.au

Property Council of Australia 2002, *Recapitalising Australia's Cities: a strategy in the national interest*, PCA National Office, Sydney.

Spiller, M. 2005a, 'Unclogging our cities is the next step', *The Australian Financial Review*, 9 June.

———— 2005b, 'What's required for a sustainable Melbourne?', Paper presented to the 'Sustainable Cities' forum convened by Green Capital 2nd June, Hilton Hotel, Melbourne.

Stilwell, F. 2006, 'Vulnerability in the Australian city: towards security and sustainability?', paper presented at Vulnerability in the Australian City symposium, Griffith University, Brisbane, 5 May.

Sydney Morning Herald 2005, 'The Sydney we deserve', editorial feature, 4 June.

Troy, P. 1978, *Federal power in Australia's cities: essays in honour of Peter Till*, Hale & Iremonger, Sydney.

ENDNOTES

[1] Some passages of text in this chapter are taken from my recent book, *Australian Heartlands: making space for hope in the suburbs* (Gleeson, 2006)

[2] In Forster (2004:3). Anti-urbanism was of course rife in nineteenth-century Europe and its new worlds. In the United States, Thomas Jefferson (1743-1826) declared, 'The mobs of great cities add just so much to the support of pure government as sores do to the strength of the human body'. What is distinctive about Australia's anti-urbanism is our deeply embedded tendency to deny that we are even urban.

[3] Many of these initiatives, such as the Land Commission Program, outlasted the Whitlam Government.

[4] I am grateful to Patrick Troy AO who helped me to compose this list

[5] Although, as Parkin (1982) observes, the quality of municipal representation was degraded in the latter years of the Board's existence.

Chapter 6: The Challenge of Coastal Governance

Mike Berwick

Introduction

The challenge for reform of regional governance within the Australian federal system, facing all of Australia, is especially sharpened in coastal communities. In these communities, increasing social, economic and environmental pressures associated with unprecedented levels of population growth and increasing levels of international and domestic tourism, all make the policy and service demands on government and communities particularly pressing and complex (NSCT 2006). The movement of people to the coast is a national issue impacting on coastal communities in every Australian State and Territory, and it is gathering pace.

Based on Australian Bureau of Statistics data, it is estimated that Australian coastal areas outside the major metropolitan areas of Australia's capital cities support more than 5.5 million people (NSCT 2006). In other words, 75% of Australia's non-metropolitan population is living in coastal areas. Moreover, these areas also continue to experience the most prominent growth in population (ABS 2007). This rapid population growth coupled with growth in tourism is impacting significantly on existing coastal communities through a variety of complex social, economic and environmental issues (Salt 2004; Burnley and Murphy 2004; Gurran et al 2005, 2006; Smith and Doherty 2006). These include:

- increasing demand for infrastructure, community facilities, public transport and human services;
- impacts of coastal development on the environment;
- social and economic impacts on the identity and character of coastal communities;
- difficulty of establishing a sustainable economic base for local communities;
- housing affordability; and
- lack of, and difficulty in attracting, human and financial resources to deal with emerging issues.

These issues brought together the CEOs of 27 high-growth coastal councils in February 2004, to a 'Sea Change Summit' to talk about the common problems they faced in relation to rapid growth in coastal areas. As an outcome of this meeting, the National Sea Change Taskforce (NSCT) was formally constituted at a meeting in Canberra in November 2004, involving more than 60 participating councils. It is still a very young organisation. The issues that brought the Councils together are all related to the impact of high growth rates on coastal communities, but it was evident that the dysfunctional system of governance that we currently have for coastal regions was central to the problem. More than a decade ago, the Resource Assessment Commission's (RAC) Coastal Zone Inquiry report identified major resource management problems in the coastal zone and the need for a national approach to improve management arrangements and meet these challenges (RAC 1993).

The NSCT believes there is an urgent need for a national response to rapid coastal development (NSCT 2006). It advocates a national policy framework and governance structure capable of delivering a triple bottom line outcome for coastal communities. Significantly, the local government sector is driving the NSCT agenda – not the State/Territory and Australian governments. The reason for this is twofold: first, in the face of the confused jurisdictional issues involved, there is a lack of political will, at both State/Territory and Australian Government levels, to deal effectively with coastal issues; and secondly, it is local governments, mostly small ones, that are confronted directly with the consequences of these issues on a daily basis.

This chapter examines these issues for coastal communities in the context of the disjointed nature of the current federal, state and local system of governance. It highlights the complex impacts of high growth rates on coastal communities, and the critical role of local government, and it explores some priorities for a more responsive federal-regional-local system of governance that embodies participatory democracy principles.

Growth pressures on coastal communities

Rapid population growth rates: amenity migration

Although not all coastal regions are growing and a few are even experiencing a decline in population (such as Port Pirie and Port Augusta in South Australia), overall population growth rates in coastal Local Government Authorities (LGAs) are consistently high in proportional and numerical terms (ABS 2004a, 2004b, 2007; Burnley and Murphy 2004). In fact, the rate of growth in many coastal LGAs is equivalent to or higher than that of metropolitan areas (ABS 2004a). In recent years, many LGAs have experienced growth rates in the range of 50% to 60% higher than the national average. For example, in the year to June 2004 the rate of growth in coastal LGAs was 2%, which is 60% higher than the national average growth rate of 1.2% (NSCT 2006).

Described in Australia as 'the big shift' (e.g. Salt 2004) or the 'sea change' phenomenon (e.g. Burnley and Murphy 2004; Smith and Doherty 2006), these rates are expected to continue for the next 10 to 15 years, driven in part due to the 'baby boomer' generation reaching retirement age and 'by factors such as the rapid increase in house prices in capital cities and a desire by many people to seek a better lifestyle away from the congestion of the cities' (NSCT 2006). Significantly, in Australia, this phenomenon is underpinned by fundamental social and economic changes which create significant planning challenges (Gurran et al 2005, 2006).

Australia's coastal areas offer an attractive quality of life and an appealing environment for people to live. The movement to locations that offer leisure opportunities and an attractive environment is known internationally as 'amenity migration' (Gurran et al 2005). People are moving to these areas because of lifestyle considerations rather than to specifically improve their financial circumstances. Other factors influencing people's decision to migrate, identified in the literature, are personal circumstances (e.g. social networks) coupled with cultural factors (e.g. perceptions about a particular place and sense of connection to 'reference groups' within it) (Stimson and Minnery 1998; Gurran et al 2005).

Population growth in Australian coastal areas is expected to continue for the foreseeable future due to several factors, including (Gurran et al 2006):

- the imminent retirement of the 'baby boomer' generation, which will produce a sizeable new market for high amenity retirement destinations;
- the global shift away from manufacturing-based economies towards information, service and consumption-based industries which are less dependent on a metropolitan location; and
- the growing flexibility of work practices associated with new telecommunications technology, which enables some workers to relocate to small coastal centres or the rural hinterland.

The growing number of people making the move to coastal communities for lifestyle reasons is now challenging traditional theories that people relocate mainly for economic considerations – which has generated most previous migrations. Moreover, the migration is not to a single destination, but to a large number of smaller and scattered destinations making it difficult or impossible for government to meet the infrastructure and service expectations and demands of this expanding population.

Tourism

Many of Australia's coastal areas are experiencing not only unprecedented population growth, but they are also attempting to deal with a rapid growth in tourism. Tourism is predicted to become our largest export earner in the next couple of years – and on many estimates will increase in revenue by 50% by the year 2020. It will be the coastal LGAs that bear the brunt of the impact of this growth. Beyond the pressures of amenity migration, tourism places additional demands on coastal communities through, for example:

- the use of infrastructure and services; and

- the impacts on the environment especially in vulnerable areas (e.g. arising from nature-based tourism and increased visitor numbers in coastal areas during summer months) (Ward and Butler 2006).

Obviously, tourism brings an economic benefit to local commercial operators and helps to generate employment opportunities in a region. But, while visitors generate revenue for local economies, they do not contribute to the cost of public infrastructure they use, such as roads, water, sewerage treatment, waste collection and recreation facilities. There is simply no mechanism for capturing tourism expenditure as a contribution to these services. Whenever anybody mentions something as radical as a bed tax, or a local tourism levy, or some other means of generating revenue to provide the infrastructure that is needed by visitors, there is an outcry from the tourism industry. So, the burden of expanding and maintaining infrastructure to meet the increasing demands of Australia's second biggest industry inevitably falls on local ratepayers. This is just one example of the issues affecting local government financing, which is the subject of the recent report by the House of Representatives Standing Committee on Economics, Finance and Public Administration on 'Rates and Taxes: A Fair Share for Responsible Local Government' (Commonwealth of Australia 2003). The report makes the case that local government is under-resourced and is not achieving a fair share of taxation revenue. In addition, the more recent NSCT 'Meeting the Sea Change Challenge' study (Gurran et al 2005, 2006) and the State of Environment paper on 'Local Government in environment and heritage management' (Wild River 2006) also identify infrastructure shortfalls and lack of capacity to fund them through existing funding sources as critical issues impacting on coastal councils.

In 2004, it is estimated that domestic and international visitors spent about $20 billion purely on recreation and tourism activities directly involving coastal and ocean ecosystems (DEWR 2006). Tourism therefore is generating enormous revenue for State and Federal Governments (e.g. capital gains tax, GST and stamp duty) but this revenue is not flowing through to local government authorities, which are bearing most of the financial burden of tourism. For example, the national accounts for 2002- 2003 show that total tourism consumption from both domestic and international tourism in that year amounted to more than $73 billion dollars (ABS 2004b). GST revenues to the States and Territories generated by that expenditure was around $6.7 billion. But the local government share of that taxation revenue is virtually nothing. The money generated by tourism is not being spent on maintaining the assets, so that eventually, of course, this will be counterproductive. How many tourists will want to revisit an area where the environment is trashed, traffic is at a standstill, the local water or sewerage systems are failing, and the social indicators are declining?

Sea change communities: a social transition

The motivating factors influencing this 'sea change' phenomenon have led to the emergence of considerable diversity in the types of communities developing in coastal regions around Australia, each with their own particular problems and needs. For example, five different profiles of coastal communities outside the Australian capital cities are (Gurran et al 2005; ABS 2004b):

1. coastal commuters: suburbanised satellite communities in peri-metropolitan locations within easy daily commuting of a capital city (for example, Wollongong, Gosford, Wyong and Port Stephens near Sydney, Pine Rivers and Caboolture near Brisbane, Casey and Lorne near Melbourne, Wanneroo, Mandurah, Rockingham and GinGin near Perth and Onkaparinga near Adelaide);

2. coastal getaways: small to medium coastal towns within approximately a three-hour drive of a capital city for day tripping and easy weekend access to a holiday home (for example, Bunbury and Busselton in south-west Western Australia, Bass Coast and Surf Coast in Victoria, and Victor Harbour in South Australia);

3. coastal cities: substantial and predominantly continuous regional urban conurbations beyond the State capitals (for example, Cairns, the Gold Coast, Sunshine Coast in Queensland, Greater Geelong in Victoria and Albany in Western Australia);

4. coastal lifestyle destinations: predominantly tourism and leisure communities generally more than three hours drive from capital sities (for example, Coffs Harbour, Byron Bay and Hasting shires in New South Wales, Whitsunday area in central Queensland, and Moyne in Victoria); and

5. coastal hamlets: small and remote coastal communities which may often be adjacent to protected natural areas (for example, Robe and Grant in the Limestone Coast area, S.A., Augusta-Margaret River area and Broome in WA, Douglas Shire and Agnes Waters in Queensland and Bellingen in New South Wales.).

Moreover, Curran et al (2005) argue that the sea change phenomenon impacting on these diverse community types does not necessarily lead to sustainable economic growth or improved socio-economic outcomes for local populations. The growth in coastal communities is associated predominantly with the creation of new jobs in lower paid occupational categories within the retail, restaurants, tourism and care-giving sectors. Such sectoral jobs are commonly part-time and many may be subject to seasonal fluctuations. Moreover, Australian coastal communities outside the capital cities have the highest proportion of low-income households, the highest proportion of families receiving income support benefits, the highest median age and highest 'elderly dependency' of Australia (Curran et al 2005). Thus, coastal communities are experiencing significant pressures not only on their social identity and character but also on their economic and environmental sustainability.

Many coastal councils have not anticipated this substantive and rapid growth in their planning and now find they do not have the human or financial resources to deal with the continuous increase in demand for infrastructure (such as roads, mains water supply, sewerage and power) or for essential services (such as public transport, health care, emergency services and education facilities) (NSCT 2006). This is a national issue requiring the urgent support and cooperation of both State and Federal Governments in identifying solutions to the complex challenges associated with coastal growth.

Coastal governance: a dysfunctional system?

The sea change phenomenon is symptomatic of a larger malaise. We have a particularly dysfunctional system of government in Australia – the 'federal-state-local' system with its complex and chaotic mix of institutional arrangements and related roles and responsibilities. As Gurran et al (2006, p.6) point out:

> Due to the environmental and strategic significance of the coast, sea change localities are subject to complex, cross jurisdictional planning and management processes relating to coastal management and protection, heritage conservation, natural resource management and utilisation, defence, and land use planning and development. Like other amenity areas endowed by highly significant natural and cultural heritage values, coastal communities are often subject to additional planning or policy requirements at state, national, and even international levels.

The blockage to better planning and the sustainable use of coastal resources is primarily an institutional one – a multitude of State/Territory and Commonwealth Government agencies, advisory bodies, statutory bodies, NGOs, regional Natural Resource Management bodies, Catchment Management Authorities, Coastal Councils and so on, all supported by reports, plans, strategies, and scattered discordant policies and legislation. As Smith and Doherty (2006, pp.6-7) identify:

> … it is possible for a range of statutory and non-statutory instruments relating to land use and environmental planning to be administered independently by any of the three tiers of government. Adding to this complexity is the nature of many planning instruments that are specific to an issue or sector, thus creating conflicting goals within and between institutions.

> Similarly, with the emergence of regional governance in Australia, there has been the creation of more institutional complexity and disconnects in some coastal areas.

With the emergence of 'new' regional governance in the last couple of decades in Australia (see Brown this volume; Bellamy this volume), there has been increasing institutional complexity that lacks any semblance of coherence. For example, the new national regional governance arrangements for natural resource management are commonly developed independently of coastal planning, regional growth management frameworks, and local government regional collective arrangements such as Regional Organisations of Councils (e.g. Smith and Doherty 2006). In this complex system of coastal governance, roles and responsibilities vertically across levels of government and horizontally across actors at each level are not clearly defined and frequently conflicting. Significantly,

- There is no clear demarcation of responsibility on major issues – health, education, environment, transport, and so on. For example, aged care is supposedly a Commonwealth responsibility, but in the Douglas Shire it is being shed to the State through the development of a Multi Purpose Health Centre. Now that the Council has bought land for this initiative, an expenditure well outside its core business, it is being blamed for the initiative not happening;
- There is waste and duplication. Notably, with the exception of defence and foreign policy, for every state function there is a corresponding federal function, with no clear boundaries;
- There is a duplication of bureaucracies (e.g. between spheres of government and amongst individual states and territories);
- The co-ordination of policy is poor, and integration is minimal;
- Blame shifting and cost shifting is rife; and
- We do not have national policy on key issues instead there are seven state/territory policies on each one.

Notwithstanding, there are some good regional initiatives like the *SEQ Regional Plan* linking infrastructure to long term land use planning in south-east Queensland (OUM 2005), and the Victorian Government's *Coastal Spaces Plan* fixing the urban footprint (DSE 2005). However, these initiatives are the exception rather than the rule, and highlight the lack of any national approach. Much of the migration is across state boundaries and therefore it cannot be dealt with in isolation by different states.

In 2006, the NSCT released the findings of a second research report it commissioned on the pressures facing Australian coastal regions, which highlights the need for a collaborative national response to the challenge of coastal growth. This report, *Meeting The Sea Change Challenge: Best Practice Models of Local and Regional Planning for Sea Change Communities* (Gurran et al 2005; 2006) documents the range of governance, environmental, community, economic, and infrastructure challenges affecting 'sea change' councils in Australia. The report identifies best practice planning models. These are reasonably obvious, and the sorts of thing with which everyone would agree, but which cannot be implemented by local governments in isolation under current legislative and institutional arrangements. There is a community will across Australia to sustainably manage the coastline. There is sufficient knowledge about how to deal with these issues. But there is no pathway to the adoption or delivery of national policy. The problem is often the failure to adopt and apply existing knowledge rather than the lack of it. Of course, disjointed planning and governance is not unique to coastal settings.

The Sea Change Best Practice report refers to calls for more integrated approaches to environmental management across ecologically, rather than administratively defined territories. These approaches include forms of 'catchment' and 'ecosystem' management, or bioregional planning, all of which have emerged in Australia over the past two decades. It is happening to some extent with regional natural resource management bodies (e.g. see Bellamy this volume; Head this volume), which is a very interesting experiment in regional governance emerging across Australia – although perhaps a little threatening to the States and Territories in some instances. Notwithstanding, as Gurran et al (2006, p.7) identify:

> At the national level in Australia, a 'Framework for a National Cooperative Approach to Integrated Coastal Zone Management' has been developed by the Natural Resource Management Ministerial Council. An important initiative, the framework identifies five issues for national collaboration: land and marine based sources of pollution, managing climate change, introduced pest plants and animals, allocation and use of coastal resources and capacity building. However, the framework does not extend to co-operative policy across agencies or jurisdictions making or strategic planning for the coast, despite the fact that this is frequently an area in which different state and Commonwealth jurisdictions collide.

So, if there is a lack coherence and consistency about jurisdictional arrangements for the coast, what is the answer? Gurran et al (2006) recommend a national level strategic framework, articulating overall objectives in line with the national and international values associated with the coastal zone. They also recommend that such a strategic framework should provide a basis for coordinating policy-making and land use planning on coastal areas with the other national interests and responsibilities that impact on coastal development (such as environmental protection and heritage, management of territorial waters, infrastructure provision and regional economic development).

A way forward?

Is there a model that could be used to guide such a framework? Yes, there is. For example, the *New Zealand Resource Management Act 1991* potentially provides a good model for the national coordination of coastal policy and planning with broader resource management and land use decisions at national, regional and local levels. However, the New Zealand system of government is not bedeviled by the same tripartite arrangement that we have here in Australia, with Commonwealth, state and local spheres of government.

In addition, research is showing that up to three-quarters of people surveyed in Queensland and New South Wales are not happy with the current three-tier system of government, and want the system changed (see Gray and Brown this volume). These surveys also suggest that the most popular option is to abolish state governments and create a two-tier structure of government. As Dr Brown has commented, such a system would see the Federal Government take over stronger policy responsibilities for key services, like health, with delivery of services at a community level necessarily occurring on a more local and regional basis. For many this resonates with suggestions made more than 30 years ago by the Whitlam government, which proposed growth in the federal government and started investing directly in regional bodies between the scale of the current state and local government tiers.

The States and Territories, however, would find some kind of federal/regional/local system difficult, because they would cease to exist. So, probably, would local governments, because they too would need fundamental and far-reaching reform. While there is growing support for this sort of framework, the pathway to adoption and the details are wide open. A few principles that could be signed off on, are:

- the federal/state/local government tripartite system is wasteful, ineffective and divisive;
- we are one country, so we need national policy on key issues – education, health, environment, infrastructure etc.;
- regardless of issue or sector, service and policy delivery has always ended up being regional in nature, but based on different boundaries and different institutional arrangements for different issues;
- there is a need for reform in practical 'bite size chunks', which allow for regional variation (one size never fits all), and which empowers and engages local communities; and
- finally, we need to move from representational to participatory democracy at the regional level.

Applying these principles, we might begin to see a proposed framework for addressing the dysfunctional state of regional governance in coastal Australia. Its first element would be that the Australian Government should raise the necessary taxes and set the necessary policies for managing this population growth, at a national level. Secondly, however, the regions should engage the community in the process of tailoring the national programs to suit local needs, feeding policy advice back up to the Australian Government, and delivering the actual programs and services.

The third element of this framework would see state and territory government phased out of any direct responsibility for regional coastal governance, and possibly phased out altogether. The fourth element, however, is that the framework of regional and local government would need to be redesigned to foster more effective participatory democracy – that is, styles of governance which better empower people to have some influence over their lives and their own areas, within the national framework.

This broad framework immediately requires a huge amount of research, options and discussion. The details to be worked out include the broad national policies; the distribution of tax income to regions; clarity about roles and responsibilities; how to engage regional communities and foster this participatory democracy; whether to rely on slow evolution or sudden change; and how to align the existing regional boundaries – in health, education, environment, transport and so on.

How to get there? This is the real question. We live with the reality of a federal system in which the Constitution continues to be built on and to protect the position of state governments, to at least some extent. Removing them is difficult. For these reasons, we need to think creatively, and acknowledge that even when we see our problems as lying in part with our current constitutional structure, at least some of the answers may well lie within it. For example, the Australian Constitution allows for a lot more states to be created, with less constitutional barriers. So the path to an effective federal/ regional/ local framework may be to go from our present eight states and territories, to 50 or 60 states and territories, and call these 'regions'. When it comes to more effective regional governance for coastal Australia, the ideology and terminology we use to describe the result matters far less than the practical workability of the outcome.

References

Australian Bureau of Statistics (ABS) 2004a, *Australian Social Trends: Population Seachange – New Coastal Residents*, Commonwealth of Australia, Canberra. Viewed 10 November 2006. http://www.abs.gov.au/ausstats/abs@.nsf/cat/4102.0

——— 2004b, 'How many people live in Australia's coastal areas?' In *Year Book Australia*, Catalogue No. 1301.0, Commonwealth of Australia. Viewed 8 March 2007. http://www.abs.gov.au/ausstats/abs@.nsf/cat/1301.0

——— 2007, *Regional Population Growth, Australia, 2005-06*. Catalogue No. 3218.0. Released 27/02/2007. Viewed 12/03/2007. http://www.abs.gov.au/AUSSTATS/abs@.nsf/productsbyCatalogue/797F86DBD192B8F8CA2568A9001393CD?OpenDocument

Burnley, I. and P. Murphy, 2003, *Seachange: Movement from metropolitan to arcadian Australia*. UNSW Press, Sydney.

Department of Environment and Water Resources 2006, 'External pressures on human settlements – Tourism' in *2006 Australia State of the Environment*, Department of Environment and Water Resources, Canberra, Viewed 09/03/2007. http://www.environment.gov.au/soe/2006/publications/drs/settlements/issue/157/index.html

Department of Sustainability and Environment (DSE) 2005, *Coastal Spaces: Inception Report*. May 2005. Victorian Government DSE, Melbourne.

Gurran, N., C. Squires, and E. Blakley, 2005, Meeting the Sea Change Challenge: Sea Change Communities in Coastal Australia. Executive Summary. The University of Sydney Planning Research Centre, Sydney. Viewed 13 November 2006. http://www.seachangetaskforce.org.au/Publications/publication.html

———— 2005, *Meeting the sea change challenge: Sea Change Communities in Coastal Australia*. Report for the National Seachange Taskforce, March 2005. The University of Sydney Planning Research Centre, Sydney.

———— 2006, *Meeting the sea change challenge: Best Practice Models of Local and Regional Planning for Sea Change Communities in Coastal Australia*. Report No. 2 for the National Seachange Taskforce. The University of Sydney Planning Research Centre, Sydney.

National Sea Change Taskforce (NSCT) 2006, *The challenge of coastal growth*. Viewed 10 November 2006. http://www.seachangetaskforce.org.au/Publications/publication.html

Office of Urban Management (OUM) 2005, *The South East Queensland Regional Plan 2005-2026*. June 2005. Queensland Government, Department of Local Government, Planning, Sports and Recreation: The State of Queensland. Viewed 08/02/2007. http://www.oum.qld.gov.au/?id=29

Resource Assessment Commission (RAC) 1993, *Resource Assessment Commission Coastal Zone Inquiry – Final Report*. Department of Environment and Heritage, Canberra.

Salt, B. 2004, *The Big Shift: Welcome to the Third Australian Culture*. 2nd edition. Hardy Grant Books, South Yarra, Victoria.

Smith, T. and M. Doherty, 2006, 'The suburbanisation of coastal Australia', Paper prepared for the 2006 Australia State of the Environment, Department of Environment and Water Resources, Canberra, Viewed 09/03/2007, http://www.deh.gov.au/soe/2006/integrative/coastal/index.html

Stimson, R. and S. Minnery, 1998, 'Why people move to the 'Sun-belt': A case study of long distance migration to the Gold Coast, Australia', *Urban Studies* 35(2): 193-214.

The Parliament of the Commonwealth of Australia 2003, *Rates and Taxes: A Fair Share for Responsible Local Government*. House of Representatives Standing Committee on Economics, Finance and Public Administration, October 2003, Canberra.

Ward, T.J. and A. Butler, 2006, 'Coasts and Oceans' in *Australia State of the Environment* (SOE) Committee, Department of Environment and Water Resources, Canberra. Viewed 09/03/2007. http://www.environment.gov.au/soe/2006/publications/commentaries/coasts/contributions.html

Wild River S. 2006, 'The role of local government in environmental and heritage management', paper prepared for the 2006 Australia State of the Environment Committee, Department of Environment and Heritage, Canberra. Viewed 09/03/2007, http://www.deh.gov.au/soe/2006/integrative/local-government/index.html

Chapter 7: Adaptive Governance: The Challenge for Regional Natural Resource Management

Jennifer Bellamy

Introduction

Concern for the sustainability of our interdependent social and natural systems is growing exponentially in policy and science arenas, both nationally and internationally, as exemplified by recent policy statements and debates on major environmental issues such as global climate change (e.g. Stern 2006; Cosier 2006; Environment Business Australia 2004), water use and management in Australia (e.g. The Wentworth Group 2003, 2006; NWC 2006) and the health of our natural ecosystems (e.g. Australian SOE Committee 2006; Morton et al 2003; Millennium Ecosystem Assessment 2005). Human induced changes are having significant impacts on our natural resources with major implications for issues such as social and economic development, sustainable livelihoods and environmental management. Peri-urbanisation, the growth of urban populations and the increase in rural non-farm economic activities are all part of a global transition that is rapidly reshaping not only our social systems but the pattern of land use and related pressures on our natural resources[1]. Diamond (2005) frames the problem in a recent book through a rhetorical question:

> Australia illustrates in extreme form the exponentially accelerating horse race in which the world now finds itself ... On the one hand, the development of environmental problems in Australia, as in the whole world, is accelerating exponentially. On the other hand, the development of public environmental concern, and of private and public countermeasures, is also accelerating exponentially. Which horse will win the race? (p. 415-416)

This paper explores the complexity of natural resource governance within the framework of sustainable development and identifies challenges to an effective, legitimate and adaptive approach in practice. It considers prospects for more adaptive regional governance frameworks within the Australian federal system to address the accelerating and long-term challenges of the sustainability of our interconnected social and natural systems.

Sustainability: an evolving policy concept

Sustainability[2] as an over-riding goal for society in general is arguably one of the greatest challenges currently facing human society. It is a complex, ambiguous and often contested concept which has generated much debate in the academic and political literature. As a concept, its focal emphasis has evolved over time. The contemporary interpretation of sustainability as an integrative concept encompassing the so-called 'triple bottom line' of environmental integrity, economic vitality and social cohesion evolved in Australian policy arenas in the 1990s (e.g. Commonwealth of Australia 1992; AFFA 1999; Bellamy and Johnson 2000; MDBMC 2001; Dovers and Wild River 2003). This interpretation places strong emphasis on:

- the interconnectedness of the triple bottom line dimensions;
- the long term nature of problem framing and of the related policy processes needed to address these three dimensions in tandem;
- equity, both within contemporary society (intragenerational) and in terms of the legacy of future generations (intergenerational); and
- the urgency of the need for action.

The 'triple bottom line' dimensions of sustainability are fundamental to progress towards Australia's preferred and sustainable future but they require considerable change in policy and institutional systems and structures.

Significantly, from local to global scales, linked social and natural systems do not respond to change in 'smooth' linear ways rather they are dynamic and characterised by accelerating complexity, uncertainty, disorganisation and irregular or sudden changes that are multilevel, difficult to predict and potentially irreversible or very difficult and costly to manage (e.g. Gunderson and Holling 2003; Berkes et al 2003). Moreover the multifunctional character of our interconnected social and natural systems involves multiple, but often conflicting, benefits (such as water supply, recreation, commerce, human health, ecosystem services), which are linked to a multiplicity of stakeholders (across governments, industry and community) with diverse and plural values, responsibilities and agendas, which may themselves be conflicting.

Contemporary interpretations emphasise sustainability as a process and a means to an end, rather than an end in or of itself. For example, Holling (2001) argues that:

> Sustainability is the capacity to create, test, and maintain adaptive capacity. Development is the process of creating, testing and maintaining opportunity. The phrase that combines the two, 'sustainable development', thus refers to the goal of fostering capabilities and creating opportunities (p. 390).

It is argued that for societies to deal with and shape change, they require 'adaptive capacity' based on shared understanding and management power through collaboration and partnerships that foster adaptation and learning (e.g. Berkes et al 2003; Folke et al 2005). Importantly such adaptive capacity resides in actors, social networks and institutions as well as ecosystems. This concept of adaptive capacity emphasises the ability of underpinning systems to adapt to or compensate for on-going transformative processes rather than just the ability of management approaches to maintain existing systems. As such, sustainability is as much about the flexibility and adaptive capacity of our underlying social and natural systems as it is about the ability of actors to manage change. Governance considerations are therefore central to an adaptive process.

Coupled with a perceived failure of top down governmental command-and-control approaches to resolving many natural resource issues, this shift in interpretation has led to increasing calls for new and more 'adaptive governance' of interconnected social and natural systems (e.g. Folke et al 2005; Scholz and Stiftel 2005; Howlett and Raynor 2006). A new generation of governance institutions is being experimented with by governments worldwide to address diverse issues relating to the uncertainties and dynamism of changing social and natural systems (e.g. Bellamy and Johnson 2000; Bellamy et al 2002; Innes and Boher 2003; Lebel et al 2006). These issues include: policy coordination and coherence; multidimensional and inequitable policy impacts (i.e. equity and social justice); power sharing; legitimacy (i.e. procedural justice and social acceptability); incomplete knowledge, technical uncertainty and ignorance; conflicting values and priorities; and urgency of response.

Addressing sustainability: through a natural resource management lens

In Australia, the current system and pattern of use and management of our natural resources has developed over a long period during times when people commonly considered these resources as largely unlimited in terms of capacity for productive use and when beliefs in people's rights to use their land as they wished were particularly dominant (e.g. Cocks 1992). For example Bates (2003) argues:

> The governmental approach to natural resource management has had to be applied in the context of a social system that hitherto placed few restrictions on the exploitation of natural resources by private owners. The common law effectively allowed landowners to do what they wished with their land and its resources, subject only to the right of other landowners not to be unreasonably interfered with by such use ... It remains true that the most significant environmental problems facing Australia today have also proved to be the hardest for governments to tackle because they force regulators to confront the traditional rights of

private landowners … Attempts to curb degradation and destruction of natural resources on private land however; for example, clearance of native vegetation and forests, land degradation and loss of biodiversity in general, have historically proved difficult to introduce, and have been inadequate in their coverage, implementation and enforcement. Water and fisheries reform have also had to grapple with the difficulties inherent in modifying or removing entitlements that over the years have come to be regarded as *de facto* property rights (p.279-280).

Institutional arrangements for managing our natural resources traditionally involve numerous individual, single-function federal and state agencies, each pursuing its own legal mandate through developing and implementing policy dominantly focused on single issues (such as sustainable production, water supply or nature conservation). Over some period of time, this system developed numerous natural resource policies and government incentives (e.g. encouraging land clearing for development) which often proved to have conflicting or unintended and environmentally-undesirable effects (e.g. ANAO 1997; The Senate Committee Inquiry 2004).

With growing recognition that the impacts of past resource use policy and practices are becoming socially, economically and environmentally unacceptable, the term 'natural resource management' (NRM) emerged in the mid to late 1990s in Australian national and state policy arenas as an integrative and systemic concept to address the complex sustainability issues of our interconnected social and natural systems. In 1999, a federal policy discussion paper on *Managing Natural Resources in Rural Australia for a Sustainable Future* on developing a national policy for natural resource management defined NRM as 'protecting, maintaining and enhancing natural resources in rural Australia to provide the basis for sustainable production, healthy ecosystems (including healthy rivers and estuaries) and viable rural communities' (AFFA 1999, p.1). It also clearly argues that 'policy approaches for NRM need to be applied in an integrated way across regions and catchments and at the local or farm levels' (AFFA 1999, p.1).

Governance for natural resource management

NRM as a wicked problem

NRM addresses issues where it is often unclear where responsibilities lie and where traditionally no one sphere of government, agency, institution, or group of individuals has sole jurisdictional responsibility, such that problem solving capacity is widely dispersed and few actors or decision-makers can accomplish their mission alone (Innes and Booher 2003; Bellamy et al 2002, 2005). In a pluralistic society, therefore, NRM policy problems are what Rittel and Webber (1973) refer to as 'wicked'; namely, problems that 'defy efforts to delineate their boundaries and to identify their causes, and thus expose their problematic nature'

(p. 167). Wicked problems are characterised by a number of inherent properties (Rittel and Webber 1973; Bellamy and Johnson 2000; Williams 2006). Firstly, they cannot be definitively described. Second, they do not respect fixed and conventional territorial or sectoral boundaries or spheres of government (i.e. bridge political, geographical and ideological boundaries). Third, they are persistent, complex, non-linear and irreversible and involve long time scales. Fourth, they are socially constructed and often disputed. Fifth, there are no optimal solutions or solutions with definitive and objective answers. Finally, they levy enormous costs and have broad consequences (social, economic, environmental).

Wicked NRM policy problems involve large and multifunctional spatial areas (i.e. rather than the use of a single resource by a local community), substantial institutional and organisational fragmentation, and require enduring and resourced collective responses across interdependent public, private and community sectors (e.g. Bellamy and Johnson 2000; Bellamy et al 2002; Connor and Dovers 2004). 'Collective action problems may occur because of a fragmented institutional setting that necessitates cooperation between a considerable number of actors with highly varying norms, interests and powers to act' (Saglie 2006, p. 9). Wicked problems therefore require coordination and cooperation across the horizontal and vertical dimensions of policy and institutional systems and structures including (e.g. Murray 2005, p. 28-29):

- horizontally across administrative boundaries;
- horizontally between agencies and departments within the same level of government when management components of a single natural system is fragmented between them;
- horizontally between government and non-government stakeholders who affect, or are affected by, natural resource management; and
- vertically when responsibility for management of the processes of an ecological or spatial natural unit rests with different levels of government and/or private actors.

Within the Australian federal system, wicked natural resource problems have profound implications for political problem framing and the design of credible and legitimate pathways towards sustainable futures. From local to global scales, the increasing and on-going challenges of wicked natural resource problems are imposing and their continuing emergence as fundamental political problems signifies the need for a new approach to their governance. Specifically, this paper argues these new approaches need to support the development of governance frameworks that encourage and support adaptation as our social and natural systems inevitably continue to evolve and change.

New NRM Governance: a response to a failed system?

The traditional hierarchical governmental institutions for NRM are increasingly identified as unable to cope with contemporary 'wicked' natural resource problems (e.g. Bellamy and Johnson 2000; Connor and Dovers 2004; Scholz and Stiftel 2005; Sabatier et al 2005). In the context of sustainability, there is also a growing recognition that government alone does not determine the future direction of sectors in society; these are shaped through the interaction of many actors. In response, there has been a global trend in government of devolving specific decision-making closer to its source or context and an emphasis on developing partnerships, strategic alliances, networks and broader consultation with those who are likely to be responsible for, or experience impacts from, decisions (Bellamy et al 2003; Brown this volume; Head this volume). As Eckersely (2003) argues:

> From a political perspective, ecological problems represent a major disjuncture in democratic accountability and control. This arises because there is no necessary connection between those who create ecological problems, those who have the expertise to understand them, those who suffer the negative consequences and those who must take political responsibility for them. If there is a general lesson from the eco-political literature, it is that many of these 'democratic deficits' in relation to political accountability and control may be remedied by new forms and styles of political communication which brings together as many disparate players as practicable (including culprits and beneficiaries, experts and laypeople, indigenous and 'settler' communities) into an open and constructive dialogue aimed at reaching broad social consensus (p. 492-3).

Stoker (1998) describes this global shift as 'the development of governing styles in which boundaries between and within public and private sectors have become blurred' (p. 17). The term 'governance' is a contested concept but it is increasingly used to signify this transition in patterns and processes of governing across a wide variety of policy areas (e.g. Stoker 1998; Bingham et al 2005; Swyngedouw 2005). Governance encompasses formal institutions of government and informal arrangements among government and non-government actors from the private sector and civil society (see Brown, this volume). In particular, governance is increasingly used within the NRM arena to refer to processes by which power is exercised and conflicts and interests are accommodated within an institutional context which emphasises participation, inclusiveness, deliberation and social and political learning. Three broad 'modes' of NRM governance commonly occur through (Bell and Park 2006):

- hierarchies (e.g. traditional forms of top-down control and regulation through the state);
- market-based forms of resource allocation; and

- networks (involving various forms of public-private collaboration).

Significantly, with the emergence of network governance and increasing community expectations for more participatory and inclusive governance arrangements, it is argued that the 'new institutional 'fixes' have begun to challenge traditional state-centred forms of policy-making and have generated new forms of governance-beyond-the-state' (Swyngedouw 2005, p. 1991). The term 'new governance' has emerged as a descriptor for this mode of governing (e.g. Howlett and Raynor 2006; Bingham et al 2005). The notion of complexity is key to understanding the perceived failures of traditional hierarchical modes and the emergence of these new more participatory and deliberative governance approaches.

Complexity and capacity

NRM governance is typically highly complex and characterised by (e.g. Bressers and Kuks 2003): multiple levels of policy implementation; multi-actor character of policy implementation; multiple perceptions of the problem and the objectives of policy implementation; multiple strategies and policy instruments for policy implementation; and a complex multi-resourced and multi-organisational basis for implementation of policy.

The complexity of these characteristics relates not only to the functioning and outcomes of linked natural and social systems but also to the capacity to subject them to adaptive administrative management. In the NRM arena, therefore, new governance approaches aim to address 'wicked' natural resource problems occurring within complex multilevel and multi-actor settings based on a more holistic approach to problem framing and policy implementation. They focus, in particular, on participation, deliberative processes, collaborative relationships, networks and consensus building processes that serve 'as mechanisms for cooperation and coordination among diverse and often rival participants in the policy process' (Bingham et al 2005, p.551). Folke et al (2005) point out that governance of linked social and natural systems 'generally involves polycentric institutional arrangements, which are nested quasi-autonomous decision-making units operating at multiple scales' (p. 449). These arrangements involve 'local, as well as higher, organisational levels and they aim at finding a balance between decentralised and centralised control' (Folke et al 2005). These complex governance systems have multiple centres or authorities and, although typically multilayered, they are not necessarily neatly hierarchical (Lebel et al 2006).

Expectations are high for the new more participatory and inclusive modes of NRM governance. For example, Bingham et al (2005) identify that:

> Advocates argue that new governance processes promote increased collaboration among government, business, civil society, and citizens; enhance democratic decision making; and foster decisional legitimacy,

consensus, citizen engagement, public dialogue, reasoned debate, higher decision quality, and fairness among an active and informed citizenry. They contend that these processes promote individual liberty while maintaining accountability for collective decisions; advance political equality while educating citizens; foster a better understanding of competing interests while contributing to citizen's moral development; and orient an atomised citizenry toward the collective good (p. 554).

Notwithstanding, there is considerable debate concerning their capacity to answer many of the pathologies of adversarial top-down policy systems and support a transition toward desired social, economic and environmental outcomes. For example, many question their capacity to:

- reduce conflicts and transaction costs (e.g. Lubell 2004; Saglie 2006);
- promote public participation and policy dialogue (e.g. Innes and Booher 2003; Leach et al 2002);
- foster deliberative processes (e.g. Connelly et al 2006; Lebel et al 2006);
- Lead to more cooperative behaviour (e.g. Lubell 2004; Scholz and Stiftel 2005; Kenney 2000; Sabatier et al 2005);
- devolve power (e.g. Lane et al 2004; Bell and Park 2006);
- be more democratic and equitable in relation to the legitimacy of process and outcome (e.g. Lane and Corbett 2005; Leach 2006; Moore and Rockloff 2006; Connelly et al 2006); or
- improve environmental and social conditions (e.g. Bellamy and Johnson 2000; Kenney 2000; Lubell 2004).

The next section of this paper examines some of these issues in the context of a shift to regional NRM governance in Australia.

NRM Governance in Australia: a complex federal system

Multi-layered, fragmented and ad hoc

The current management of Australia's natural resources is multi-jurisdictional involving cooperative arrangements of the three spheres of government – national, state/territory and local (e.g. Bates 2003; WalterTurnbull 2006). Under the Australian Constitution, responsibility for the legislative and administrative framework within which natural resources are managed lies with the State and Territory governments, who in turn have traditionally devolved some responsibilities particularly relating to land use and development planning to local governments. The Australian Government's involvement in NRM focuses dominantly on matters of national environmental significance and fulfilling Australia's international obligations. The laws that are made for NRM matters by the federal government draw their validity from other heads of power in the

Constitution, such as taxation power, trade and commerce or external affairs power (HRSCEH 2000). But as Bates (2003) points out:

> It has been clearly established through a number of decisions of the High Court of Australia, over the past 25 years, that the Commonwealth Government has undoubted constitutional powers to override state decision-making on the use and management of natural resources. In practice, however, since the heyday of federal intervention in the 1980s, political constraints have influenced any decision to use these powers. The Commonwealth and States have now adopted a more cooperative approach to environmental protection and natural resource management ... This 'co-operative' federalism has been reflected in recent years through the Commonwealth Government basically adopting an initiation and co-ordination role with respect to the development of national policies for resource management and environmental protection (p. 284-5).

The shared responsibility between the Commonwealth and the States referred to as 'cooperative federalism' is reflected, for example, in the *Intergovernmental Agreement on the Environment* which was signed by the Commonwealth and all States and Territories in 1992. The purpose of this agreement was to achieve sound environmental management through a system of parallel and complementary legislation. Under this agreement, consultation between the Australian, State and Territory governments in practice is formalised through ministerial councils, standing committees and a range of consultative committees that also include key industry, scientific and local government representatives. Since the late 1980s, however, a fourth regional tier of responsibility for NRM has been introduced by state and territory governments through a broad range of different statutory and non-statutory arrangements within each jurisdiction (e.g. Bellamy et al 2002, 2003; Dovers and Wild River 2003). Although particular responsibilities can vary according to the legislative environment and the administrative arrangements within a particular jurisdiction, the traditional division of responsibilities between the levels of government, regional authorities and individual land owners in Australia for natural resource management are summarised in Table 7.1.

Table 7.1. Typical division of responsibilities for natural resource management in Australia

Jurisdiction Activity	Commonwealth	State	Region (i.e. Catchment Management Authority)	Local govern-ment	Individuals / corpor-ations
Adherence to international / national conventions	* * *	* *	*	*	*
Leadership and catalysing change	* * *	* * *	* * *	* * *	*
Administer land and water legislation and regulation	*	* * *	-	* *	-
Undertake regional and local planning	*	* *	* * *	* * *	*
Support for research and development	* * *	* * *	*	*	-
Development of national NRM policy	* * *	* *	*	*	*
NRM extension and community capacity building	*	* * *	* *	* *	*
On-ground management (except for crown lands)	-	-	* *	* *	* * *
On-ground management of crown lands	* * *	* * *	* *	*	-

Levels of responsibility

- Not relevant

* Low

** Medium

*** High

Source: HRSCEH 2000, p. 27

Although in practice all three spheres of government in Australia (local, state and federal) have demonstrated a significant involvement in NRM policy initiatives, such initiatives have generally developed independently of each other in an ad hoc way (Bellamy et al 2002; Connor and Dovers 2004). This has led to a diversity of NRM institutional arrangements existing across Australia and within any state/territory or region (see Bellamy et al 2002; The Senate Committee 2004; Keogh et al 2006; WalterTurnbull 2006). Not only does each level of government typically adopt its own NRM governance approach but state and federal governments often continue to develop policy as well as design and implement program-specific arrangements that differ in scale, style, resourcing and accountability standards within themselves. These fragmented institutional arrangements may well involve competing objectives and interests.

NRM governance within Australia's federal system, therefore, involves a complex system of multiple 'nested' or polycentric decision-making arrangements (versus neatly hierarchical) being carried out concurrently across a range of political decision-making levels (e.g. national, state, region, local) and horizontally across a fragmented array of territorial and sectoral areas. It is presented diagrammatically in Figure 7.2. This system is continually evolving at all political and sectoral levels. For example, each state or region is evolving in different ways, for different reasons, in varying contexts and at different rates. At each level of this complex multi-layered and polycentric system, there are different emergent properties and problems to be addressed. Moreover, the different levels may be coupled by a diverse range of relationships that involve an iterative process of devolution and feedback of functions and outcomes within and between different decision-making levels (e.g. federal to local and vice versa).

Figure 7.2. NRM governance – a complex multi-layered and polycentric system

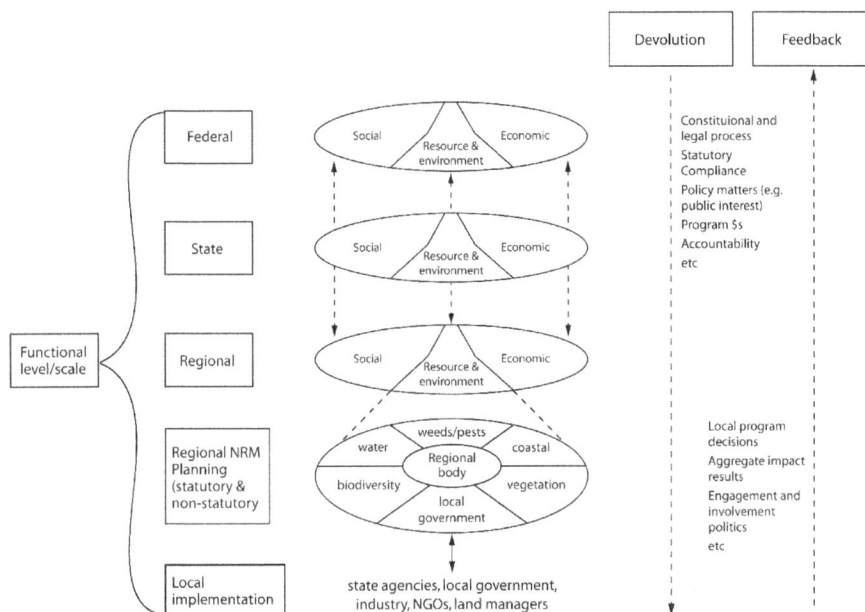

Source: Bellamy and McDonald (2005)

As a consequence of this ad hoc, polycentric and multi-layered development, constitutional constraints and fragmented institutional arrangements have obstructed an integrated and systemic national approach to managing Australia's natural resources. The result is a national agenda for NRM operating through a mix of parallel arrangements (i.e. cooperative federalism) that involve (Maher et al 2001, p.25):

- high level multi- and bi-lateral agreements between Commonwealth and State governments usually about specific aspects of NRM;
- leverage exerted by the Commonwealth Government through making State government access to Commonwealth financial resources based on meeting specified conditions;
- issue-based parliamentary inquiries; and
- an emerging Commonwealth presence in impact assessment in relation to matters of national environmental significance.

This national agenda is increasingly emphasising a regional focus for NRM, which in practice is fundamentally dependent on a cooperative approach involving all three spheres of government, as well as relevant industry and other private actors.

Shift to a regional focus: regional delivery for NRM

Over the last two decades, Australian governments and regional communities have make considerable investments in NRM governance experiments at the regional scale grounded in the underlying assumptions of an emerging sustainability paradigm of change, adaptation and learning (e.g. AFFA 2002; Bellamy et al 2002, 2003; Head and Ryan 2004). These new regional governance approaches focus on wicked natural resource problems and emphasise broad participation and deliberation through the development of partnerships, strategic alliances and broader consultation between those with policy authority and those with significant stakes in decisions.

Significantly, a major shift in the framework of the federal NRM program delivery in Australia has occurred since 2000 with critical implications for adaptive NRM governance. This shift involved the introduction of a succession of Australian Government NRM policy initiatives emphasising joint regional delivery arrangements for the second phase of the National Heritage Trust (NHT) and the National Action Plan for Salinity and Water Quality (NAP). These new regional delivery arrangements are an example of cooperative federalism involving attempts by the Australian Government to devolve the management of natural resources to a more integrated and cohesive NRM approach through the creation of mechanisms for community-based NRM based on the establishment of accredited regional NRM bodies (see AFFA 2000, 2002; WalterTurnbull 2006).

Through the new regional delivery arrangements, 56 NRM regions are defined across Australia by spatial boundaries relating largely to natural biophysical characteristics (e.g. catchments and bioregions) and their intersection with state and territory boundaries. The primary purposes of the regional bodies are to guide NRM planning strategy and investment priorities within their respective regions, and to provide the mechanism for greater community-based NRM. The core elements of the institutional arrangements supporting regional NRM delivery include (e.g. WalterTurnbull 2006; Bellamy et al 2005):

- *Bilateral agreements* between the Australian Government and each of the State/Territory governments signed off progressively over a number of years (2001 to 2004). They include requirements for policy and institutional reforms consistent with national priorities and the relationship between the State/Territory governments for the delivery of regional funding. Each State/Territory has negotiated agreements with variations in accordance with State NRM policy requirements and NRM delivery arrangements;

- *Partnership agreements* signed between respective state/territory governments and each regional body in their jurisdiction;
- *Joint Steering Committees* established separately for each state/territory and which are the main vehicle for bilateral decision-making and development of recommendations to Australian and State/Territory ministers in relation to regional delivery of NRM;
- *Lead NRM State/Territory agency* nominated to facilitate the delivery of the regional component of the NAP and NHT within each State and Territory jurisdiction; and
- *Financial resourcing* through parallel NAP and NHT programmatic 'block funding' mechanisms based on accredited regional investment strategies developed collaboratively by each regional body.

As Head and Ryan (2004) argue, this new form of regional governance 'changes the role of government to framework-setter, co-funder and facilitator, representing an adaptive form of public management. Governance is managed through a strategic framework of cooperation rather than primarily through regulatory and legal mandate' (p. 377). The role of federal and state governments however remains critical in establishing program direction, boundaries and resourcing.

Importantly, the regional delivery model is a new governance approach that operates within, and does not replace, an overarching framework of legislation, policy, and defined stakeholder responsibilities implemented by multiple, overlapping (and often competing) formal and informal NRM arrangements. Rather, the new regional NRM delivery approach operates concurrently with the existing polycentric system of nested arrangements, both 'horizontal' and 'vertical', between different actors (e.g. business/industry groups, community organisations, government agencies and politicians) and between different spheres and functional areas of government. The outcome is a unique regional NRM governance system for each State and Territory each operating through a different set of institutional arrangements. For example, there is considerably variation across the States and Territories in terms of the statutory status (and powers) of regional NRM bodies themselves, the membership and resourcing arrangements of these bodies and the role and powers of local government in relation to NRM and their linkages to regional NRM bodies and delivery processes. Importantly, overall these systems require cooperation of all three spheres of government, industry and other private actors and, in practice to-date, they largely involve more representative democratic structures rather than truly embracing participative democracy.

Not surprisingly, the implementation of the new regional NRM governance is proving a difficult challenge for the individuals, the institutions and the communities concerned and as a consequence, actual impact is often perceived to fall short of expectation (e.g. Bellamy and Johnson 2000; Lane et al 2004; Lane and McDonald 2005; Farrelly 2005; Moore 2005; Moore and Rockloff 2006). There are numerous and often conflicting social and institutional challenges imposed by the complex and fragmented polycentric character of Australia's federal system for NRM. Many of these challenges reflect on the capacity for more adaptive regional governance for NRM within the Australian federal system. Key challenges include:

- balancing traditional business and industry development interests with social and environmental constraints.
- competing or contradictory statutory and policy objectives and strategies arising from the breadth of sectoral concerns involved in regional NRM systems and the complex interrelationships between them;
- contest over the optimum degree of openness and inclusiveness in the setting of regional objectives and priorities to foster community ownership and commitment;
- complex transboundary problems (territorial and sectoral) and the related challenge of creating linking and bridging devices (that is structures, processes, mechanisms and people) to enable an integrated and collective perspective;
- developing whole-of-government responses to regional demands;
- turf issues, including the need to balance cooperation and competition because organisational self-interest is still heavily engrained in regional systems;
- conflicting values, including competing influences of industry groups and non-governmental groups or organisations on legislation and policy outcomes;
- conflicting approaches to the recognition of cultural diversity and difference;
- resource constraints including the adequacy of regional shares of public revenues, resources and regulatory powers; and
- knowledge sharing including the application of a more holistic and integrated science that crosses traditional knowledge boundaries and gives greater status to 'grass roots' or societal knowledge.

These challenges provoke a vital question about where the implementation of regional NRM within the Australian federal system is heading in terms of institutional arrangements, adaptive capacities and technical performance.

The way forward: a question of adaptive capacity?

Notwithstanding the fact that, as a wicked policy problem, NRM poses significant governance challenges, it is increasingly evident that a regional and systemic focus in NRM is a critical mechanism for addressing the sustainability of our interconnected natural and social systems. So what are the essential elements of 'good' adaptive regional NRM governance? Essential attributes recognised both nationally and internationally include (e.g. Folke et al 2005; Bellamy et al 2006; Lebel et al 2006; Davidson et al 2006):

- *Participatory*: engagement with stakeholders being inclusive of the range of values of people involved or affected by NRM decision-making. Critical for building trust and legitimacy;
- *Deliberative:* accommodating debate, dissent, mediation and negotiation. Critical for developing shared understanding and trust and enhancing adaptive capacity;
- *Multi-layered*: not necessarily neatly hierarchical but able to handle scale-dependent governance challenges and territorial or sectoral cross-boundary interactions and coordination. Critical to adaptive responses at appropriate levels;
- *Nested*: multiple centres or authorities for creating opportunities for understanding and for servicing needs in spatially heterogeneous contexts. Critical for providing flexibility for adapting to local contexts (i.e. knowledge, values, community capacity for action and social and environmental conditions) and creating appropriate learning and decision-making opportunities;
- *Accountable and responsive*: relating to both local communities and higher authorities in terms of decisions and actions that are responsive to changing circumstances, performance, knowledge and societal objectives and preferences. Critical to efficiency and adaptive capacity of regional NRM governance to respond to and shape change in the long term;
- *Just*: that is, social justice in relation to the distribution of benefits and involuntary risks. Critical to enhancing the adaptive capacity of vulnerable groups and society as a whole; and
- *Well informed:* embracing new forms of knowledge to deal with complexity and uncertainty associated with change in interconnected social and natural systems. Critical to social acceptability and adaptive governance capacity.

Is it possible to design and implement such an adaptive regional NRM style of governance within the Australian federal system that is effective, legitimate and durable in delivering sustainable outcomes for our linked social and natural systems? Although the 'jury is still out' on the outcomes of the new regional NRM delivery experiments, the multi-layered and polycentric nature of Australia's federal system for NRM is revealing some opportunities for a more adaptive, participative and deliberative regional style of governance.

A number of key lessons are emerging from current regional NRM practice that are critical elements necessary for enhancing adaptive capacity of NRM governance within Australia's federal system. Firstly, the regional focus is broadening the scope and scale of the collaboration on NRM (that is, both geographically large and institutionally broad and multi-levelled). Second, it is fostering new forms of participation of regional communities in NRM policy decision-making through changing the roles of state and societal actors and allowing social actors more capacity to coordinate amongst themselves and make collective decisions on action in the pursuit of societal goals with less central government control. Third, it is enabling the emergence of new network configurations or arrangements that connect individuals, organisations, agencies and institutions at multiple organisational or political levels. These inevitably have potential to enhance cooperation amongst the different spheres of government, communities and individual decision-makers who all act or have influence at multiple political scales. Fourthly, a clear recognition is emerging of the central role of local government in regional NRM and its delivery; although to date there has been very limited devolution of powers and limited capacity present in local government to enable this increasing role to be realised (see Bell this volume, Berwick this volume). Finally, it is encouraging new mechanisms for linking science, policy and society in which 'science' is more 'nested' in decision making, rather than external to it. Such mechanisms have greater capacity to value and engage multiple sources of knowledge and also the potential to provide improved opportunities for collaborative learning.

Although regional NRM governance is not the sole solution or panacea for NRM within our complex federal system (see Head and Ryan 2004; Lane and McDonald 2005; Moore 2005; Bell and Park 2006), these emerging attributes have promising implications for the potential of more participative and deliberative regional governance approaches to enhance adaptive capacity in our interconnected social and natural systems.

Undoubtedly, as Brown (this volume) proposes, substantive reform in Australia's complex federal system of government is ultimately critical to the move towards social, economic and environmental sustainability. Given the urgency for response posed by the sustainability challenge, in the short to medium term, what is evident is the need for an enabling environment for the regional NRM agenda that moves beyond the current limited focus on an adaptive form of public management (i.e. administrative adaptiveness) towards a more adaptive NRM governance system that enables social and political learning at multiple levels and 'nested' centres of decision-making across public and private sectors. At the most basic level, such an NRM governance system would need to:

- encompass the existing and emerging regional NRM roles and functions (including powers, responsibilities and resources) of the current three spheres of government;
- enable a cooperative and deliberative (rather than hierarchical) governance style;
- accommodate diversity in NRM policy development and implementation strategies (e.g. a mix of networks, hierarchies, and market-based instruments);

- be sufficiently flexible to allow adaptation to diverse and changing local regional contexts and circumstances; and
- value and enable the sharing of multiple knowledge systems.

Substantive structural reform of our Australian federal system to a two, alternative three or a four tiered federal system is inevitably a long term agenda. Any decision for such reform however must recognise the interconnectedness of social and natural systems and involve consideration of all sectoral policy arenas concurrently (i.e. health, education, economic development, infrastructure, environment, etc.) to more effectively and legitimately enhance the adaptive capacity of society and its related institutions to deal with and shape inevitable change.

References

Agriculture, Forests and Fisheries Australia (AFFA) 1999, *Managing Natural Resources in Rural Australia for a Sustainable Future: A discussion paper for developing a national policy*. December 1999, AFFA, Canberra.

——— 2000, *Our Vital resources: National Action Plan for Salinity and Water Quality in Australia*, October 2000.

——— 2002, *Framework for the Extension of the Natural Heritage Trust*.

Australian National Audit Office (ANAO) 1997, *Commonwealth natural resource management and environment programs. Australia's land, water and vegetation resources*, The Auditor General, AGPS, Canberra.

Australian State of Environment Committee 2006, *Australian State of the Environment 2006*. Independent Report to the Australian Government Minister for the Environment and Heritage, Department of Environment and Heritage, Canberra, viewed 7 December 2006, <http://www.deh.gov.au/soe/2006/publications/report/index.html>

Bates, G. 2003. 'Legal perspectives' in S. Dovers and S. Wild River (eds), *Managing Australia's Environment*, The Federation Press, Sydney, pp. 255-301.

Bell, S. and A. Park, 2006, 'The problematic metagovernance of networks: Water reform in New South Wales', *Journal of Public Policy*, vol. 26 (1), pp. 63-83.

Bellamy, J. 2006. 'Appendix A. Development of a case study synthesis framework' in G. McDonald, S. Hovermann, S. Heyenga and B. Taylor (eds), *Case Studies in Regional Natural Resource Management in Northern Australia. Milestone Report 5*. Healthy Savanna Planning Systems Project. Tropical Savanna Management CRC. June 2006, pp. 110-117. <http://savanna.cdu.edu.au/research/projects/healthy_savanna_pla.html>

Bellamy, J.A. and A.K.L. Johnson, 2000, 'Integrated Resource Management: Moving from rhetoric to practice in Australian agriculture', *Environmental Management* Vol. 25 (3), pp. 265-280.

Bellamy, J. and G. McDonald, 2005, 'Through multi-scaled lenses: A systems approach to evaluating natural resource management policy and planning', in J. Bellamy (ed.), *Regional natural resource management planning: the challenges of evaluation as seen through different lenses*, CIRM Monograph Series, June 2005, The State of Queensland, Department of Natural Resources and Mines, Indooroopilly, pp.3-10, viewed 20 January 2007, <http://www.cirm.org.au/publications/Monograph.pdf>

Bellamy, J., H. Ross, S. Ewing and T. Meppem, 2002, *Integrated Catchment Management: Learning from the Australian Experience for the Murray-Darling Basin. Final Report. January 2002.* A Report for the Murray Darling Basin Commission, CSIRO Sustainable Ecosystems, Brisbane, viewed 20 January 2007, <http://www.mdbc.gov.au/naturalresources/icm/icm_aus_x_overview.html>

Bellamy, J., T. Meppem, R. Gorddard and S. Dawson, 2003, 'The changing face of regional governance for economic development: Implications for Local Government', *Sustaining Regions* vol. 2 (3) Winter 2003, pp. 7-17.

Bellamy, J., D. Metcalfe, N. Weston, and S. Dawson, 2005. *Evaluation of invasive species (weeds) outcomes of regional investment. Final Report to the Department of Environment and Heritage and Department of Agriculture, Fisheries and Forestry.* November 2005. CSIRO Sustainable Ecosystems and the Rainforest CRC. <http://www.nrm.gov.au/monitoring/national-evaluations/weeds.html>

Berkes, F., J. Colding and C. Folke (eds) 2003, *Navigating Social-Ecological Systems. Building resistence for complexity and change*, Cambridge University Press, UK.

Bingham, L. B., T. Nabatchi and R. O'Leary, 2005, 'The new governance: Practices and processes for stakeholder and citizen participation in the work of government', *Public Administration Review*, vol. 65 (5), pp.547-558.

Bressers, H.T. and S.M.M. Kuks, 2003, 'What does 'governance' mean? From conception to elaboration', in H. A. Bressers and W.A. Rosenbaum (eds), *Achieving Sustainable Development*, Praeger, Westport, Connecticut, pp. 65-88.

Cocklin, C. and J. Dibden (eds) 2005, *Sustainability and change in rural Australia*, UNSW Press, Sydney, Australia.

Cocks, D. 1992, *Use with Care: Managing Australia's natural resources in the Twenty First Century*, NSW University Press, Kensington, Australia.

Commonwealth of Australia 1992, *National Strategy for Ecologically Sustainable Development*. December 1992, AGPS, Canberra.

Connelly, S., T. Richardson and T. Miles, 2006, 'Situated legitimacy: Deliberative arenas and the new rural governance', *Journal of Rural Studies*, vol. 22, pp.267-277.

Connor, R. and S. Dovers, 2004, *Institutional Change for Sustainable Development*, Edward Elgar Publishing, Cheltenham, UK.

Cosier, P. 2006, 'Will Climate Change Cost Us the Earth', paper presented at The Green Capital Conference, Sofitel Wentworth, Sydney, 8 November 2006, viewed 20 November 2006, <http://www.wentworth-group.org/docs/Will_climate_change_cost_us_the_Earth1.pdf>

Davidson, J., M. Lockwood, A. Curtis, E. Stratford and R. Griffith, 2006, *Governance principles for Natural Resource Management*, Report No. 1 of the Project Pathways to good practice in regional NRM governance, viewed 20 January 2007, <www.geog.utas.edu.au/geography/nrmgovernance/>

Diamond, J.M. 2005, *Collapse: how societies choose to fail or survive*, Penguin Group, Camberwell, Victoria.

Dovers, S. and S. Wild River (eds) 2003, *Managing Australia's Environment*, The Federation Press, Sydney.

Eckersley, R. 2003, 'Politics and Policy', in S. Dovers and S. Wild River (eds), *Managing Australia's Environment*, The Federation Press, Sydney, pp. 485-500.

Environment Business Australia 2004, *New Tools and Old Myths: Climate change action – a toolkit for transition*, A discussion paper issued by Environment Business Australia at CoP10, Buenos Aires, December 2004, viewed 18 November 2006, <http://www.environmentbusiness.com.au/conference_papers/the%20toolbox.pdf>

Eversole, R. and J. Martin (eds) 2005, *Participation and Governance in Regional Development: Global Trends in and Australian Context*, Ashgate, Hampshire, England.

Farrelly, M. 2005, 'Regionalisation of environmental management: A case study of the Natural Hertitage Trust, South Australia', *Geographical Research*, vol. 43(4), pp.393-405.

Folke, C., T. Hahn, P.Olsson and J. Norberg, 2005, 'Adaptive governance of social-ecological systems', *Annual Review of Environmental Resources*, vol. 30, pp.441-473.

Gunderson, L.H. and C.S. Holling (eds) 2003, *Panarchy: Understanding Transformations in Human and Natural Systems*, Island Press, Washington.

Head, B. and N. Ryan, 2004, 'Can co-governance work? Regional natural resource management in Queensland, Australia', *Society and Economy,* Vol. 26 (2/3), pp.371-393.

Holling, C.S. 2001, 'Understanding the complexity of economic, ecological, and social systems', *Ecology*, vol. 4, pp. 390-405.

House of Representatives Standing Committee on Environment and Heritage (HRSCEH) 2000, *Co-ordinating Catchment Management. Report of the Inquiry into Catchment Management*, The Parliament of the Commonwealth of Australia, Canberra, December 2000.

Howlett, M. and J. Rayner, 2006, 'Convergence and divergence in 'New Governance' arrangements: Evidence from European Integrated Natural Resource Strategies', *Journal of Public Policy*, vol. 26 (2), pp. 167-189.

Innes, J.E. and D.E. Booher, 2003, *The impact of collaborative planning on governance capacity*. Working Paper 2003-03, Institute of Urban and Regional Development, University of California, Berkeley.

Keogh, K., D. Chant and B. Frazer, 2006, *Review of Arrangement for Regional Delivery of Natural Resource Management Programmes*, Report prepared by the Ministerial Reference Group for Future NRM Programme Delivery, Final Report, March 2006, viewed 20 December 2006, <http://www.nrm.gov.au/publications/regional-delivery-review/index.html>

Kenney, D.S. 2000, *Arguing about consensus; Examining the case against Western watershed initiatives and other collaborative groups active in natural resource management*, Natural Resource Law Centre, University of Colorado School of Law, Boulder.

Lane, M.B. and T. Corbett, 2005, 'The tyranny of localism: Indigenous participation in community-based environmental management', *Journal of Environmental Policy and Planning*, vol. 7(2), pp.141-159.

Lane, M.B. and G. McDonald, 2005, 'Community-based environmental planning: Operational dilemmas, planning principles and possible remedies', *Journal of Environmental Planning and Management*, vol.45 (5), pp. 709-731.

Lane, M.B., G.T. McDonald, and T.H. Morrison, 2004, 'Decentralisation and environmental management in Australia: A comment on the prescription of the Wentworth Group', *Australian Geographical Studies*, vol. 42, pp.398-403.

Leach, W.D., N.W. Pelkey, and P.A. Sabatier, 2002, 'Stakeholder partnerships and collaborative policy-making: Evaluation criteria applied to watershed management in California and Washington', *Journal of Policy Analysis and Management*, vol. 21 (4), pp. 645-670.

Leach, W.D. 2006, 'Collaborative public management and democracy: Evidence from Western watershed partnerships', *Public Administrative Review*, vol. 66, Special Issue December, pp. 100-110.

Lebel, L., J.M., Anderies, B. Campbell, C. Folke, S. Hatfield-Dodds, T.P. Hughes and J. Wilson, 2006, 'Governance and the capacity to manage resilience in regional social-ecological systems', *Ecology and Society*, Vol. 11(1), 19 [on-line] URL: <http://www.ecologyandsociety.org/vol11/iss1/art19/>.

Lubell, M. 2004, 'Collaborative environmental institutions: All talk and no action?', *Journal of Policy Analysis and Management,* vol. 23(3), pp. 549-573.

Maher, M., J. Nevill, and P. Nichols, 2002, *Improving the legislative basis for river management in Australia – Stage 2 Report*, Land and Water Australia, Canberra.

Millennium Ecosystem Assessment 2005, *Ecosystems and human well-being: Synthesis*, Island Press, Washington, D.C.

Moore, S.A. 2005, 'Regional delivery of natural resource management in Australia. Is it democratic and does it matter?', in R. Eversole and J. Martin (eds), 2005, *Participation and Governance in Regional Development: Global Trends in and Australian Context*, Ashgate, Hampshire, England, pp. 121-136.

Moore, S.A. and S.F. Rockloff, 2006, 'Organising regionally for natural resource management in Australia: Reflections on agency and government', *Journal of Environmental Policy and Planning*, vol. 8(3), pp. 259-277.

Morton, S., G. Bourne, P. Cristofani, P.Cullen, H. Possingham and M. Young, 2002, *Sustaining our natural systems and biodiversity: an independent report to the Prime Minister's Science, Engineering and Innovation Council*, CSIRO and Environment Australia, Canberra.

Murray, D. 2005, 'A critical analysis of communicative rationality as a theoretical underpinning for collaborative approaches to integrated resource and environmental management', *Environments Journal*, vol. 33(2), pp. 17-34.

Murray-Darling Basin Ministerial Council (MDBMC) 2001, *Integrated catchment management in the Murray-Darling Basin 2001-2010: Delivering a sustainable future*, Murray-Darling Basin Commission, Canberra.

National Water Commission (NWC) 2006, *Australia's Water Supply Status and seasonal outlook October 2006*, Australian Government, National Water Commission, Canberra, viewed 20 January 2007, <http://www.nwc.gov.au/publications/docs/SeasonalOutlook.pdf >

Rittel, H.W.J. and M.M. Webber, 1973, 'Dilemmas in a general theory of planning', *Policy Sciences*, vol. 4, pp.155-169.

Saglie, I.L. 2006, 'Fragmented institutions: The problems facing natural resource management', in Y. Rydin and E. Falleth, E (eds), *Networks and institutions in natural resource management*, Edward Elgar Publishing, Cheltenham, UK, pp. 1-33.

Sabatier , P. A., W. Focht, M. Lubell, Z. Trachtenberg, A. Vedlitz and M. Matlock (eds), 2005, *Swimming Upstream: Collaborative Approaches to Watershed Management*, MIT Press, Cambridge, MA.

Scholz, J.T. and B. Stiftel (eds), 2005, *Adaptive Governance and Water Conflict: New institutions for Collaborative Planning, Resources for the Future*, Washington D.C.

Stern, N. 2006, *Stern Review on the Economics of Climate Change*, viewed 18 November 2006, <http://www.hm-treasury.gov.uk./independent_reviews/stern_review_economics_climate_change/stern_review_report.cfm >

Stoker, G. 1998, 'Governance as theory: five propositions', *International Social Science Journal*, vol. 50(155), pp. 17-28.

Swyngedouw, E. 2005, 'Governance innovation and the citizen: The Janus-face of government-beyond-the-state', *Urban Studies*, vol. 42 (11), pp.1991-2006.

The Senate Committee Report 2004, *Turning back the tide– the invasive species challenge, The Senate Environment, Communications, Information Technology and the Arts References Committee Inquiry into the regulation, control and management of invasive species and the Environment Protection and Biodiversity Conservation Amendment (Invasive Species) Bill 2002*, The Commonwealth of Australia, December 2004.

The Wentworth Group of Concerned Scientists 2003, *Blueprint for a National Water Plan*, 31 July 2003, WWF, Sydney, viewed 20 November 2006, <http://www.wentworthgroup.org/docs/blueprint_national_water_plan.pdf >

———— 2006, *Australia's Climate is Changing. The State of Australia's Water*, November 2006, viewed 20 November 2006, <http://www.wentworthgroup.org/docs/Australias_Climate_is_Changing_Australia1.pdf >

WalterTurnbull 2005, *Evaluation of current governance arrangements to support regional investment under the NHT and NAP. Final Report*, Departments of the Environment and Heritage and Agriculture Fisheries and Forestry, Australian Government, December 2005. <http://www.nrm.gov.au/monitoring/national-evaluations/governance.html>

Williams, P. 2006, 'The governance of sustainable development in Wales', *Local Environment*, vol. 11(3), pp.253-267.

ENDNOTES

[1] The term natural resources refers to the soil, water, plants, animals and micro-organisms that maintain our ecosystems (AFFA 1999, p. 1)

[2] In Australia, most legal definitions are based on the definition of ecologically sustainable development (ESD) agreed to by the Australian/Commonwealth, States and local government and embodied in the *National Strategy on Ecological Sustainable Development 1992* and the *Inter-Governmental Agreement on the Environment 1992*; namely 'using, conserving and enhancing the community's resources so that ecological processes, on which life depends, are maintained, and the total quality of life, now and in the future, can be maintained.' (Commonwealth of Australia 1992: p.6).

Chapter 8: Regionalism and Economic Development: Achieving an Efficient Framework

Andrew Beer

Introduction

Economic development remains an aspiration of governments across Australia at the national, state and local levels. Both communities and governments seek growth with respect to their population, gross regional product, average income and the quality and quantity of their infrastructure. The impetus for economic development has, in large measure, dominated Australian politics and society over the last two decades, contributing to the reform of labour markets, the amalgamation and restructuring of local governments, changes to education and higher education, shifts within the public sector and a recasting of immigration. Central governments have been a major catalyst for economic growth, with the federal government in particular pushing for change in order to lift gross national product. Initiatives such as the National Competition Policy and WorkChoices legislation have sought to achieve microeconomic reform as a mechanism for delivering a more competitive position within the global economy. State and territory governments have also awarded priority to policies intended to achieve economic growth. Across the jurisdictions, there has been an emphasis on achieving 'AAA' credit ratings (Spoehr 2005) as a way of demonstrating business credentials and in some instances governments have implemented innovation strategies – such as Queensland's 'Smart State' program – as a way of enhancing their long term competitiveness.

While economic development has been an important driver of policy, the programs and actions of government have largely ignored regional impacts. The focus on the national economy or the state economy *per se* has given scant attention to the distribution of growth opportunities at the regional or local level. This has meant that the gap between prosperous regions and those that struggle has widened (Baum et al 2005), and that insufficient attention has been paid to the development of an adequate infrastructure for economic development at the local or regional scale (Beer et al 2003).

This chapter considers the current state of regional economic development in Australia, drawing attention to significant shortcomings in current structures. The chapter then draws upon the example of the responses of government to the loss of employment in the automotive industry in Adelaide during 2004, to illustrate the adverse impact of policy responses developed and implemented at an inappropriate scale. Finally, the chapter outlines some ideas on how a far stronger system for local or regional economic development could be implemented, and the benefits of such a system for both vulnerable communities and the national economy.

Regional development in Australia: small scale, fragmented and non-metropolitan

Regional development is an avowed aspiration of governments in Australia, but it is a goal that is often inadequately funded and of lesser priority in the long term. Regional development is not as prominent in the agendas of state governments as health and education, and, while governments recognise the need to pay attention to non-metropolitan issues, their engagement tends to be piecemeal and opportunistic rather than strategic and comprehensive. The small-scale nature of political engagement with regional issues engenders substantial challenges at a policy level, as policy debates are dominated by portfolios and Ministers with the most substantial budgets and influence within Cabinet. This section of this chapter considers the broad challenges confronting regional development in Australia, focussing in particular on the issues of fragmentation, the small scale of regional development efforts and the practice of defining regional issues as non-metropolitan issues.

A fragmented framework for regional development

Fragmentation in responsibility for regional development presents a major challenge for the practice of economic development in Australia. Fragmentation is evident in a number of ways: first, responsibilities for regional development are commonly distributed between the federal, state and local governments and it is common to see all three tiers of government engaged in regional development activities in any locality (see Beer, Maude and Pritchard 2003, p. 45). There is fragmentation also on a territorial basis with each State and Territory largely shaping the institutional architecture for regional development via their own agencies, the requirements they place on local government and through their funding policies (Beer and Maude 1997, 2002). There is, therefore, no uniformity across the States and Territories, and while there are common elements to the practice of regional development in Australia (Beer, Haughton and Maude 2003), there are also significant differences (Beer and Maude 2002).

As a number of academics and pundits have argued, the Federal Government is probably the only tier of government in Australia with the necessary resources to sustain a coherent and viable program of local or regional economic development (Logan 1978; Beer 2000). As the collector of 75% of public sector revenues it has greater financial capacity than either state or local governments. But federal governments have long shied away from an explicit involvement in formal regional development initiatives. Throughout the 1960s an Inter-Departmental Committee sat for eight years considering whether the Federal Government should act to promote decentralisation of people and economic activity. There was a brief flurry of activity in the early 1970s under the Whitlam Labor Governments, and then virtually nothing for almost 20 years. The Keating Government's Regional Development Program was hastily jettisoned by the newly-elected Howard Coalition Government, because it considered it had no constitutional role in the area, and that federal involvement would result in overlap and duplication with state and local government efforts. In the year 2000 the Howard Government re-engaged with local and regional development issues – admittedly at an initially modest level – via the Regional Solutions Program. More recently, the Federal Government has promoted regional issues through the reformulated Bureau of Transport and Regional Economics, the establishment of the Sustainable Regions Program focussed on 10 regions across Australia, and the Regional Partnerships Program.

While the Howard Coalition Government has not formally enunciated a major regional development program, it has intervened in the functioning of regional economies in many ways. For example, drought relief is a major regional intervention, as are the arrangements for guaranteeing the quality of telecommunications infrastructure in 'the bush' after the full privatisation of Telstra. Other research (Beer, Haughton and Maude 2003) has shown that Federal funding – from a variety of sources – typically makes up 40 per cent of the budgets of regional development bodies. And while this contribution to regional development efforts is welcome, regional development practitioners are only too aware that funding priorities are established centrally, not locally. Area Consultative Committees (ACCs) are an important part of the Federal Government's engagement with regions. ACCs were originally established as labour market organisations, but have been gradually transformed and refocussed on regional development issues, broadly defined. ACCs can be a source of funding for other regional development bodies and are often perceived to reflect the political interests of the government rather than genuinely reflecting the needs and interests of local community. Importantly, ACCs have not been part of a wider political project by the Australian Government – say, comparable with Cities Commission or the Department of Urban and Regional Development - and therefore their engagement with regional issues has been disjointed.

State governments are probably the most visible participants in regional economic development, and in aggregate would make the largest investment in encouraging growth locally. State governments are substantial investors in the infrastructure and services that sustain economic activity in metropolitan and non-metropolitan regions. Many state governments have a long history of involvement in formal regional development initiatives and in the immediate post-War period decentralisation programs were favoured. In line with the growth pole theory of the time, state governments used tax breaks and financial incentives in an attempt to create growth centres. Paul Collits (1995) has suggested that the period 1965 to 1975 was the high water mark for these initiatives, and this reflected the preference for dispersed development in Australia, recognition of the rising costs associated with the growth of Australia's biggest cities, evidence that the rural population was in decline, and the strength of the Country Party. Significantly, the regional development policies of state governments have continued to reflect the decentralisation debate, despite the demise of growth pole theory within the regional economic development literature and the rise of new dynamics within national and global economy. Many states continue to promote regional development within non-metropolitan regions, with South Australia, Western Australia and NSW essentially funding regional development boards outside the capital cities only.

Most local governments have some formal role in economic development activities, though participation varies considerably by state and location. Local governments have been the primary agents for economic development in Victoria since the mid-1990s, while local governments in Queensland have always played a much broader role within their communities than elsewhere in Australia. Their participation in the provision of major infrastructure – such as water supply, roads and electricity – has given them a greater capacity to influence growth. Local government remains the smallest and poorest tier of government in Australia and its circumstances are worsening (Hawker Report 2003). Over the last two decades, the real value of financial support to local government from the Federal Government has fallen – as has state financial support in most jurisdictions – while the tasks required of local governments by the other tiers of government have grown. Despite these pressures, local governments have not shied away from promoting their region or local economy. Many provide cash incentives or infrastructure to attract firms, and the majority would employ at least one staff member with responsibilities for economic development. In some places – notably Victoria – there are large Economic Development Units within individual local governments. While there is considerable variation around Australia, it is common for them to join state governments in funding regional development agencies, Business Enterprise Centres and or initiatives. Often they host special events designed to draw in tourists and will market their region nationally and internationally. It is worth noting that the national awards in local government explicitly recognise the role of local government in working for economic development. In 2004, Burnie City Council was recognised for its role in revitalising the city's airport and developing adjacent land as an industrial estate, while the town of Cressy in Tasmania's central highlands was recognised in 2005 for its 'Troutarama' festival.

It is important to acknowledge, from the discussion above, that responsibility for regional development in Australia is divided across the three tiers of government and that each – to a greater or lesser degree – has an equivocal attitude to the development of regions. For central governments (state and federal) there is a strong imperative to be perceived to be delivering real outcomes for regions, but this does not necessarily translate into a systematic engagement with regional development. Collits (2003) has noted the 'tyranny of the announceable' within regional development, with governments favouring regional initiatives that have a high media profile, a short time-frame and limited impact on the budget, over those policy measures that attract less public interest but are more likely to deliver growth in the long-term. Local governments are too often an ineffective participant in regional development because their resources are limited and their responsibilities wide-ranging. Overall, the very structure of Australian federalism makes the achievement of an efficient framework for regional economic development difficult. Financial power is concentrated in the Australian Government, constitutional power is held by state and territory governments, while local government has, in large measure, been left to 'muddle through' as best it can.

Scale and regional development

One of the challenges for regional development in Australia is the small scale of policy interventions. Over the last 20 years, Labor and Coalition Federal Governments have transformed the Australian economy but they have relied upon policy levers that operate at the level of the whole economy to achieve their objectives. These have included: the floating of the Australian economy; lifting of control on exchange rates; a reliance on monetary policy to regulate the economy; national competition policy; micro economic reform; and de-regulation of the labour market. Australian governments have not embraced direct interventions in the economy – at either a national or regional level – via wholesale investment in infrastructure or wide-ranging business development programs. The failure to engage in these measures has had significant consequences, as reflected in the fact that, by 2006, Australia's exports were retarded by a shortage of port infrastructure. At the same time, a skills shortage has emerged, largely as a result of inadequate programs for skills development and enhancement. Other nations faced with the challenge of reforming their economy have teamed conventional national policy measures with explicit regional development initiatives. In the Republic of Ireland, for example, economic reform through the 1990s was matched by substantial investment in transport infrastructure, environmental programs and labour market training (MacSharry et al 2000). The combination of national policy change and strategic investment in regional development catapulted development in the Republic of Ireland, such that in 1990 Ireland's per capita income stood at less than 80% of the European Union average, but by 2006 incomes in the Republic of Ireland exceeded the EU mean.

The absence of large scale interventions in the economies of regions significantly reduces the ability of regional development agencies to achieve substantial outcomes. Other research has shown (Beer, Haughton and Maude 2003) that regional development agencies in Australia largely play a facilitative role: assisting business projects pass through the development approval process; lobbying for infrastructure; co-ordinating economic development strategies; networking with businesses and other development bodies and promoting tourism. By contrast, regional development agencies in England and the United States have, on average, much larger budgets and engage in a different range of activities (Beer, Haughton and Maude 2003). In the US, agencies are often locally funded, have a strong business orientation and report very high levels of achievement (Beer, Haughton and Maude 2003). In England, regional development bodies are much more likely to engage in state-of-the-art economic development practices – such as business incubators, supply chain associations, technology diffusion strategies etc. – and in large part this reflects their more generous funding.

It is important to acknowledge that governments across Australia often offer up small-scale policy solutions to the large-scale problems confronting regions. In part this is justified by the 'self help' philosophy embedded within neo-liberalism (Gray and Lawrence 2000), but it also reflects a new, and cynical, set of tendencies within government to be spatially selective (Jones 1997) and to reinforce the success of prosperous regions while ignoring the demise of the less fortunate. As will be discussed in the case study below, governments increasingly have a tendency to offer up politically expedient, short-term, responses to regional economic crises, while ignoring the long term implications and the strategies needed to provide solutions into the future.

Regions: an ex-urban phenomenon?

In Australia, regional development is usually equated with non-metropolitan or rural development. It is as if regions start at the metropolitan boundary – or to view this phenomenon in another way, it is as if regions exist up to the edges of the capital cities and then disappear. Evidence of this trend can be seen in the Australian Government's most recent regional policy statement, by the former Deputy Prime Minister and Minister for Transport and Regional Services, John Sharpe. In his foreword to this policy statement, the Deputy Prime Minister noted that:

> A thriving Australia needs growing and vibrant regions. The Federal Government is committed to ensuring a strong and resilient regional Australia now and in the future – supporting community ideas, leadership and development. We are committed to a regional Australia recognised by us all for its contribution to our great nation.

> The Liberal-National Government believes that Australia needs strong and prosperous regions – now and into the future. We want regional Australia recognised and respected by all Australians for its enormous contribution to the nation's identity and to our national economic and social wellbeing.

> Over the past five and a half years we have done much to rebuild country Australia and today there are real signs of better times. Nonetheless, as we look to the future, much remains to be done. (Anderson, nd, p. 2).

A number of assumptions and values are embedded in this pronouncement. First, there is a clear link in the Deputy Prime Minister's statement between 'regional Australia' and country Australia. Second, there is an overt political dimension to the policy document, with the 'Liberal-National Government' explicitly canvassed rather than more inclusive language around the role of the Australian Government. Third, and relevant to the discussion in the section above, the Deputy Prime Minister's foreword establishes the rhetoric of regional development – including recognition of the symbolic importance of 'regional Australia', the need to support communities ideas and build leadership, but offers few substantive programs of assistance.

Similar spatial biases are evident in the formal regional policies of state governments, with an emphasis on non-metropolitan regions and, in large measure, an absence of discussion about the development of metropolitan regions. The exclusion of cities from the discussion of regions in Australia has profound implications, and, perhaps counter-intuitively, in the long term, it disadvantages the communities that might be seen to benefit from this assistance. The focus on non-metropolitan regions ensures there is no political consensus around the need for a spatial development strategy or a comprehensive regional development framework. At a political level, both sides of politics perceive regional development policy as serving the interests of National Party or Liberal Party electorates, while the metropolitan corollary – urban policy – is viewed as serving the immediate electoral interests of the Labor Party. In both cases, the perception that locationally-focussed policy interventions equate to 'pork barrelling' (McFarlane 2002) weakens the case for their continuation in the long term and contributes to disruption when governments change. At a policy level, the alignment of political interests with regional policy weakens the case for large scale programs in debates with Treasury or other central government agencies. It makes it more difficult to justify larger programs and creates an apparently insurmountable hurdle to arguments that systematic policy interventions are required.

At a more immediate level, it is often the case that regions – such as large peri-urban local governments – are eligible for funding for half their jurisdiction on the grounds that they are defined as rural, while the other half is seen as metropolitan and is therefore excluded from financial support.

Regional policies? Mismatch in the scale of delivery and the scale of need in responding to job losses in the automotive industry

The discussion so far has focussed on the broad dimensions of regional development in Australia and the structural and institutional processes that have made the system both inefficient and, on occasion, ineffective. It has been argued that the Australian system of federalism, in conjunction with neo-liberal policy instruments, has resulted in a fragmented approach to regional development, and one which is dominated by the politics of regionalism rather than a systematic concern with addressing spatial inequalities and improving the quality of life of all Australians. This section examines government responses to the loss of jobs at Mitsubishi Motors Australia Ltd (MMAL) in 2004 and uses this example to illustrate the issues of fragmentation, scale and the inadequate conceptualisation of regions canvassed above.

Employment loss at Mitsubishi Motors Australia: a regional crisis?

In April 2004, Australia's Prime Minister John Howard – flanked by South Australian Premier Mike Rann and Mr Tom Phillips, the serving CEO of Mitsubishi Motors Australia Limited (MMAL) – announced that the Lonsdale plant of MMAL would be closed with a loss of 700 jobs, with a further 400 voluntary redundancies from MMAL's Tonsley Park assembly plant. The factory had been in operation since the mid 1960s and performed a number of roles, including a foundry where engine blocks were cast, as well as hosting the assembly of some components, such as brake knuckles. The Tonsley Park plant has remained a site for vehicle assembly, but functions such as inventory and upholstery manufacture have been further outsourced.

The loss of just over 1,100 jobs in the southern part of metropolitan Adelaide was recognised as a major setback to the regional economy. The Federal Government responded by announcing a $45 million assistance package for the region – called the Structural Adjustment Fund (SAF) – as well as enhanced employment assistance for retrenched workers. This assistance was to be delivered via the Jobs Network, Australia's network of federally-funded labour market providers. In addition, the South Australian Government committed $10 million of assistance to displaced workers, mainly in the form of enhanced access to services. The loss of employment from MMAL in 2004 can be seen to be part of the longer term restructuring of the automobile industry, and manufacturing more generally, in Australia (House of Representatives Inquiry into the Automotive Component Manufacturing Sector, 2006). In the mid-1970s manufacturing employment accounted for 25% of the workforce but by 2001 it had declined to 12% of the labour force, even though the value of production had increased (Forster 2003). Where once car-making plants could be found in all state capitals except Perth, by the year 2000 motor vehicle production had consolidated into a limited number of sites with Toyota and Ford assembling vehicles in Melbourne, Mitsubishi and General Motors Holden building cars in Adelaide, and General Motors Holden building engines in Melbourne.

The southern region of Adelaide – defined as the jurisdictions of the City of Onkaparinga and the City of Marion – was perceived to be at risk economically as a consequence of the MMAL job losses. Its potential vulnerability reflected a number of structural factors, including the fact that the region has a relatively unskilled and under-qualified workforce (City of Marion and City of Onkapringa 2006); regional incomes are lower than the national average (ABS 2001); and a significant proportion of the workforce is employed outside the region. The further loss of local employment had the potential to undermine the viability of the region's small businesses. More specifically, the workforce being made redundant was mature and tended to be concentrated in neighbourhoods close to the MMAL factories. There was, therefore, a real prospect that those who left Mitsubishi would not find paid employment and that the consequences of employment loss would be concentrated in a relatively small area. In addition, the region as a whole has lagged behind the expansion of manufacturing – and especially advanced manufacturing – in other parts of the metropolitan area, as the majority of new manufacturing enterprises have established in northern Adelaide. Businesses within the southern region of Adelaide tend to be small-scale and relatively mature (Kearins 2002). The Mobil (Exxon) oil refinery at Lonsdale had closed two years previously with significant loss of employment; and the wine industry in the southern part of the City of Onkaparinga (Southern Vales/McLaren Vale) faltered in 2004 and 2005 as the national supply of grapes for wine production exceeded demand. Finally, it is worth noting that the southern region of Adelaide is relatively poorly served in terms of access to infrastructure, with transport, power and telecommunications of a poorer standard than its competitor regions.

Regional responses

The announcement of job losses from MMAL was accompanied by the establishment of a new institutional structure to deal with the consequences of the plant closure and employment loss. A new body was established – the South Australian Government Advisory Group – to provide the government with industry-relevant advice under the chairmanship of a former President of General Motors Japan. Four sub-committees were also established:

- Lonsdale Facility Assets to advise on the best possible use of the vacated Lonsdale Plant;
- Outplacement Opportunities to provide guidance on labour market programs and issues;
- The Southern Suburbs Industry Development Working Group (SSIDWG) to assist with the further development of the southern region economy, and
- Tonsley Park Utilisation which was charged with identifiying strategies to ensure the on-going financial viability of MMAL's remaining factory.

From its inception, considerable importance was attached to the work of SSIDWG as it was the only sub-committee to involve representatives of the region and it had a mandate to shape a new future for the region. SSIDWG commenced meeting fortnightly in May 2004 and began to address an ambitious program of work including: planning for a Southern Summit to raise the profile of the challenges confronting the Southern Region; preparation of a regional economic development strategy that embraced the two council areas (The Blueprint for the Future); research into the availability of land for further industrial development; contact with businesses and other organisations interested in investing in southern Adelaide or in applying for money from the Structural Adjustment Fund (SAF); and planning for an Innovation Centre in the south.

SSIDWG's role needs to be viewed within the context of the broader processes of government, as well as the overall response to the closure of the Lonsdale plant. It is important to emphasise that the $45 million of funds made available through the SAF was by far the most significant response to economic restructuring. Limited, or no, resources were committed by the State and Australian governments to other initiatives such as SSIDWG. This stands in stark contrast to policy responses in other regions – such as Birmingham, UK – where governments have invested substantial resources in the institutions managing the processes of change at the regional level. The MG Rover Task Force, set up when MG Rover announced that it has entered administration, had £175 million allocated to deal with the impact of the MG Rover closure and to assist further modernisation and diversification of suppliers (MG Rover Task Force, July 2005).

The SAF was the most significant response by central governments to the loss of employment at MMAL, and we must recognise that it does not fit easily within contemporary paradigms of regional development (see, for example, OECD 2001; Rainnie 2004) because the program consisted of grants – effectively capital subsidies – to firms willing to invest in South Australia. The SAF supported firms that were able to make a 'business case' that the injection of additional capital would allow for the expansion of business and would result in a significant number of new jobs. Firms had to match the grant awarded to them and complete a substantial application which was assessed by the advisory group. Two issues are critical here: first, SAF monies were not targeted exclusively to the southern region of Adelaide; and, as Table 8.1 shows, more grants were awarded to firms outside the region as within southern Adelaide. In other words, the SAF was intended to assist firms within the South Australia region, rather than focus on southern Adelaide. This meant that approximately half the funding went to the booming northern Adelaide region.

In part this decision was justified on the basis that workers from the south would commute to the new opportunities in the north, but as other research (Beer et al 2006) has shown, many retrenched workers were reluctant to undertake such time-consuming journeys to work, with a number choosing to leave the formal labour force rather than seek work in the north. Second, grants of this nature are a relatively blunt policy instrument and one which has fallen out of favour in most developed economies (Haughton et al 2003). Commonly, subsidy programs of this nature do not achieve the employment outcomes forecast – and committed to – by businesses (Beer, Maude and Pritchard 2003) and the diverse firms able to take up these opportunities effectively precludes the targeting of those industries considered to have the best long term prospects. In this instance, as shown in Table 8.1, the single largest grant was awarded to a chicken processing plant (Ingham Processing) in northern Adelaide.

Table 8.1: Grants Awarded under the Structural Adjustment Fund

Company	Amount	Location (in Adelaide)	Jobs created
Redarc Electronics	$1.6 million	Lonsdale (Southern)	60
Alloy Technologies International	$1.8 million	Wingfield (Northern)	100
Resource Co	$3 million	Lonsdale (Southern)	120
Cubic Pacific	$0.95 million	Edinburgh Park (Northern)	75
Fibrelogic Pty Ltd	$5.9 million	Lonsdale (Southern)	140
Ingham's Enterprises	$7 million	Edinburgh Park (Northern)	245
Intercast and Forge	$2.5 million	Wingfield (Northern)	68
PBR Australia	$1.5 million	Lonsdale (Southern)	?
Normanville Export Meatworks	$3.5 million	South (Southern)	80
SAGE Group Holdings	$1 million	Holden Hill (Northern)	73
ScreenCheck Australia Pty Ltd	$500,000	Melrose Park (Southern)	22
BD Farms Paris Creek Pty Ltd	$900,000	Adelaide Hills (Northern)	40
True Life Creations	$1 million	Adelaide city	46
Origin Energy Solar Pty Ltd	$2 million	Regency Park (North West)	53
Jumbo Vision International	$1.8 million	Mawson Lakes (Northern)	39
Inpak Foods	$2.1 million	Royal Park (North West)	37

Critically then, government responses to the loss of employment at MMAL included a high profile grant program from the Australian Government that was not targeted to the affected region, and which the evidence suggests is likely to be ineffective in the long term. The South Australian Government response was restricted and did not include ongoing measures to assist the adjustment of regional businesses. Local governments – the junior tier of government within Australian federalism (Troy and Stilwell 2000) – were left with responsibility for developing and implementing a more strategic approach to advancing the wellbeing of the southern region. SSIDWG emerged as an important avenue for local government to articulate its vision for the future of the region, as it adopted the roll of a 'clearinghouse' whereby ideas and issues were raised and tested against the opinions and attitudes of central government agencies. SSIDWG was the catalyst for a number of regional development strategies that attempted to present a new 'vision' for southern Adelaide and these are discussed in more detail in the section below.

The Australian Government chose to implement a Structural Adjustment fund that operated at the scale of all of South Australia. Effectively this decision saw the region affected by the redundancies as the entire state, and privileged that scale of intervention over a more tightly targeted intervention in the southern region. Critically then, the SAFSA allocated more monies to enterprises outside the southern region than within it. This outcome reflected both a neo-liberal ideology in which governments place priority on assisting private industry to expand in the wake of economic shocks, and an emphasis on market processes that operate on a wide geographic scale. It is quite possible that SAFSA funding would not have been fully allocated within the two year time period if had been restricted to the southern region. Instead, central governments would have been forced to think – more imaginatively – about other forms of assistance and support for the region. Such approaches could have included the provision of infrastructure that would have enhanced the competitive position of the region; comprehensive labour market training and education; and small business development programs. The approach adopted by the Australian Government assumed that workers displaced from MMAL would be willing and able to find employment in other regions, including northern metropolitan Adelaide. Other research (Beer et al 2006) challenges this assumption.

The strategic priorities of both the Australian Government and the Government of South Australia must be reviewed in order to understand the scale at which governments chose to act. For the Federal Government, the southern region of Adelaide is not a strategic priority as the nation's medium to long-term growth prospects are tied to mining and the expansion of knowledge-intensive industries along the eastern seaboard. The South Australian Government, also, had priorities that lay elsewhere. During the period of redundancies at MMAL the South Australian Government was bidding for, and won, a substantial expansion in its defence industries and was at the same time promoting the growth of mining in the northern part of the state. Indeed, the State government's priorities in the expansion of manufacturing capacity lay in northern Adelaide, in and around Edinburgh Park, where there was significant state government investment in road, rail and land development.

Conclusion: can Australia achieve an efficient framework for regional development?

Through this chapter I have argued that regional development in Australia is hampered by the outcomes of our system of federalism, by political ideologies grounded in neo-liberalism that are wary of direct interventions in regional economies, and by an emphasis on short-term political responses, rather than longer term strategic interventions. As the case study of the response to the loss of employment at MMAL has shown, governments often choose to act at scales that do not coincide with the scale of need: the closure of the Lonsdale plant and the loss of jobs at Tonsley Park generated challenges for the southern region of Adelaide, but the major response was directed to all of South Australia. This mismatch resulted in the leakage of a considerable percentage of assistance out of the region, often to localities where governments had other priorities. In large measure this failure of scale reflects a flawed understanding of regional issues and regional policies. In the case study presented here, the failure of either the Australian or State government to articulate regional policies that embraced both metropolitan and non-metropolitan regions meant there was no formal structure in place to serve as a mechanism for the delivery of assistance, and gave governments room to manoeuvre in directing assistance to where funding would best suit their political ends, rather than the real needs of affected regions.

Australian federalism lies at the heart of the failure to develop appropriate regional policies. As noted above, the Australian Government has the funding that would empower an effective regional development framework, the State and Territory governments have the constitutional power, and local governments have neither the funding or the power, but have the commitment needed to bring about change. As the discussion of the response to job losses at Mitsubishi Motors has shown, the division of powers between the three tiers of government contributes to a clouding of the lines of responsibility and accountability. While leader of the Opposition, Kim Beazley noted that:

> buckpassing between Commonwealth and the States isn't a new problem. But it has reached absurd heights in recent years ...

> John Howard's federalism has failed. Failed to tackle Australia's challenges. Failed to seize special opportunities. Failed to lay foundations for future prosperity (Beazley 2006, p.1).

In a similar vein, the Business Council of Australia has described our federal system as 'chronically blurred and confused'. It would be false to expect that Australian federalism would operate more efficiently if Labor was in power nationally, because the fundamental tensions between the revenue raising powers of national government and the substantial expenditure and service provision responsibilities of state and territory governments would remain unchanged. State governments must also shoulder their share of the blame for the parlous state of regional policy in Australia. The new-style state populism pioneered by Bob Carr in NSW is dominated by slogans such as being 'tough on crime' and emphasises health and education expenditure over other fields. There is little scope for systematic and comprehensive regional economic development strategies – that would focus on non-metropolitan and metropolitan regions alike – within this political and policy framework.

Finally we should ask, is it possible to achieve an efficient framework for regional development in Australia? At a technical level the answer must be yes, we know that other nations have more rational and comprehensive approaches to regional development than that evident in Australia. We are also aware of the strategies and techniques that could deliver better economic development outcomes (see, for example, Beer, Haughton and Maude 2003) but such technical solutions are of little merit unless there is fundamental change within Australian federalism. We need a system of government that recognises the importance of regional development and that allocates resources and responsibilities appropriately. Until that time, Australia is likely to continue to experience the impact of partial and inadequate regional development policies.

References

Anderson, J. (undated), *Stronger Regions: A Stronger Australia,* Department of Transport and Regional Services, Canberra.

Australian Bureau of Statistics 2001, *Census 2001*, ABS, Canberra.

Beazley, K. 2006, 'Modern Federalism: Beyond States' Rights and States' Wrongs', Address to the *Economic and Social Outlook Conference*, Melbourne, November.

Beer, A. 2000, 'Regional Policy in Australia: Running out of Solutions?' Chapter 10 (pp 169-194) in Pritchard, B. and McManus, P. (ed.) *Land of Discontent*, University of New South Wales Press, Sydney.

Beer, A., F. Baum, H. Thomas, C. Lowry, C. Cutler, Guangyu Zhang, G. Jolley, A. Ziersch, F. Verity, C. MacDougall and L. Newman, 2006, 'An Evaluation of the Impact of Retrenchment At Mitsubishi Focussing on Affected Workers, Their Families and Communities: Implications for Human Services Policies and Practices', Department of Health, Adelaide, Unpublished.

Beer, A., G. Haughton and A. Maude, 2003, *Developing Locally: Lessons in Economic Development from Four Nations*, Policy Press, Bristol.

Beer, A. and A. Maude, 1997, *Effectiveness of State Frameworks for Local Economic Development*, Local Government Association of South Australia, Adelaide.

———— 2002, *Local and Regional Economic Development Agencies in Australia*, Local Government Association of South Australia, Adelaide.

Beer, A., A. Maude and B. Pritchard, 2003, *Developing Australia's Regions: Theory and Practice,* University of NSW Press, Sydney.

City of Marion and City of Onkaparinga 2006, *Southern Region Economic Diversification Plan Draft*.

Collits, P. 1995, 'Balanced State Development in NSW Policy Making – Past Glories and Future Prospects', Paper presented to the Australian and New Zealand Regional Science Association, Brisbane, December.

————. 2003, 'The Tyranny of the Announceable', Paper presented to the Australian and New Zealand Regional Science Association, Fremantle, September.

Forster, C. 2003, *Australian Cities, Continuity and Change*, Second Edition, Oxford University Press, Melbourne.

Haughton, G., A. Beer and A. Maude, 2003, 'Understanding International Divergence and Convergence in Local and Regional Economic Development' in Beer, A. et al (eds) *Developing Locally*, Policy Press, Bristol, pp. 15-36.

House of Representatives, Standing Committee on Employment, Workplace Relations and Workforce Participation, 1st May 2006.

House of Representatives Standing Committee on Economics, Finance and Public Administration (The Hawker Report) 2003, *Rates and Taxes: Fair Shares for Responsible Local Government,* The Parliament of the Commonwealth of Australia, Canberra.

Jones, M. 1997, 'Spatial selectivity of the state?' *Environment and Planning A,* 29, pp. 831-64.

Kearins, B. 2002, 'Exporting Locally: A Strategy for Regional Small Business Growth', *Sustaining Regions*, 2(1), pp. 17-28.

MacSharry, R., P. White, and J. O'Malley, 2000, *The Making of the Celtic Tiger,* Mercier Press, Cork.

McFarlane, D. 2002, 'Deputy Prime Minister Serves Up More Pork', *The Australian*, p. 3, 12 June.

MG Rover Task Force, 2005, 'Closure of MG Rover: Economic Impact Assessment', July, Birmingham.

OECD 2001, *Best Practices in Local Economic Development,* OECD, Paris.

Rainnie, A. and M. Grobelaar (eds) 2005, *The New Regionalism,* Ashgate, Aldershot.

Spoehr, J. 2005, *The State of South Australia,* Wakefield Press, South Australia.

Chapter 9: Reconceiving Federal-State-Regional Arrangements in Health

Andrew Podger

Introduction

Australia has a generally good health system, but it is changing in response to existing challenges and it faces new challenges which require substantial reform if the system is to remain affordable and effective. The system is huge, with expenditure in health accounting for around 9.7% of Australia's annual gross domestic product (GDP). It is difficult to imagine an area of public policy and service delivery with which the average Australian citizen would have more contact, or of greater importance to the community. As a result, substantial reform is difficult – politically, financially and logistically.

This chapter examines some of the options for reform and restructuring of the health system to meet new challenges, in the context of our current federal system. Most of my perspectives are from practical experience at a federal level, rather than any particular theory of how our federal system should work. First I will examine some of the principles of effective and responsive government including some new ways in which government can and often does achieve results, working across traditional institutional boundaries. But despite improvements in whole-of-government collaboration, for major ongoing national priorities like health, poor institutional structures can still present major practical obstacles to achieving efficient and effective outcomes. This is explained in the second part of the chapter. The challenges lie at both the national level, where we need the accountability and efficiency of a system based on national funding and national standards – and at the regional and local levels – at which health services need to be adapted and delivered, but where our institutional infrastructure is comparatively weak: there is a need for greater directness, simplicity and clarity in the relationships between these levels.

The third part of the chapter talks a little more about what is needed at each level of the health system, particularly the local and regional levels. It becomes clear that we have to start considering some new institutional options, within our current federal context, if we want to maintain the best possible health system into the future. The model I propose would be more patient-focussed than the one we have now, but would also have in-built incentives to improve efficiency. It would also more effectively address equity, in my view, giving more resources to regions and communities (including Indigenous communities) that most need additional support.

The choice facing governments is not one between theoretical, idealised models of new systems, on the one hand, and small practical incremental solutions to immediate problems on the other. It is a mixture of both. If a more incremental approach is pursued, it is important also to have a clear strategic direction to avoid *ad hocracy*; if government is willing to consider systemic change, it must include measures that deliver tangible improvements along the way as well as lead to structures with better in-built incentives for improved performance. Clearly my preference is for the latter approach.

Principles for more effective governance

A first general principle for helping make government effective and responsive is the 'subsidiarity principle' – also mentioned by other authors in this volume (see Brown, Head, Wiltshire, Smith this volume). Based on what our national Productivity Commission has said over many years (e.g. Productivity Commission 1998), my own definition of the subsidiarity principle is that 'power should be devolved to the lowest level of government where there is shared community interest'. The principle is about distinguishing clearly who should be responsible for what, as well as supporting vertical fiscal balance, so that each level of government is able to raise and control the funds necessary to meet the policy requirements for which it is accountable.

In practice, however, 'subsidiarity' is not an absolute principle – it has to fit into the pragmatic realities of day-to-day government. As a former head of Commonwealth Government departments, including Health as well as Housing and Regional Development, I learned it was very useful, in a practical sense, to understand that the relationships between different parts of the federal system were much like the relationships between any set of organisations. A Canadian expert once distinguished between those matters that you can control; those you can only influence; and those matters which lie in the control of others, which it is wise to appreciate as you decide how to go about your own business (Smith 1992). While there are advantages in clarifying responsibilities – that is, who controls what – there are still always boundary areas and grey areas, where one jurisdiction wants to influence another. As boundaries shift over time, it is also wise to have an appreciation of those areas that are under the control of the other party, to ensure that attempts to influence are based on informed judgments.

So, if the Commonwealth wants to influence aspects of health or housing or city planning or community services it needs a real appreciation of those fields of social policy and management. Equally, it is important for state or local governments to have an appreciation of national policy concerns that might affect the areas that are under their control, such as international obligations or national equity issues. It is not just a matter of setting who controls what, but thinking carefully of how you influence and appreciate the things that other levels of government have to control.

Another practical reality, which can assist the ability of government to work across traditional institutional boundaries, is 'horizontal' rather than 'vertical' management of programs and projects. Horizontal management means 'connected government', or 'joined-up' government, in which we find new ways to ensure that all the different parts of government overcome their institutional separations and come together to efficiently and effectively play their part. The greater interest in connectivity and horizontal government in recent years should not be seen as just a fad – it has many recognised long-term drivers, across many policy areas, on a worldwide basis. These include the increasing demands of citizens; the complexity of modern social problems; the pressure on public budgets; the impact of new information and communications technologies, giving both the increased technical capacity to connect and a related increase in expectations that we will use that capacity; and active experimentation by governments in new ways to meet these challenges and deliver services (Lindquist 2000).

Again, however, there are limits and risks to using horizontal approaches. We identified some of these in a recent major report on 'connecting government' at a Commonwealth level (Management Advisory Committee 2004). If you try to connect everything to everything else, all the time, it can be very costly and time-consuming, and not very efficient. A great deal of effort can be put into cooperative efforts that were always doomed to fail, because there were competing political and community agendas within the control of other parties. Alternatively, if those agendas are not taken seriously and are instead overridden in the push to consensus, there is the danger of 'groupthink' – that is, of pressuring everyone involved to agree, rather than to ensure that the different perspectives are robustly considered. This can result in lowest common denominator solutions. Finally, establishing complex arrangements to involve many parties in a solution, may not be the most efficient and effective way of dealing with a routine, straightforward issue.

Of the many issues relevant to deciding when and how to apply the principles of connected government, two are particularly important when thinking about the problems with our current federal system – the structures and processes to be used, and the imperatives for external engagement, meaning direct engagement with the community and others outside government. Table 9.1 sets out that there is no fixed approach, when it comes to structures and processes. Different whole-of-government tasks require different structures.

Table 9.1. Matching Whole-of-Government Structures to Different Tasks

Task Structure	Policy Development	Program Design / Review	Program Management/ Service Delivery	Cross Jurisdiction/ Cross Sector	Crisis Management
Inter-Departmental Committee (IDC)	H	M	L	M	H-M
Taskforce	H	H	H	H-M	M-L
Joint team	H-M	H-M	M	M-L	L
Agency arrangements	L	L	H	M-L	L
Frontier agencies	H	H	H	L	L

H = high relevance

M = medium relevance

L = low relevance

Source: Management Advisory Committee 2004, p.42 (Table 2.6)

The Management Advisory Committee report from which this table is drawn, focussed primarily on whole-of-government activity within a single level of government. But the message from this table would apply equally to inter-governmental structures and processes. The message is that horizontal management is easiest and most effective when dealing with time-limited projects. If you want to move away from traditional agency arrangements, and instead use IDCs and taskforces (or inter-governmental committees), for example, it is better when you are dealing with individual projects. In a modern world, in most government departments, there is also growing interest in thinking about program management as a series of projects. Accordingly, this approach to policy implementation – implementing policy project by project – also lends itself to being able to more easily pursue 'connectedness'. However, if you are dealing with ongoing programs – such as health programs in general, or natural resource management programs in general – then more traditional agency arrangements still tend to remain a better arrangement, in which a deliberate attempt is made to line up who is responsible for what, and where inter-agency (or inter-governmental) committees play more of a support role rather than a direct management role. So, notwithstanding the interest and the great potential of 'connected' or 'joined up' government in many areas, there are practical limits to this *horizontality* approach, and there are still advantages in trying to define the differing roles and responsibilities of different agencies reasonably firmly, where you can.

Because 'connected government' is partly a response to community demands, there are also serious issues about how connected government then deals with community engagement. These issues relate particularly to the political accountability and legitimacy of new types of structures. Whole-of-government initiatives, including ones involving multiple levels of government, often entail commitments to take into account the views of particular stakeholders more seriously than before – yet they must also preserve the responsibility of government(s) to the broader public interest. This can be a difficult exercise, especially for structures or institutions that have been formed on a relatively temporary and flexible basis.

An important part of community engagement is careful assessment of the views of the different interest groups that are presented. There are challenges involved in balancing complexity and consistency, where there is a need to respond to individual or community needs and preferences, while adhering to the policy objective of the broader – possibly national – community interests involved. Of particular relevance to reform in the health system, and some other service delivery areas, is the growing challenge of being responsive to a community or area or to individuals in ways that traditional services have not been able to achieve. An important success factor highlighted in the Management Advisory Committee report is having 'clout on the ground'. At the end of the day, there must be somebody there with authority and capability in local management, and with the necessary legitimacy and standing in the local community, to carry the outcomes into effect. Connected government can help provide these local actors – be they public servants or community representatives or both – with the authority from 'on high' to be able to act, but the local resources still need to be there, to have local legitimacy, and usually to be there longer than the lifespan of any single project.

This has been particularly demonstrated in Aboriginal affairs, but from my own experience it is important in any area of regional development. If you want to have regional development of a Commonwealth interest, you need to have a Commonwealth person at that regional level who has some clout and the capacity to negotiate and be able to act.

What lessons do we draw from these principles, for the current structures of public administration in our federal system? First, even in the age of cooperation and intergovernmental collaboration, we should not throw out the subsidiarity principle. It is important to clarify who is responsible for what, when talking about ongoing responsibilities, to the extent this is possible. But secondly, there will always still be boundaries between levels of government in any system, however it is reformed; and so we will need to have ongoing consultative machinery to ensure appreciation as well as management of those boundaries. Third, whole-of-government approaches can be used to improve government responsiveness, and share responsibility, where it is important and efficient to use these approaches to deal with challenges in a timely fashion – especially in relation to project management crises. But fourthly, the political pressure for these 'joined-up' solutions is also more long-term and enduring than can simply be met by shorter-term collaborations. And fifthly, in all of this, there is a need, however we do it, for greater capacity at the local/regional level – including

Commonwealth capacity at that local/regional level – to develop and deliver better outcomes in the many areas where important national interests are at stake, along with those historically regarded as local and state ones.

New approaches in health policy and services

When we apply these principles to Australia's health system, the need for a new strategic approach becomes clear. Health is as much an industry as a system. In most countries, and certainly in Australia, health is certainly not a centrally designed, or hierarchically managed system. Participants, both consumers and providers, exercise a considerable degree of independence. The health system nonetheless is dominated by government, as funder and regulator, and frequently as the provider of health services themselves. While the system should, and will, remain a mixed 'public' and 'private' system, some of the key issues surround what it is best for government to do, with the focus on regulating, funding and purchasing health services. Under a reformed system, it would continue to matter less whether services themselves were provided privately or publicly, provided these regulatory, funding and purchasing arrangements were effective and more directly accountable.

Elsewhere I have set out some of the evidence that our health system actually performs quite well, on international standards (Podger 2006a and b). However this provides no room for complacency, because the challenges continue to mount. Indeed the system is already changing in response to these challenges, which increases our need to map clearly where we want it to go, rather than risk some of our current advantages by responding in ways that are disorganised or *ad hoc*. There are at least five major structural problems with the current system:

- *A lack of patient-oriented care* which crosses service boundaries easily, with funds following patients, particularly those with chronic diseases, the frail aged and Indigenous people. This is becoming increasingly important with our increasing life expectancy, and the big change over the last 30 years in the proportion of our population that is living longer after reaching the age of 50. The consequence is that there are many more frail aged people in our population, and many more people surviving heart disease, or cancer, and then living on under complex health regimes. A key issue for Australia's health system concerns people who are chronically ill or frail aged who move about the whole system – in and out of hospitals, on and off pharmaceuticals, receiving support in nursing homes, and getting support in their community. An increasing proportion of citizens cross all the traditional boundaries that have separated different service providers in the health system, both organisationally and geographically. Boundary issues are becoming far more important these days than they ever were in the past.

- *Allocative inefficiency*, in which the allocation of funding between different types of care is not always geared towards achieving the best health outcomes possible, including in the ability of communities to invest directly in prevention and community health strategies as opposed to simply receiving funding for medical services (Menadue 2000, 2003). There are presently obstacles to our ability to shift resources within the system to enable individuals or communities to allow different mixes of service that reflect different needs.
- *Poor use of information technology*, where better investments and usage could not only reduce administrative costs and costs of duplicate testing, but also support more continuity of care, better identification of patients at risk, greater safety and more patient control.
- *Poor use of competition*, with an uneven playing field in acute care, a reluctance to use competition to ensure best access to medical services at reasonable cost, and less choice than should be possible, particularly in aged care.
- *Workforce supply constraints*, and increasing demand.

Every one of these structural problems is exacerbated by the institutional framework that we currently use to run the health system, and in particular, by Australia's current division of roles and responsibilities between the Commonwealth and the States. Therefore, even though our health system is performing pretty well on the whole, and changing the system cannot be without cost or risk, it is important to examine the options for where we want the system to end up – not as a distant pipe dream, but as a realistic alternative given practical realities and our history, culture and institutions.

Applying the principles in the last section to our current health system, two important shifts in the structure of the system become not only desirable, but probably inevitable. When we apply the subsidiarity principle, it becomes clear that the Commonwealth Government is going to continue to increase its responsibility for health policy and services, rather than reduce it. Quite apart from issues of funding, this is because of the strength of our national community interest in ensuring that there is equity throughout Australia in the availability and quality of health services; because health industries increasingly operate on a national basis, and both the health workforce and health service consumers are increasingly mobile; and because there are economies of scale to be captured in administering health services as a national system. The private health insurance industry and the pharmaceutical industry, for example, operate at the national level. Some of the services that have to be handled at a national level include cord blood banks and organ donations. Health education and medical training are national needs and are largely nationally funded. Recent crises in some state health systems over the qualifications and accreditation of health professionals highlight the increasing inappropriateness of trying to monitor and police such issues at a provincial level. If you think about who should be responsible for what, subsidiarity principles leave a great deal of responsibility with the Commonwealth.

The extent of the Commonwealth interest is then further underscored, of course, by the fact that two-thirds of all the public spending on health is already spending by the Commonwealth Government. Unlike other areas of public policy, where the Commonwealth has expanded its influence by stealth, in health it has been done by the express will of the Australian people – voting in 1946 to amend the Constitution to give the Federal Parliament power over the provision of pharmaceutical benefits, sickness benefits, hospital benefits, and medical and dental services (Constitution, section 51 (xxiiiA)). The present level of Commonwealth expenditure aligns with this historical reality, and public expectations about an efficient, seamless national health system that have only continued to strengthen.

The importance of the Commonwealth in the system is then further reinforced by pressure for movement towards a single funder arrangement. Faced with the current challenges, most economists agree that we would be better off moving from an arrangement where multiple governments provide the funds, tied to at times competing and conflicting priorities and accountabilities, to a single funder who can bring simplicity, consistency and efficiency. Most reformers in the health sector agree that a single funder would be better able to track the money so as to ensure that it follows the patient, rather than being constrained by strict functional or jurisdictional boundaries, or lost or redirected as it filters down through the system. In these ways, a single funder would facilitate more integrated and comprehensive planning, enhance the coordination of service delivery, improve value for money, increase the opportunity for seamless, patient-oriented services, and reduce cost-shifting and blame-shifting. These are highly relevant advantages for our system today.

There are four main options for who this single funder could be. The first would be to revert 100 years to a system where state governments are the single funder in their jurisdiction, but few regard this as realistic or desirable. A form of this option could work along the lines of the Canadian model, with a revenue-sharing agreement with the national government but all purchasing and delivery left to the States, but the fact is that, given all our history, we are not like Canada. Second, we could 'pool' Commonwealth and state funds, to then be administered by a 'joint' national health administration, which is a solution in the tradition of cooperative federalism, under the Council of Australian governments (COAG) framework. However, applying what we know about the strengths and weaknesses of 'connected government', this has all the problems of trying to have a shared arrangement for ongoing programs, which is very difficult to manage in practice, and is likely to be extremely hard to operate efficiently. The third option, involving other massive transformations of the system, is a 'managed competition' or voucher-based insurance system such as proposed by Scotton (2002), which I discuss elsewhere. Importantly for advocates of this option, it could not be introduced without the Commonwealth first becoming the single government funder (option four below), and then redirecting that funding into a system of insurance vouchers.

The fourth option – in my view, by far the most logical given all of the above – is that the Commonwealth Government move the relatively short distance from its current role, to that of also being the single funder. In practice, funding the entire system would mean retention by the Commonwealth of its current specific purpose grants to the States for health, plus around 37% of the $35 billion (2003-04) paid annually to the States in the form of Goods and Services Tax (GST). This could be achieved by renegotiation of the GST agreement. State governments would be left in the same financial position as currently, since they would no longer have to spend the $13 billion (2002-03) of their own-source funding currently expended annually on hospitals and other health services.

However, an important second structural shift is also implied in the evolution of our health system. Again applying the principle of subsidiarity and the other issues reviewed in the previous section, it is clear that even if we move towards a single national funder and clear Commonwealth regulatory control over the health system, the case remains for stronger regional and local involvement in the purchase and provision of these centrally-funded health services. Indeed, the case only becomes stronger. Therefore, while the subsidiarity principle translates into a very strong argument for a lot of health responsibilities to be handled at the national level, it also translates into an equally strong argument for most service delivery to be handled lower down, at the local or regional level. This includes all manner of delivery, including general practitioners, baby health clinics, pharmacies, hospitals, and nursing homes. Alongside the national government accepting the leadership role in setting the overall design principles of the system, and monitoring its performance, the problems of our current system would be addressed by introducing greater flexibility in the system at a lower level – lower than that of most of our present state governments. For these reasons, local and regional-level institutions would only become more important in the future.

Taking these two shifts together, Figure 9.2 sets out the structure of what a Commonwealth-funded public health system might look like. This structure would more clearly distinguish between who is funding the services, and the roles of purchasers and providers. It also remains a three-tiered system – national, regional and local – because local-level provision of health services remains vital. Essentially the Commonwealth would have the funding responsibilities at the national level and the oversight of the purchasing, but most purchasing would be at the regional level, and most of the services would be delivered either at the regional or local level. The major structural difference with current arrangements, in terms of service delivery, would be that these regional purchasers and/or providers, who control much of how services are designed and delivered in practice, would be unlikely to be a state government – other than perhaps in the case of Tasmania. In my view, they should be Commonwealth authorities, with a 'region' defined in line with the criteria already used by governments to determine the best scales at which to deliver these services.

Figure 9.2. What should a Commonwealth funded Public Health System look like?

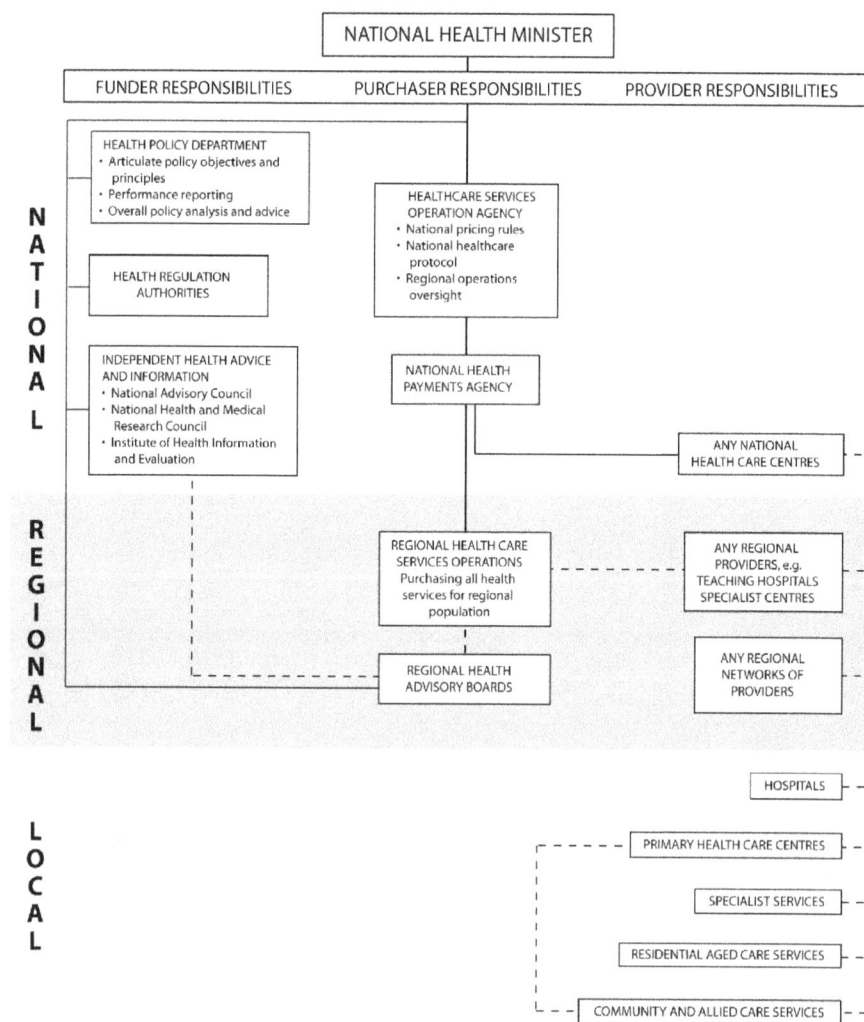

The next section discusses what this would mean in practice. Clearly there is little value in pretending that simply restructuring the system in these terms would suddenly fix all its problems or, in itself, meet all its challenges. A range of supplementary measures would be needed to ensure that *any* system works well, including this one as proposed. Some of these are already under way, such as the separation of funding, purchasing and providing – in ways that reinforce the need for a larger blueprint. What is clear is that if we ignore the options for systemic and institutional reform, we limit our own capacity to improve the system, whereas by considering them, we can hope to achieve sensible reforms including national principles for purchasing; greater ability to reallocate resources across and within regions in more flexible ways; increasing local involvement in service delivery; strengthening primary health care where it is needed; increasing the investment in preventive health strategies; strengthening cost control and accountability; and maximising the benefits of competition.

The new regional level in health: new institutions?

How would a reformed health system work in practice, particularly at the regional level? It goes without saying that it would mean institutional reform, but not constitutional reform, as it would rely on an existing range of familiar institutions. Even at the national level, there would be the need for new institutional infrastructure, rather than simply entrusting an increased range of responsibilities to the existing Commonwealth department.

The national administrative framework needs to be designed to meet a number of key requirements:

- political oversight and accountability;
- policy-advising capacity, well-informed by health and medical expertise;
- professional integrity in setting and administering regulatory standards;
- dedicated effort, appropriate management and technical expertise for operational matters, particularly for oversight of the nation-wide purchasing function.

The scale of these responsibilities would demand a number of separate agencies performing key roles, while working together within the policy framework set by the political leadership. The options for the national structure might include:

- a policy department responsible directly to the Minister for Health, advising expertly on the various health functions, health infrastructure, broad strategic issues, and general policy coordination;
- a suite of regulatory authorities, some of which already exist, overseeing separate but related areas of regulation including licensing of health products and providers, food standards, nursing home and residential facility standards, and the private health insurance industry;

- an operational or executive agency, responsible for purchasing services at a national level and oversighting regional health service purchasers (see further below); and
- a strong national advisory body having links to advisory bodies associated with each of the major regulators, resources for independent research and independent reporting.

This national-level arrangement could draw very heavily on existing organisations, which would all be best placed in one portfolio, to aid policy coherence and coordination.

At the other end of the system – the local level – many institutional arrangements would not be substantially changed, even though the availability and quality of services should continually improve. At this level, the focus is on service provision. Most doctors and other professional health providers would continue to operate as independent private businesses and hospitals and aged care providers would continue to operate with a degree of independence as private or charitable organisations, or as public institutions with substantial management autonomy. However, some important changes could be expected over time. For example, a more integrated and patient-focussed approach will require further strengthening of primary care arrangements, with GP practices becoming increasingly multi-skilled, supported by nursing staff and linked more closely with allied health professionals as well as specialist medical practitioners. GP practices might effectively exercise increasing responsibility for the health care budget for their patients within the framework developed by regional purchasers. In rural and remote areas and for Indigenous communities, primary care services may be provided in more flexible and community-responsive ways, to address their particular needs and/or their unique problems in attracting skilled workers.

Similarly, while hospitals would need to comply with minimum national standards and supervision, and be supported by the simplicity of uniform national purchasing requirements, they could ultimately be managed more flexibly according to the needs of the particular region. In community aged care services, there would be increased opportunity for regional purchasers to negotiate prime contracts with organisations responsible for networks of service providers delivering services in line with individuals' care assessments and customer-responsive authorisation. Over time, there would be opportunities for closer integration of community and residential aged care, and for services that allow more 'ageing-in-place' including more choice for the individuals concerned about their accommodation and services. For all major local publicly-owned facilities, there is a choice of governance models for delivering greater local responsiveness. The management of public hospitals should involve some direct interaction with the community, and ensure good community access; it should have the full confidence of clinical and professional staff; it needs to have sufficient critical mass to deliver acute care services safely and efficiently; and it needs the flexibility to go with the accountability for delivering services efficiently and effectively. The options include trusts within the framework of the national operations agency, with executive boards that include health expertise, business acumen and local community representation; or separate agencies each managed by a CEO appointed by the national operating organisation and responsible to it, with a strong advisory board. Indeed, governance models might vary between regions. Major local facilities might be Commonwealth-owned, regionally-owned, locally-owned or indeed privately owned; in any case, they would be subject to clear national regulation and their roles and requirements as service providers determined by contract with the regional purchasing authority.

The crucial link in obtaining the gains envisaged by a truly Commonwealth public health system of this kind, is at this regional level. The regional purchasers of health services would carry much of the responsibility for the increased flexibility under the new system. They provide the key to improving allocational efficiency in the system, through the incentive framework created by these regional purchasers having responsibility for the health objectives for their own population, and the flexibility to allocate funds according to their most cost-effective use. There would also be constraints: for example, national policy requirements such as co-payment limits and safety nets, nationally negotiated prices for particular services and oversight to guard against risks of poor management or inefficient responses to short-term pressures. However, consistent with these constraints is the clear scope for regional authorities to provide:

- close connections with providers and community organisations to ensure the purchasing is well-informed and responsive to regional requirements;
- clear accountability back to the national operational agency, and compliance with national policies; and
- sufficient clout to negotiate cost-effective deals with providers, including hospitals, nursing homes and specialists.

A crucial factor is that the regional population would be large enough for the authority to accept responsibility for the vast majority of health risks, thus driving the development of a holistic regional health strategy and integrated approaches to service design and purchase. The actuarial evidence is that purchasers could cover most variations in health risk if the population they are responsible for is around 200,000 or more. Given the variations in Australian demography, there is the possibility of around 20-30 regional purchasers, with the possibility of sub-regional arrangements to assist community responsiveness. This also has the advantage of being not too great a number of purchasers for the national operational agency to oversee.

There are a number of options for the constitution of this regional health authority. My own preference would be for each regional purchaser to be under the direct control of the national operational agency, but with each also having a strong advisory board involving, in particular, the relevant GP Division(s) and other regional providers, and community organisations, possibly including local government representation. Some individual nominees selected by the Minister could also ensure a consumer voice and a sensible balance, without unduly politicising the board. The precise structure could draw heavily on current state regional health authorities and state and Commonwealth regional planning arrangements (e.g. for aged care); and draw upon – and, in time, influence – the structure and role of Divisions of GPs.

In time, the manner in which the regional purchaser is constituted might be influenced by, or evolve in line with, other regional governance arrangements within the federal system. It is not necessary, however, for the regional purchaser to be a constitutionally-recognised regional government in order to capture the benefits of competitive federalism, in which you still get the advantage of competition between different regions to provide better services to citizens. The efficiency and performance of regional health purchasing authorities, designing and contracting for services on behalf of the Commonwealth, would still be monitored and reported in the same way that the Productivity Commission now reports on the performance of state governments. It is, therefore, not clear that the purchaser needs to be a level of government, provided it is an agency with both flexibility and authority.

Clearly the staff of the regional authority would need to include health expertise as well as management expertise. The purchasing authority would have responsibility for paying for all services provided to residents in the region, wherever those services are provided (including, for example, high level acute services in a national centre outside the region). It would have a 'soft-capped' total budget based on the population's risk profile, with access to some specific national risk pools where the region cannot be expected to manage the risk on its own. The soft cap would also allow budget over-runs if necessary, where the consequences would be some form of performance review rather than penalising the regional population. The regional budget would identify estimates for component parts, but with specified levels of discretion where the regional purchaser can substantiate claims of savings in one component that might be better employed elsewhere, or can substantiate claims of the positive impact of a proposed investment on both health and costs. The degree of discretion might be widened in the light of proven performance over a period of several years. Regional purchasers could be expected to develop increasingly sophisticated approaches to managing the risks of sub-populations, particularly the various categories of chronically ill, drawing on the nationally developed protocols of best-practice, cost-effective care. Substantially increased funding of Indigenous communities could be expected, subject to monitoring improved health performance.

Regional purchasers would be required to publish annual reports on performance including health outcomes, service levels and financing, preferably supplemented by broader information reports by the national health statistics organisation for all regions.

As outlined earlier, the key advantages delivered by this arrangement would be not simply increased efficiency but, more importantly, increased responsiveness and flexibility. The regional authority might consider contracting with Divisions of GPs not only to provide support for GPs and for primary care planning in the regions, but also to manage the delivery of some allied or specialist services where the local (private) supply is not adequate. The regional purchaser may find it cost-effective to establish (or re-establish or restructure) associated primary care services such as maternity and child health clinics. It would be expected to move reasonably quickly to consider options for 'contracting out' or for 'centres of excellence' for particular procedures and activities to improve efficiency. It would explore with GPs, hospitals and other non-hospital providers the options for reducing the need for hospital care and building, or rebuilding hospital outreach services as a more cost-effective way of supporting patients. This may lead to reversing the decline in rehabilitation services, and in various outpatient services particularly in fields such as dialysis and cancer remediation.

What would this new or reconstituted regional level mean for the current state governments? In most cases, there would no longer be particular purpose or value in the state government attempting to own or run hospitals or other major health services, when these can be more efficiently run either privately, locally or as Commonwealth-owned facilities within the streamlined national system. Section 51 (xxiiiA) of the Constitution not only provides the Commonwealth with the power to make laws with respect to the provision of sickness and hospital benefits, but with respect to the provision of medical services, including owning and managing hospitals itself. Indeed its powers would extend to compulsory acquisition of state facilities for this purpose. However it would clearly be wise for the Commonwealth to negotiate the transfer of responsibility from the States, either to itself or to alternative local or regional providers, rather than attempting a compulsory take-over. The objective of a more seamless patient-oriented system would also suggest the transfer not only of hospitals, but other elements of state health systems. Of course, new boundaries would arise between the Commonwealth system and ongoing state and local community services systems, but these boundaries would not generally be as disruptive to patient care as the boundaries that currently exist within health. The model does not preclude the States from delivering health services purchased by a

(Commonwealth) regional purchaser, and particularly in the medium term there could be benefit in drawing on state expertise in establishing the regions and supporting the planning work of regional purchasers. But, over time, the state role could be expected to fall away.

Importantly, the system would not be managed entirely from Canberra. It would have regional purchasers with the responsibility and flexibility to purchase the mix of services most appropriate to the region. They would be required to work closely with local community leaders and providers such as the GP Divisions. They would, however, work within the policy framework established nationally. Most services would be provided locally with a considerable degree of professional independence; services such as public hospitals would have management boards or trusts. Geographically large regions would need to have sub-regional planning structures and associated flexibility to allocate resources within the local area.

The potential benefits are clear, especially for rural and remote communities (see Podger 2007), but also less-advantaged urban communities. There would be transparency about the allocation of resources across regions and the ability to highlight regions receiving significantly less than their population needs deserve (relative to other regions). There would be greater flexibility to find local solutions to regional problems, blurring the current boundaries between hospitals, general practice and other forms of primary health care, and between medical services and aged care services. There would be room for informed choice by communities about services to be provided locally, and those to be accessed from specialist providers outside the area – making the trade-off, for example, between access and quality. These are all advantages that should be considered standard in a modern world-class health system. In Australia's case, strategic investment in orderly change and new institutions is needed to achieve them.

Conclusions: systemic reform or *ad hocracy*?

Reform of the kind advocated in this chapter would take time to implement, with many details open to debate and refinement. Moreover, there will be costs and risks in the transition. Accordingly, it is sensible to keep pursuing incremental changes in parallel with exploring the systemic change options. There are also natural limits to structural solutions and to the pace of reform, requiring attention also be given to the 'people issues' that will make a difference, including leadership and collaboration, and supporting systems and processes such as better information and transparency and genuine consultation. It is also important to remember that any new system will still have boundaries to manage, and is likely to involve all levels of government, even if some clearer division of responsibilities can be achieved.

However, we should not be satisfied with incremental reforms alone, particularly if they smack of political *ad hocracy* rather than a clear and coherent longer term strategy that might make systemic reform easier in the future.

The shift towards a truly national health system, with new regional institutions and frameworks as one of its cornerstones, is not predicated on abolition of the federal system nor does it necessarily imply that the State governments disappear. State governments could choose to remain in the area of providing services, and continue to receive Commonwealth funding accordingly, but through the more transparent, accountable and efficient regime provided by the new national system. Equally, however, local government could become a much more major provider of local health services, again taking its funding direct from the Commonwealth through a single purchaser arrangement. Whoever provides the services, the focus of reform needs to be on improving the effectiveness and efficiency of the system when viewed nationally *and* when viewed from the regional level. The necessary financial resources need to be both centralised in the Commonwealth as the national funder, *and* then decentralised to regional purchasing authorities in a way consistent with genuine devolution of these important areas of public policy and services.

All of this is both necessary and achievable in the area of health, without constitutional reform, but with appropriate vision and commitment. Whether the lessons of subsidiarity and the limits of connected government, discussed earlier, also make similar reform appropriate to other areas of Australian public policy, is a question worth considering, but which is best left for others to answer.

References

Lindquist, E. A. 2000, 'Preconceiving from the centre: leadership, strategic review and coherence in public sector reform', in Organisation for Economic Cooperation and Development, *Government of the Future*, OECD, Paris, pp. 149-84.

Management Advisory Committee 2004, *Connecting Government: Whole of Government Responses to Australia's Priority Challenges,* Management Advisory Committee Report No. 4, Australian Public Service Commission, Canberra.

Menadue, J. 2000, *Report of the NSW Health Council*, NSW Government, Sydney.

—— 2003, *Better Choices, Better Health*, Final Report of the South Australian Generational Health Review, Government of South Australia, Adelaide.

Podger, A. 2006a, 'Directions for Health Reform in Australia', in *Productive Reform in a Federal System: Roundtable Proceedings* 27-28 October 2005, Productivity Commission, Canberra, pp. 133-60.

———— 2006b, *A Model Health System for Australia*, Inaugural Menzies Health Policy Lecture, Menzies Centre on Public Health Policy, 3 March 2006; also published in three parts in *Asia Pacific Journal of Health Management*, 2006.

———— 2007, 'Rural and Remote Implications of a New Structure for Australia's Health System', Presentation to National Rural Health Conference, Albury NSW, 10 March 2007.

Productivity Commission 1998, *State, Territory and Local Government Assistance to Industry*, Final Report, Canberra.

Scotton, R. 2002, 'The Scotton Model', in Productivity Commission, *Managed Competition in Health Care*, Workshop Proceedings, Canberra.

Smith, W. E. 1992, 'Planning for the Electricity Sector in Columbia', in Weisbord, M. R. (ed.), *Discovering Common Ground*, Berrett-Koehler Publishers, San Francisco.

Part 3. New Institutions? Approaching the Challenge of Reform

Chapter 10: Taking Subsidiarity Seriously: What Role for the States?

Brian Head

Introduction

This chapter focuses on the issues and challenges for State governments in reforming Australian federalism. It proposes the more effective use of subsidiarity principles as a benchmark for assessing various reform proposals recently put forward from a range of perspectives. It examines some of the possible roles of state governments within an evolving federal system that has recently been characterised by a series of national agreements on major policy issues. The various proposals for fundamental redesign of the federation, including abolition of the States, are rejected. An argument is made in favour of a practical focus on effective and responsive governance, including a closer focus on more effective regional service delivery. This practical approach to 'good governance' would thus require continuing along the path of negotiating national agreements, taking subsidiarity more seriously, further clarifying roles in improved service delivery, and allowing greater flexibility and capacity for innovation at the sub-national levels. Having seriously embraced this path, more research needs to be done on the institutional arrangements that would most effectively sustain it in the long term.

As a prelude to analysing preferred solutions, we need to understand the nature of the problems with the Australian federal system as it has operated over recent decades. Concerns about the 'crisis of federalism' are raised in different ways by each generation (e.g. Greenwood 1946, Patience and Scott 1983). These are variously identified as problems with structures, problems with revenue-raising, problems with the allocation of powers, problems with coordination, problems with relational or political processes, problems with poor outcomes/performance in certain areas, or all of the above. The pressures for change come from many sources – some come indirectly through external and systemic pressures such as the global economy, and other sources of change are closer to home, such as political disputes over directions in important areas of policy. The federal system, at any given time, reflects its complex history. It offers a range of constraints, opportunities and incentives for the actors at three levels of government, and also for those major business and community groups that seek to influence policy arrangements. The variable identification of problems naturally gives rise to different prescriptions for change.

It is important to understand that there are widely divergent views about what needs to be fixed in relation to the current *three-tiered* federal system. Among the many sources of criticism, it is useful to note five sectoral perspectives: local government, state government, the national government, business lobbies, and the larger non-government organisations (NGOs). The alleged deficiencies and preferred solutions are defined in different ways.

Perspectives

Local government

The local government sector sees itself as inherently closer to the people than the other levels of government. It also sees itself as deprived of the necessary powers and resources to undertake a full range of services (see Bell this volume). Local governments, being entirely dependent on state legislation, have a poor revenue base and have also been subjected to 'cost-shifting' (i.e. required to undertake tasks for which sufficient funding is not provided). In principle, this latter problem has now been recognised and addressed by an intergovernmental agreement (ALGA 2006). However, the ongoing reality may be a different story, and there are strong claims by local government leaders that the state governments are the oppressive and unnecessary layer in the current federal system. The Federal Government, for its part, has sometimes encouraged this viewpoint, by including local authority representation in inter-governmental forums, providing some funding programs directly to local government, and establishing various local and regional 'partnership' arrangements which minimise the role of the States.

State governments

For the eight states and territories, the problems of the federal system over the last forty years arise from three inter-related features of federal government power:

- fiscal centralisation (Head and Wanna 1990) – noting, however, that the massive redistribution of GST funds to the States since 2000 has greatly changed the political dynamics of this issue;
- overlap and duplication of federal and state powers in key policy areas, with increasing federal intrusion into traditional state areas of service delivery; and
- increasing centralisation of policy controls (regardless of the political party in office) through applying financial leverage (tied grants) and through expansion of the legal scope of federal powers through international treaties and High Court rulings (Court 1994).

Conservative defenders of a federal 'balance' (e.g. Gibbs 1993) are generally concerned about an increasing centralisation of power. Market-oriented defenders of federalism are also suspicious of centralisation and seek to encourage flexibility and competition among the constituent governments (e.g. Kasper 1993, Moore 1996). The solutions offered by state leaders (e.g. Goss 1994) have usually centred on reducing the incidence of tied grants, and seeking clearer demarcation between federal and state roles in key policy areas. Recent state leaders have recognised changing political and economic realities, by acknowledging that national economic efficiency requires a national approach (e.g. corporations law, competition law) rather than separate state regulatory frameworks; and even the recent movement towards a single industrial relations system is tacitly accepted.

Commonwealth Government

For the Commonwealth, the problems of the federal system over recent decades arise from the behaviour of the States, including:

- their capacity to delay or frustrate sound initiatives for improved performance standards, e.g. national standards for schooling;
- their failure to spend wisely on key services or economic infrastructure (Howard 2005, Abbott 2003, Abbott 2005); and
- their failure in some instances to support reforms to cut business costs by reducing regulatory inconsistencies and taxation on business transactions.

Federal politicians have a long history of supporting, in principle, the creation of a two-tier federal system without the current array of states (Hawke 1979, Macphee 1993), while acknowledging that this would be difficult to achieve. However, many commentators have noted that the diminution of state roles can proceed without constitutional change through the assertion of federal fiscal and legal powers (e.g. Craven 2005).

Big business

For large business organisations and associations, e.g. the Business Council of Australia (BCA), the federal system creates a higher regulatory burden and business imposts. The multiple layers of government produce unnecessary complexity, higher levels of taxation, a lack of uniformity or consistency in business regulations, complex project-approval processes, and higher compliance costs. Business lobbies – especially those representing larger firms operating across borders – are concerned to have uniform business regulations. They also want to ensure that economic issues affecting competitiveness (including the major areas of micro-economic reform, infrastructure and trade) are able to be addressed rapidly and decisively (Deveson 2006, Chaney 2006). During the debates of the early 1990s the BCA supported, in principle, a shift towards two-tier federalism (BCA 1991). However, the BCA has more recently supported national regulatory reform within a cooperative federal/state model with very strong leadership by central government (BCA 2006a, 2006b).

Other major national interest groups

For the other major national interest groups (e.g. NGOs concerned with family and community services, Indigenous issues, and the environment), there is often an impatience with fragmentation of responsibility for key outcomes and a preference for a national approach to major issues of program design. National approaches can be achieved either through federal imposition or through patient negotiation with the States; but the national NGOs often prefer centralised clarity over pluralist uncertainty. Calls for greater federal powers to over-ride the States on some social and environmental issues have been common over the years.

Solutions: incremental or radical?

These five critical perspectives define and locate the problems in different ways. Some place more emphasis on structural inequalities among the spheres of government, others focus on the inefficiencies of our complex system, and others on the lack of clear responsibilities for improving outcomes for citizens and business. While the diagnoses and prescriptions are diverse, there is a more fundamental distinction that can be drawn between those who support *incremental* models for change (adjust and improve current arrangements) and those who support *radical* models (fundamental reconstruction of governance systems including abolition of the current array of states).

The radical case for abolishing the States and building up the local or regional level of government has been proposed from two main viewpoints, which I will term the 'top-down rationalist' approach and the 'regional-responsiveness' approach. The top-down rationalist model for change is largely shared by both political centralists and the advocates of economic efficiency. Both argue for abolishing the States in order to cut wasteful duplication, cut costs of 'surplus' politicians and bureaucrats, and promote national standards. Massive benefits (up to $30 billion annually) are suggested (Drummond 2001b), of which half arises from lower public sector running costs (simplified machinery of government), and half from boosting economic productivity (lower taxes and reduced regulatory costs for business). Former Brisbane Lord Mayor, Jim Soorley, claimed some years ago that the costs saved by abolishing the States (and thereby removing 'duplication, bureaucratic red tape and waste' between the three levels of government), could be used to eliminate Australia's foreign debt within 20 years (Soorley 1994).

As with most top-down models of change, proponents have given little consideration to the full range of issues. One problem is the lack of attention to likely *costs* as well as benefits – for example, the medium-term organisational costs of transitional arrangements, the difficulties of maintaining and building legitimacy and support while large-scale changes are underway, and the practicalities of leadership and change management where there are dispersed winners and losers. A second problem is the lack of attention to ensuring that the alleged deficiencies of states (fragmentation, inefficiency, appropriate powers, etc.) would not be *repeated*, and indeed on a much wider scale, among the new regional entities. It is very difficult to ensure that major changes do not create unintended dis-benefits.

A third set of problems is the lack of clarity about how many local/regional authorities are required to achieve the right balance between organisational capacity or effectiveness and democratic responsiveness – obviously somewhere between the current number of States/Territories (8) and the current number of local authorities (700). The answer has varied widely. Soorley (1994) claimed that 'about 20' new regional governments would suffice. On the other hand, a federal report on regional development identified 67 regions from the viewpoint of economic development characteristics (Kelty 1993), fewer than the 80 regions proposed much earlier by the Department of Urban and Regional Development (DURD 1973). Two Federal Labor MPs (Tanner and Snow) who proposed abolition of the States, in Federal parliamentary resolutions tabled in 1993-94, proposed to substitute 'less than 100' new local/regional bodies. Drummond (2000, 2001a) has more recently proposed 'between 40 and 60' as the optimal number with a preference for the larger number; around 30 of these would be based on metropolitan and provincial cities.

An alternative to the top-down systemic approach is the regional responsiveness approach, which draws its strength from a sensitivity to regional identity, interests and sense of place (see Berwick this volume). Regional champions argue that 'communities of interest' are not sufficiently recognised in the current arrangements for state-level politics and administration. This sentiment underlies the 'New States' movements (discussed in Brown this volume) that have emerged in some areas of rural and remote Australia, especially in the larger States – Queensland, New South Wales and Western Australia. Here, a distrust of metropolitan governments is closely linked with arguments that the historical boundaries of the large states are quite inappropriate. Support for greater devolution of powers to the regional level is stronger in such areas. This is a case-by-case approach, generated by local and regional sentiments and local leadership rather than by systems theory.

In terms of the ideal *scale* for coherent and effective regional entities, it might seem plausible to assume that some existing smaller jurisdictions such as Tasmania and the Australian Capital Territory are perhaps about the optimal size in terms of population and coherence. However, it is an open empirical question as to whether they are actually seen as more legitimate in eyes of their citizens than the larger jurisdictions.

In terms of the appropriate *powers* required by regional entities, there is no agreement among the advocates of two-tier federalism about whether new regional governments should have the same powers as the existing States (and thus the same conflicts with the Federal Government over roles and responsibilities) or should become largely service delivery arms of the national government. There is a distinct possibility in two-tier federalism that centralisation could be even greater, with many of the more important state powers flowing to Federal Government and with regional governments being more fragmented and weaker than the current States.

Subsidiarity revisited

Lower levels of government usually favour the devolutionist principle of 'subsidiarity' – the concept that decisions should be taken as close as possible to the citizens by the lowest-level competent authority. Some established definitions of subsidiarity have already been supplied in this volume (see Brown, Podger this volume). As a principle, subsidiarity is widely invoked and supported, but in practice it is highly contested and could be used to justify a variety of practical outcomes in different circumstances. In principle, subsidiarity would entail that a central (or higher) level of government would perform only those essential tasks that (for reasons of scale, capacity or need for exclusive power) cannot be effectively undertaken at lower levels of administrative decision-making. In practice, subsidiarity has not supplanted power-politics in which the devolution of tasks is seen as a contractual arrangement between principal and agent.

In Australia, the principle of subsidiarity has attracted widespread support but without leading to long-term political and institutional changes. It has been invoked, firstly, by the States against the Federal Government; and secondly, but more recently, by local and regional entities against the State level. This sequence of acceptance is significant because, taking the second case first, the situation of local authorities can be quite parlous, with many being close to financial incapacity. The states have not seriously tried to devolve either revenue-raising powers or well-funded new functions to local government. Some cost-shifting has occurred and that has worsened the position of local authorities, even though, as already noted, such practices have recently been addressed by an intergovernmental agreement. The states have generally been content for local authorities to have a narrow role, and have not supported proposals for the recognition of local government in the Australian constitution. The states have taken some interest in regionalisation of their administrative arrangements for the delivery of services, but their links with local government remain problematic in most program areas.

However, the States have endorsed the principle of subsidiarity as a weapon in their ongoing arguments with the Federal Government aimed at reducing the

States' financial dependency on the Commonwealth. This argument has been tightly interwoven with the long-running debate about how to reduce duplication and overlap of roles in the federation. Australia seems to have rejected traditional ideas about rational allocation of service functions to particular levels of government, since there are about ninety program areas in which the Commonwealth makes specific-purpose payments (SPPs) to other levels of government. Attempts to reduce duplication of roles during the Special Premiers Conferences of 1990-91 and in Council of Australian Governments (COAG) debates since 1992 have not led to clearer separation of roles. There is also no reduction in the political impetus, at federal level, for continuing expansion of SPP agreements.

While noting the lack of progress in implementing subsidiarity, it may be suggested that this principle could provide a useful benchmark for assessing, and for reforming, program design and funding arrangements. One approach, as recommended by the Victorian Government (ACG 2006), would entail the following elements:

- governments should focus on what really matters to the community – better outcomes, not bureaucratic arrangements between themselves;
- state governments should have the fullest scope for developing diverse ways to deliver improved services for their own communities and their own circumstances, within a broader national framework;
- SPP arrangements should be reformed in the mould of a partnership in which governments ensure that all of the related programs contributing to, say, health outcomes are well coordinated and complementary; and
- diversity in the ways that outcomes are achieved among the States is a fundamental driver of policy, program and service innovation – a key spur to improved effectiveness and efficiency (ACG 2006: 7).

This approach essentially attempts to marry a strategic partnership approach – for setting objectives and for coordination – together with ensuring major opportunities for innovation, diversity and competition at lower levels of service delivery to reflect different circumstances.

This approach requires the Commonwealth to 'let go' some of its detailed controls. However, this remains difficult to achieve at the *political* level, where the incentives are for the Commonwealth decision-makers to retain all their power and control. The Commonwealth retains the key role in the design, funding and governance arrangements for future patterns of service delivery in many program areas. However, the Commonwealth has gradually abandoned the traditional administrative model of direct control of service delivery through a large federal workforce. In most policy fields, the Commonwealth now prefers to work through other providers and mechanisms (Head 2005). The pattern of recent decades has been to gain control through agreements, standards, and accountabilities leveraged by tied funding. There has been a strong trend towards greater use of contractual controls, linked to a variety of service providers:

- other levels of government (state, local, regional);
- private sector contractors; and
- community not-for-profit organisations.

Contract-based service delivery is not, however, a robust model for developing partnerships based on shared thinking and devolution of authority and resources.

Regional approaches

Both the Commonwealth and the States have been experimenting in recent decades with regional planning and program administration. The emergence of a new suite of policy initiatives that place more emphasis on devolution, is perhaps a sign that subsidiarity is finally being recognised as important and that without it, real change in services on the ground may be difficult to achieve. These now extend to everything from natural resource management (e.g. see Bellamy this volume), to transport infrastructure. Indeed, if regional policies and programs were well designed and based on local consultation, they might go part way to deflecting some of the hostile views held by the regions towards the metropolitan centres.

However, it is instructive that neither the Federal nor the State governments have been able to 'let go' in relation to empowering regional areas to develop their own agendas. In other words, subsidiarity remains problematic and largely rhetorical even in regional policy. For the States, regional administrative offices and special regional entities (e.g. catchment management authorities) are part of the State apparatus even though they are required to have close connections with local and regional interests. The role of local governments in these state-led arrangements varies widely around Australia. To the extent there is some devolution, it is not necessarily to the next (lower) level of government. For the Commonwealth, new regional bodies have been established as an *alternative* to state-sponsored bodies, e.g. in policy areas such as economic development and natural resource management.

The Federal Government in recent decades has claimed credit for serious work on some regional-scale planning and development activities. Examples include the mapping of 'regions' under the Whitlam government (DURD 1973), diverse plans and forums for regional economic development, regional forestry agreements in the 1990s, the Natural Heritage Trust regions developed since 1997, and various social policy programs aimed at 'place management' in and for disadvantaged communities. Yet in all these examples the Commonwealth model is generally contractual, retaining regulatory and funding power, while strongly promoting the involvement of non-state actors at local and regional levels. There is also a risk that both state and federal programs with a 'place' or locational emphasis are open to unfortunate political pressures such as pork-barrelling. Another problem is that so many regional programs have limited time-frames, exacerbated by being subject to short budget cycles, lack of bi-partisan support, or lack of genuine federal-state cooperation. Initiatives are thus vulnerable to changes in direction owing to political conflict or ministerial changes. The challenge is to develop program design principles that are durable, supported by communities, and institutionally robust.

The current half-hearted attempts at regional policy and programs need to be made more genuinely cooperative and involve real devolution if they are to achieve ownership at lower levels. This would require both the Commonwealth and the States taking subsidiarity more seriously, although within agreed national policy frameworks. It is likely that our current system lacks the political incentives necessary for this to occur. The system currently tends to respond to power and conflict rather than new strategic thinking. Conflict and tension is built into the federal system. Differences are not always a bad thing in a dynamic evolving system. Indeed, the negotiation of different viewpoints can sometimes be a useful catalyst for innovation and progress. In a rigid power-based system, however, the conflict becomes either a passive symbolic ritual or else becomes a polemical exercise in blame-shifting and confrontation (worse if complicated by party political differences). Under these conditions, conflict is not a creative force for developing better solutions.

The system thus needs specific machinery to encourage genuine negotiation and to facilitate innovation and excellence. Cooperative federalism, despite its legal and constitutional complexities (Saunders 2002), is the way forward on most large policy issues. The question becomes, how can efforts towards cooperative federalism – which tend to focus on relations between federal and state governments, and even then have a problematic history – be extended to pursue more genuine devolutionary models at the local and regional levels.

Institutionalising cooperative federalism

There is a strong case for a substantial Commonwealth role in strategic coordination (or 'steering') in key policy areas (Head 1989). Since the 1990s there have been some impressive results from 15 years of attempting to improve policy outcomes on national issues through federal/state agreements. Negotiation of national policy frameworks is an economical and effective way of achieving benefits without structural redesign of federalism. The Special Premiers Conferences and the Council of Australian Governments (COAG) forum have a solid record of achievement, as noted below. The political leadership of 'first Ministers' has been important for reform – the track-record of portfolio-based ministerial councils has been much less impressive. The availability of financial incentives from central government has also been an important tool in inducing support and achieving a number of national agreements. The States for their part have demonstrated their willingness to cooperate to resolve interstate anomalies and inefficiencies, and to cooperate with the Commonwealth in achieving important national goals in the public interest. Each level of government has made considerable progress with the efficiency and effectiveness agendas inside their own jurisdictions.

Some national problems have been so large that cooperative solutions among the governments have been seen as essential. This was recognised in 1990 with a new decision-making forum for Heads of Government, the Special Premiers' Conferences, to deal with overarching issues such as microeconomic reform, principles of environmental management, government roles in service delivery, and the efficiency of regulatory regimes. This was renamed the Council of Australian Governments in 1992. For those who doubt whether a cooperative approach can produce results, the achievements of the 'golden' period 1990-95 were considerable (Head 1994; Painter 1998):

- national framework legislation for non-bank financial institutions;
- mutual recognition of interstate standards for goods and occupational qualifications;
- standardised data on the comparative efficiency of government business enterprises;
- establishment of National Rail Corporation to manage interstate rail freight;
- establishment of Australian National Training Authority to coordinate vocational training;
- establishment of National Grid Management Council to coordinate electricity supply and distribution protocols;
- agreement on uniform road transport regulations;
- establishment of National Food Authority to coordinate food standards;
- agreement on national approach for distribution and pricing in the gas and water industries;
- agreement on balanced approach to ecologically sustainable development and a national approach to greenhouse issues;
- inter-governmental Agreement on the Environment (IGAE) to establish a consultative approach on relevant national issues and agreement to establish a National Environmental Protection Council to determine quality standards for air, soil and water;
- agreement on strategies for disability services;
- rationalisation of structure and operation of ministerial councils;
- agreement on a national approach to teaching Asian languages and cultures in our school curriculum;
- principles for National Competition Policy following from the Hilmer Report;
- a national approach to reform of legal services and the legal profession; and

- national approach to performance indicators for benchmarking the provision of government services were considerable.

State leaders have insisted that if the federal system is run as a centralised hierarchy, there is little incentive for innovation and cooperative problem-solving. If the system is run as a team event, albeit with a special role for the central government, it is likely that better results will be produced. The states remain responsible for very substantial issues of service delivery and business efficiency. In some cases, it is appropriate that the States should compete for citizen support by offering attractive packages of social and economic policies, tailored to regional needs and preferences. Cooperative federalism can be successful with a degree of goodwill, even where the 'first Ministers' include leaders of different political parties. Difficulties remain in seeking to determine what system of government will best facilitate joint problem-solving for genuinely national challenges and encouraging innovation and diversity at each level of government while tackling the major issues of service quality and economic productivity. The Business Council (BCA 2006b) has argued that progress should not depend on the 'accident' of whether political leaders have sufficient goodwill to engage in constructive debate and reform. The BCA proposes a strengthening of national strategic capacity by establishing a Federal Commission to identify key issues requiring a collective response, and to report on progress in implementing previous COAG agreements. Despite the manifest failure of previous exercises to reduce duplication and overlap, the BCA also proposes a Federal Convention to examine re-assignment of roles and responsibilities on key policy arenas and to achieve a more uniform approach to national markets.

The States have been increasingly willing to enter into national agreements on many policy areas concerning the economy and cross-border issues: e.g. corporate business regulation, competition policy, trading enterprises, mutual recognition, energy, water, transport, environment, and benchmarking of service delivery. The States, it must be said, should continue to lift their game at a strategic level, as is being attempted through the second wave of productivity reforms and human capital reforms being considered by COAG with strong input from Victoria (Glover 2006; Wilkins 2006). For the States, the political necessity of developing a more coherent 'collective' position to balance the power of the Federal Government, has led (after many false dawns) to the establishment of a states-only forum, the Council for the Australian Federation, in mid-2006. Its key role, apart from information-sharing, is to discuss strategic issues without the presence of the Commonwealth. If it can focus on strategic long-term issues (e.g. the COAG productivity agenda) rather than tactical skirmishes with the Commonwealth, it may prove to be useful.

Intergovernmental agreements supported by tied grant programs have often been too rigid and overly focused on detailed operational controls. Agreements have often failed to reflect a genuinely cooperative national approach to policy development, let alone facilitate state or regional differences in policy settings. The States have argued for many years that the federation would be better managed if the following occurred:

- National strategic objectives should be cooperatively negotiated with the States in policy areas genuinely requiring a national approach. COAG should be the ongoing forum for debate and decision on major strategic issues including regional policy frameworks;
- However, except in Commonwealth-only service areas, program implementation should be essentially a matter for the States and regions, with financial accountability lying primarily through State Parliaments and State Auditors-General;
- National agreements should increasingly focus on the goals and outcomes expected by governments, with less emphasis on detailing quantitative inputs. The availability of consistent and reliable performance information on the major areas of service delivery in the last decade has reinforced the strength of this position. However, it remains an educational challenge to convince the media, interest groups and federal politicians that an outcomes focus, anchored in published comparative performance information, is really a superior form of accountability;
- Review the role of 'tied grants' in jointly-funded government programs. Commonwealth SPPs, which might be a minority of total program funds, are used as leverage to influence the goals and components of the whole program area. A significant proportion of tied grants could be converted into either block-funding for the agreed policy purpose (e.g. school education) or converted into general revenue grants, providing that agreed goals and performance measures are in place; and
- Progress should be made in redefining the spheres of policy and service responsibility for each level of government. While there can never be precision in dividing roles in our federation, there has been insufficient effort to assign certain functions more clearly to one level of government (e.g. universities to the Commonwealth). Canberra has found it difficult to agree that school and vocational education should largely be a matter for the States, subject to broad national agreement on coordination, equity, and performance indicators. Healthcare, the other large-spending area of overlapping federal/state roles, remains a political and administrative minefield (see Podger this volume). The Commonwealth has recently backed away from radical plans for structural reform in favour of 'incremental reforms' (Abbott 2006).

Conclusions

It is true that, if the Australian people were confronted with a 'greenfields' choice between alternative paper plans for good government, they might choose a more simplified structure than the current complex three-tier model. The attitudinal research set out by Gray and Brown (this volume) certainly tends this way. However, the two-tier option, despite its apparent simplicity and rationality, is ultimately impractical for the foreseeable future. The business case for moving rapidly towards two-tier federalism, with the current array of states displaced or absorbed in various ways, remains rhetorical and impractical; especially the radical version of constitutional change to abolish the States. It is therefore more productive to apply our imagination and political goodwill towards addressing the apparently high level of public interest in federalism reform, by making our system work a lot better.

This should not be seen as a defence of archaic 'States' rights', a rhetoric whose time has truly passed. Rather, this is an opportunity for existing state jurisdictions to recognise they can play an important role in purposeful reform of policy and administrative arrangements – even if this means being prepared to share power with local and regional bodies in more serious and durable ways than previously achieved, or indeed previously tried.

Instead of their historical preoccupation with resisting the Commonwealth, the state governments should focus their attention on program areas that deserve to be organised at a state level (i.e. on the spatial scale between national and local). They should divest themselves of matters that can better be handled federally, regionally or locally. Areas that are directly concerned with national economic regulation should be ceded to the federal level. Some matters that the States largely control should be devolved, with appropriate authority and funding, to lower levels for planning and action. Matters for such consideration might include urban and regional development, and improved service integration for residents of provincial and rural areas. The state level could assist by ensuring good governance, equitable treatment of local areas, and support to address skills shortages.

Insofar as structural changes to improve the federation deserve further consideration, more research and policy development is needed on options, transitional arrangements, and the testing of public support for various objectives and institutional options. In the meantime, three-tier federalism should be improved by innovative attempts to deliver better services through a combination of national agreements, clear responsibilities for service arrangements, and a more robust approach to regional-level policy and programs that involves genuine devolution. This would require both the Commonwealth and the States taking subsidiarity more seriously, within agreed national policy frameworks. The States need to take this opportunity to rethink their core business (what works best at state level?) and support both sensible devolution and national frameworks. Half-hearted attempts at regional policy and programs (by both the Federal Government and the States) need to be made more genuinely cooperative, and involve genuine devolution.

References

Abbott, Hon T. 2003, 'Responsible Federalism', Norman Cowper Oration, Sydney, June; see also 'Responsible Federalism' in W. Hudson and A. J. Brown (eds) 2004, *Restructuring Australia: Regionalism, Republicanism and Reform of the Nation-State*, Federation Press, Sydney.

———— 2005, 'A Conservative Case for Centralism', *The Conservative*, No.1, pp.4-5.

———— 2006, Ministerial address to conference on *Making the Boom Pay*, cited in *The Australian*, 3 November.

Allen Consulting Group (ACG) 2006, *Governments Working Together? Assessing Specific Purpose Payment Arrangements*. Report to the Victorian Government, ACG, Melbourne.

The Australian, editorial 5 June 2006, 'Profligate Premiers'.

————, editorial 14 July 2006, 'Federalism a Test of Leadership'.

————, editorial 30 October 2006, 'Less Talk, More Action'.

Australian Local Government Association (ALGA) 2006, 'IGA on Cost-Shifting: historic agreement to ease cost shifting burden on councils', media release, Canberra, 12 April.

Business Council of Australia 1991, *Government in Australia in the 1990s*, BCA, Melbourne.

———— 2006a, *Modernising the Australian Federation: A Discussion Paper*, BCA, Melbourne.

———— 2006b, *Reshaping Australia's Federation: A New Contract for Federal-State Relations*, BCA, Melbourne.

Chaney, M. 2006, 'Make a Federal Case of it', *The Australian*, 10 July.

Court, R, 1994, *Rebuilding the Federation: an audit and history of State powers and responsibilities usurped by the Commonwealth in the years since Federation*, WA Government, Perth.

Craven, G. 2005, 'Federalism and the States of Reality', *Policy* 21 (2), pp.3-9.

———— 2006, 'Business gets its Absolutes out of Order', *The Australian*, 17 October.

Department of Urban and Regional Development (DURD) 1973, *Regions*, AGPS, Canberra.

Deveson, I. 2006, 'One Step from Best in World', *The Australian*, 14 July.

Drummond, M. 2000, 'Regional government can transform Australia', *Online Opinion* 15 July. www.onlineopinion.com.au

——— 2001a, 'Towards a best-possible new system of government', *Online Opinion*, 15 January. www.onlineopinion.com.au

——— 2001b, 'A $30 billion annual boost that better government can deliver', *Online Opinion* 31 January. www.onlineopinion.com.au

Gibbs, Sir H. 1993, 'The Threat to Federalism', in Samuel Griffith Society, *Upholding the Australian Constitution Vol 2: Proceedings of the Second Conference of the Samuel Griffith Society*, Samuel Griffith Society, Melbourne, pp.183-193.

Glover, R. 2006, 'Collaborative Federalism: Getting More from the Competition of Ideas', *Public Administration Today*, No.7, pp.4-7.

Goss, W. 1994, 'Reinventing the States', paper to the *2020 Vision* Forum, Brisbane.

Greenwood, G. 1946, *The Future of Australian Federalism*, Melbourne University Press, Melbourne.

Hawke, R.J. 1979, *The Resolution of Conflict*, ABC Boyer Lectures, Sydney.

Head, B.W. 1989, 'Federalism, the States and Economic Policy', in B. Galligan (ed.), *Australian Federalism*,Longman Cheshire Melbourne, pp.239-259.

——— 1994, 'The Federal Imagination: Making the System Work Better', paper for University of Melbourne conference on *Australian Federalism*, July.

——— 1999, 'The Changing Role of the Public Service: Improving Service Delivery', *Canberra Bulletin of Public Administration*, No.94, pp.1-3.

——— 2005, 'Governance', in P. Saunders and J. Walter (eds), *Ideas and Influence: Social Science and Public Policy in Australia*, UNSW Press, Sydney, pp.44-63.

Head, B.W. and J. Wanna, 1990, 'Fiscal Federalism', in J. Forster et al (eds), *Budgetary Management and Control*, Macmillan, Melbourne, pp.22-40.

Howard, Hon J.W. 2005, 'Reflections on Australian Federalism', address to Menzies Research Centre, Melbourne, April.

Kasper, W. 1993, ;Making Federalism Flourish;, in Samuel Griffith Society, *Upholding the Australian Constitution Vol 2: Proceedings of the Second Conference of the Samuel Griffith Society*, Samuel Griffith Society, Melbou, pp.167-181.

Kelty, B. 1993, *Regional Development: report of the taskforce*, Department of Industry etc., Canberra.

Lewis, D. 2005, 'Altered States', *Sydney Morning Herald*, 25 January.

Macphee. I. 1993, Address to the Samuel Griffith Centenary Seminar, Brisbane.

Moore, D. 1996, 'Duplication and Overlap: An Exercise in Federal Power', in Samuel Griffith Society, *Upholding the Australian Constitution Vol 6: Proceedings of the Sixth Conference of the Samuel Griffith Society*, Samuel Griffith Society, Melbourne, pp.37-64.

Painter, M. 1998, *Collaborative Federalism: Economic Reform in Australia in the 1990s* , Cambridge University Press, Melbourne.

Patience, A. and J. Scott (eds) 1983, *Australian Federalism: Future Tense*, Oxford University Press, Melbourne.

Saunders, C. 2002, 'Collaborative Federalism', *Australian Journal of Public Administration*, 61 (2), pp.69-77.

Soorley, J 1994, Address to the Centenary of Federation Advisory Committee, May.

Steketee, M. 2006a, 'Unwanted, but State Governments are here to stay', *The Australian*, 27 April.

————. 2006b, 'A Federal State of Recalcitrance', *The Australian*, 24 June.

Wilkins, R.B. 2004, 'Federalism: Distance and Devolution', *Australian Journal of Politics and History*, 50 (1), pp.95-101.

————2006, 'A New Era in Commonwealth-State Relations?' *Public Administration Today*, No.7, pp.8-13.

Chapter 11: How Local Government Can Save Australia's Federal System

Paul Bell

Introduction

The debate about federalism is gathering momentum. Australia's system of government is facing renewed scrutiny as we enter an era where blame-shifting, cost-shifting and duplication between the three spheres of government have become part of the public debate (e.g. House of Representatives 2003; LGI 2006; Dollery 2005; Wild River 2006). As a nation, we have already passed up two prime opportunities to reflect on the nature of our federation and how it should evolve to meet the nation's needs. The Centenary of Federation was a lost opportunity; something we did not take sufficient advantage of. So, too, was the constitutional debate on whether or not Australia should become a republic or retain the monarchy. On that occasion, we worked ourselves into lather about symbols – not substance.

More than 10 years ago, then Queensland Premier Wayne Goss posed the question: 'Will the States survive as viable political entities into the 21st century?' (Goss 1995). Goss called for a national debate on the future of our federation, including a reallocation of responsibilities between different spheres of government and argued '[u]nless this debate is vigorously taken up, what we will witness within a generation is the de facto, if not de jure, abolition of the States'.

Wayne Goss' warnings sound prophetic now. Federal Governments have been encroaching more and more on state territory. It is a trend seen through both the Hawke and Keating Governments and which is accelerating under John Howard. As mentioned earlier (see Brown, Peters this volume), the recent High Court decision upholding the Federal Government's powers to legislate in the area of industrial relations is a case in point (WorkChoices 2006). States' powers are being challenged in the policy areas of the environment, water, health and education. Local government is providing a broader range of services. The Labor State Premiers across Australia have recently formed the Council for the Australian Federation (CAF) based on the Canadian Council of the Federation model. This is a political response to the increasing centralism of federal governments.[1]

But where are we heading – under what terms, and what conditions? More importantly, what will the outcome be? It is timely for a really good look at how we govern ourselves. We – the people – need to be masters of our own destiny.

If we were drawing up government in Australia from scratch, we would not pick the 'dog's breakfast' we have today. Yes, Australia is doing well. But we're doing well in spite of our governance arrangements, not because of them.

This chapter demonstrates the importance of the local government sector to regional governance in Australia's federal system of government. It puts the case that, although there has been substantial reform within the federal governance system in the last 20 years, there has been a failure to establish enabling institutional arrangements for strengthening local government's capacity to work together to deliver regional outcomes. In the context of current shifting roles and responsibilities for local government, this paper argues the case for constitutional reform to recognise local government within the Australian federal governance system.

Local government and federalism: a need for change

From a local government perspective, we now have three spheres of government in Australia that should operate in a cooperative and cohesive way. All three spheres should be treated as equal and valued partners, working together to achieve the best possible governance outcomes for the people they collectively serve; the Australian public.

Galligan (1996: 55) refers to local government's greatest strength, 'in the democratic character of the Australian polity', as being to 'represent and serve people in local communities'. Galligan also points out that 'the Australian States have been, and in various degrees remain, dominant and dictatorial in their treatment of local government and will concede to its representatives no part of their constitutional rights which they so vehemently claim for themselves'. Herein lies the rub. There is no mention of local government at all in the Australian Constitution, the document that sets out the way the nation is governed. This is because in 1901 local government was regarded as 'residue', for which the States were responsible. Constitutional responsibility for local government lies with the State and Territory governments with formal roles, functions and responsibilities established in state-level laws that differ across the different jurisdictions in Australia. Local government was 'established by state parliaments to exercise delegated powers and, as such, it is part of the States' administrative apparatus (whose) powers can be readily changed and the manner in which it exercises them is subject to overall control by the State' (Advisory Council for Inter-government Relations 1984: 23).

Importantly, local government is dependent on the States and the Federal government for resourcing. Though it has its own ability to raise revenue through rates, these are capped in NSW, and it does not have access to a growth tax such as the States and Territories have with the GST. Local government has also become a convenient dumping ground for costly and onerous state government services. This led to the historic signing of the Intergovernmental Agreement on cost shifting between the States, the Federal Government and local government in April 2006 (IGA 2006).

Councils have been amalgamated or sacked by state governments without apparent cause or what many would consider a reasonable process and without the councils having the ability to appeal against unfair treatment. The campaign catch-cry for local government in 2007 is 'Fair Funding, Fair Treatment and Formal Recognition', which I will explain further below. But this catch-cry is a response to the fact that in Australia today, we have a federation with four distinct features:

- an increasingly dominant and centralist Federal Government;
- state governments that are still strong, but whose power has peaked;
- a complete absence of regional government, but a growing mish-mash of inter-government regional arrangements that are largely ad hoc and lack any real cohesion; and
- local government that continues to deliver services for communities despite being seriously under-resourced and increasingly over-regulated.

Notwithstanding, on the positive side, we are witnessing a greater degree of cooperation when it comes to our key forum for the resolution of intergovernmental challenges – the Council of Australian Governments (COAG). Local government is represented on COAG by the Australian Local Government Association (ALGA), the peak national body for local government in Australia. As a peak government body, COAG brings together the Prime Minister, State Premiers, Territory Chief Ministers and the ALGA President to develop responses to issues of concern to all three spheres of government. COAG at the very least is a willing spirit to address issues of mutual national importance that affect all three spheres of government. However, we have perhaps the personalities of the day to thank – not the system of governance that surrounds them.

Strengthening regional governance: empowering local government

In seeking to reconfigure our federation, first and foremost we need to strengthen local government. In doing so, we will empower councils to work together more effectively at the regional level. We must also overcome the problems confronting the diverse range of intergovernmental regional arrangements by making sure local government is at the centre – not the side – of these activities. We must empower local government to play a larger and fuller role in our governance arrangements by:

- embracing the principle of subsidiarity;
- eliminating cost shifting;

- fully addressing the problem of vertical fiscal imbalance; and
- providing local government with greater autonomy through full constitutional recognition.

The need to find better regional governance arrangements is clear. Communities and councils in coastal regions are facing dramatic demographic change. Their problems are compounded by the fact that their populations are not only growing at a rapid rate, but are also ageing at a rapid rate (see Berwick this volume). In rural and remote areas, communities are crying out for a greater emphasis on regional development to generate robust economic growth and counter the drift of young people to the major metropolitan centres (as shown by Mal Peters in this volume). Meanwhile, councils on the fringe of major cities face particular difficulties as the rapid expansion of suburbia into the rural fringe has increased demand for public infrastructure (see also Gleeson this volume). These are just three issues of critical concern to councils that have a regional dimension.

So, how do we get a greater focus on the problems that confront our regions? Some advocate a two-pronged approach: first, abolish the States, and second, amalgamate local government into regional governments; and 'hey presto – fewer spheres of government, better regional arrangements'. Unfortunately, this approach is fundamentally flawed. Despite our best wishes, the States are not going to roll over and die – at least, not in the short to medium term. More importantly, by merging local government into regional government you will destroy the one sphere of government that is genuinely part and parcel of our communities.

This does not mean that local government should not be prepared to reform, in order to better represent and serve those communities. Experience has shown that reform, accepted by councils and supported by communities, such as voluntary amalgamations, boundary changes, regional arrangements, shared services and doing things more collectively, achieves the best outcomes. However, it is clear from compulsory reform programs such as the State-imposed new boundaries in Victoria and South Australia, that reform based simply on 'top-down' ideas of amalgamation will risk the current benefits of local governments' connectedness with the community, and may make them less, not more financially sustainable. In Victoria, 12 to 14 of the councils created through the Kennett government's amalgamation program are now financially unsustainable. In South Australia, where the number of local governments was cut in half – to 69 – the indications are that about 29 of those are financially unsustainable. The decision by the Queensland Government in April 2007 to abandon its collaborative approach to reform with local government, and unilaterally attempt to impose new boundaries, is a backward step unlikely to achieve the benefits promised through a more considered partnership.

Local government reform is both a part – and a creature – of moving forward, therefore, all options for reform need to look beyond artificial financial indicators, and look at the ways in which communities change, and the ways in which they link and work together. There are eight or nine significant indicators for what makes 'community', not simply financial indicators and finances. Under any option, the existing strength of local government must be maintained and built, and local government's great strength lies in the fact that is part of and close to the people. It is the most transparent, responsive and accountable form of democracy that we have. It can respond to local need in a way no other sphere of government can, be it regional, state or federal. Local government embodies the spirit of subsidiarity, a principle which holds that the functions of government should be exercised as closely as practicable to the affected citizens. Local government delivers services and facilities on a human scale. It is responsive to local need, provides local leadership and advocacy, fosters civic pride and reflects local priorities in a way state and federal governments never can.

So, how can we in local government address our lack of solid, regional governance arrangements? Local government already works closely together at the regional level in a number of important ways. Firstly, for example, for some years local government has worked together through Regional Organisations of Councils, that is ROCs (see http://www.alga.asn.au/links/regionalOrgs.php). ROCs provide an opportunity for councils to exchange ideas, develop a sense of regional identity, promote common objectives and share resources.

Secondly, councils also work together on specific projects. For example, in NSW, councils in the Hunter and Central Coast have developed a comprehensive regional environmental management strategy (http://www.hccrems.com.au/about.html). This very successful regional initiative is being implemented through the collaborative efforts of fourteen councils to facilitate a regional approach to ecologically sustainable development. This has been achieved through a package of natural resource management initiatives. It encourages greater co-operation between member councils, state and federal authorities, industry and community groups, and it's led by local government. Now regarded as a model for integrating local government planning and environmental management at the regional level, it provides a framework for co-ordinated action, addresses those environmental and natural resource issues that are best managed at a regional level, and facilitates regional partnerships and resource sharing to address key environmental management issues in a co-ordinated, pro-active and efficient manner.

A third example comes from Queensland, the South East Queensland Regional Plan and its accompanying Infrastructure Plan (OUM 2005; 2006), which together are considered an outstanding achievement for regional planning in Queensland and Australia. In short, these plans establish collaborative, top down and bottom up processes that will deliver tangible and lasting benefits for the region's communities.

Finally, local government also participates in the development of better regional governance through direct partnership with Federal agencies. As recognised in the submission by the Department of Transport and Regional Services to the House of Representatives inquiry on local government and cost shifting, local government is central to regional development and the delivery of the regional policy objectives of the Australian Government on a national scale (SCEFPA 2003, p.91). As DOTARS recognised, local government offers a wide and well-established national network of public administration which may be capable of taking on extra responsibilities and functions, especially in rural and regional Australia. In some cases local government is the only institutional presence in small rural and remote areas. Its strong links to the community, accountability to the communities it represents and its legislative basis make it both durable and financially stable – unlike some community or interest groups. The integrated structure of councils can allow a high level of co-ordination between different activities; and the links between local government and local business and industry puts councils in a good position to foster a 'bottom up' approach to regional development. As DOTARS said, local government plays an increasingly important role in providing information to support Commonwealth regional policy development, and as a key stakeholder in the implementation of Commonwealth regional policy initiatives.

A national reform agenda for local government

When it comes to regional cooperation, councils are getting on with the job. But if councils are to work more effectively at the regional level, they need to be better resourced individually. Strengthening councils individually enhances their capacity to work together regionally. But how can we do this? The peak national representative body for local government in Australia, the Australian Local Government Association (ALGA), is pressing for three objectives – fair funding, fair treatment and formal recognition.

Fair funding

The need for fair funding is the top priority. The Australian Government collects the lion's share of Australian taxation revenue. It is the Australian Government's duty to share these funds with its state and local government counterparts to ensure they meet their service and infrastructure obligations to communities. By doing so, the Australian Government can counter the destructive impact of vertical fiscal imbalance.

A Coalition Government in the late 1970s linked payments to local government to a share of taxation revenue – in that case, personal income tax. This gave local government, for the first time, access to a fair share of revenue – that is access to growth funding. This sensible and fair arrangement unfortunately was axed in the 1980s by the Hawke Government as a cost cutting exercise. Since then, local government has been steadily losing ground. Federal financial assistance grants have failed to match the increasing demands made on councils in the 21st century. The value of these grants, as a proportion of total Commonwealth revenue, has fallen from 1.2% in the early 1990s to less than 1% in 1996-97 (ALGA 2006). In two years time, it will have fallen to less than 0.8% (ALGA 2006). Local government's share of the Australian tax base has fallen from around 6% in the 1970s to about 3% today (PwC 2006). In fact, local government in Australia now has the fourth lowest share of taxation among the 30 industrialised nations of the OECD, and as shown at the outset (Brown this volume), a far lower share than in most other federations. And yet, councils have undergone a period of profound change over the past 40 years. Traditionally, local government has provided property-based services – the old 'roads, rates and rubbish'. To these traditional 'three R's' we can now add regulation, recreation, relief (as in welfare, childcare, aged care and health care services), regionalism and regional development, and retail services such as water, sewerage and transport services.

Local government continues to perform its traditional roles. But there is now much greater demand for councils to provide a growing range of human services. In recent years, councils have acquired new responsibilities including arts and culture, management of health, alcohol and drug problems, community safety and accessible transport. Local government is also playing a growing regulatory role in areas such as development and planning, public health, and environmental management, to name a few. Like a hungry caterpillar, these new services are now gobbling up the expenditure once reserved almost exclusively for traditional services and infrastructure maintenance. In the 1960s, around 50% of local government expenditure was allocated to the maintenance of roads. By the 1990s, this had fallen to just over 25% and local governments now have a significant issue in maintaining infrastructure (see PwC 2006). In the early 1960s, just 4% of expenditure was allocated to education, health, welfare and public safety activities. By the late 1990s, this had risen to 12% – a threefold increase.

These changes have been partly driven by community demand and partly by a range of other factors beyond the control of local government. Significantly, these factors have not only added to the range of services required of local government – they've also come largely without new or adequate sources of revenue.

ALGA argues that financial assistance grants should be replaced with a share of Commonwealth taxation revenue. This is supported by the recent Pricewaterhouse Coopers report into local government funding which recommends revising the escalation methodology for Financial Assistance Grants from a mix of population growth and Consumer Price Index to a new escalation formula tailored to local government cost movements (PwC 2006). The funding provided to local government through Financial Assistance Grants should also be fixed at a rate of at least 1% of taxation revenue, providing councils with funding that grows as the economy grows.

Fair treatment

Apart from the need for fair funding, we also need to ensure fair treatment – and that means putting an end to cost shifting. Local government has been on the wrong side of cost shifting for decades, with state governments and – to a lesser extent – the Australian Government, passing functions to local government with inadequate or no off-setting revenue source. The Australian Government, for example, transferred responsibility for a large number of regional airports to local government in the early 1990s. The PricewaterhouseCoopers report (PwC 2006) shows that while some initial funding was made available, councils have been substantially out of pocket in their efforts to maintain and upgrade these important economic assets. The total infrastructure backlog for local government across Australia is estimated at between $11 billion and $16 billion. PricewaterhouseCoopers' conservative estimate is that between 10% and 30% of councils have financial sustainability issues. It recommends a new infrastructure fund for local government – a Local Community Infrastructure Renewals Fund – to provide a source of revenue to upgrade existing community assets, many of which were built in the 1950s and 1960s and are deteriorating, such as swimming pools, ovals, community centres, libraries and health centres.

In many rural communities, local government is the last man standing. Once the federal or state governments withdraw services, if local government doesn't step in, no one will. That's why we are seeing more and more councils buying doctors' surgeries and accommodation, and entire hospitals in some cases, in a bid to keep medical services available to people in rural communities.

In essence, cost shifting amounts to theft, diverting scarce council dollars to fund a function imposed on it by another sphere of government. The impact of cost shifting on local government has been estimated to be somewhere between $500m and $1.1 billion each and every year (House of Representatives 2003). Importantly, all three spheres of government – the Australian Government, the State and Territory governments and local government – have recently come together and signed an intergovernmental agreement in an attempt to set up some guidelines and principles to put an end to cost shifting (IAG 2006). Essentially, this agreement seeks to ensure that when agreements are made by a state or federal government which wishes to transfer a function or service to local government, then the cost of that function or service will be taken into account. It is possible that this historic agreement will pave the way to greater cooperation between all three spheres of government, ensuring proper consultation and negotiation takes place over the movement or shifting of responsibilities and functions between spheres of government. Time will tell — but it's a promising start.

A further welcome initiative has been the Tripartite Partnership Agreement on Population Ageing that has recently been reached between the Australian Government, Tasmanian State Government and Tasmanian Local Government (Tripartite Partnership Agreement 2006). This Agreement is the first of its kind, and seeks to achieve a coordinated and cooperative approach to ageing in Tasmania. This would include joint work on planning, services and facilities to meet demands of an ageing population.

Formal recognition

The third element of ALGA's campaign is formal recognition: that is, constitutional recognition. Councils should not be merely creatures of state and territory governments. They should be seen as expressions of Australia's commitment to community democracy. This is why recognition of local government in the Australian Constitution is so important. A milestone towards local government's long-term goal of constitutional recognition was reached with the Commonwealth parliamentary resolution on recognition of local government, which passed the Senate on 7 September 2006 and the House of Representatives on 17 October 2006. The resolution stated:

> That the House/Senate:

> Recognises that local government is part of the governance of Australia, serving communities through locally elected councils

> Values the rich diversity of councils around Australia, reflecting the varied communities they serve.

> Acknowledges the role of local government in governance, advocacy, the provision of infrastructure, service delivery, planning, community development and regulation.

> Acknowledges the importance of cooperating with and consulting with local government on the priorities of their local communities.

> Acknowledges the significant Australian Government funding that is provided to local government to spend on locally determined priorities, such as roads and other local government services.

> Commends local government elected officials who give their time to serve their communities.

ALGA has representation on 14 ministerial councils; so local government is at the table but not formally recognised. Local government should not only be recognised and valued, but should also be recognised and protected as a sphere of government.

Conclusion: reconfiguring the federation

In summary, the need to reform our federal system of government is very clear. So what is the way forward? The debate has already begun. In a major speech on 14 July 2005, before he became Labor leader, Kevin Rudd outlined his commitment to 'co-operative federalism':

> The challenge for a future Labor government will be to rebuild the federation. And it is my argument that the federation can be rebuilt based on the principles of co-operative (rather than coercive) federalism. If Federal Labor succeeds in this enterprise, it will create a sustainable political and constitutional mechanism to deliver lasting reform to the nation; to implement a progressive policy agenda that is likely to endure beyond subsequent changes in the political cycle at either a Commonwealth or state level (Rudd 2006).

Mr Rudd also emphasised the importance of local service delivery: 'Arguments in favour of a federal structure include the classical idea of 'subsidiarity' – that is, devolving decision-making to the lowest level of government as possible so that decisions are as sensitive as possible to local circumstances and those responsible for these decisions are readily accountable to local communities.'

Fixing federalism has also been listed by the Federal Treasurer, Peter Costello, as one of the key criteria for future greatness. Addressing a dinner to mark the announcement of *The Bulletin* magazine's top 100 most influential Australians, Mr Costello said individuals who made their way onto the list in future would include 'the person who can solve the problem bedevilling Australian political life in every area, the problem of federalism'. He said federation was a great success in 1901 as 'the coming together of colonies in a customs and economic union within an empire':

> But the empire has faded and the nation now has consciousness of itself. We are no longer dealing with self-governing sovereign colonies. I believed that by giving the States a revenue base – a financial free kick – we would restore that sense of sovereignty. It was a failed hope. States are moving towards the role of service delivery more on the model of divisional offices than sovereign independent governments. Legally, constitutionally and practically we must fix the problem of federalism (Costello 2006).

The Shadow Minister for Federal-State Relations, Bob McMullan MP, outlining his vision in a recent speech suggested some form of 'Performance Partnerships' between the States and the Federal Government and that 'there must be enhanced recognition of local governments as delivery agencies for programs'. His approach is 'fund nationally, act locally' (McMullan 2007).

We need to reform our federal system of government and we need to do it quickly. We have one sphere of government that is being slowly bled dry by the others. And we have a lack of sensible regional governance arrangements to really ensure that the decisions that we are making regionally are community-based and are linked to proper governance arrangements. But this is a vacuum that a properly-funded and properly-resourced local government sector can fill, and do so in a manner that will ensure the principles and benefits of local democracy are preserved and enhanced. The ALGA has been pressing for a review of federalism to better recognise the increasingly important role local government plays within the Australian federation. However, we need bipartisan support for constitutional change in order to achieve our long-cherished goal of constitutional recognition. After two unsuccessful referenda, the most recent in 1988, we cannot afford to fail again. To this end, local government is working towards holding a constitutional summit to highlight this issue and to ensure it maintains its prominence in the national agenda.

Finally, in considering the necessity for bipartisan support for reform, the most important thing of all is that leaders of all political persuasions understand the relationship between local government and community. It was very interesting that when the Prime Minister last spoke on federalism at the Menzies Institute (Howard 2005), on one occasion he mentioned local government, on three occasions he mentioned state governments, but on four or five occasions he mentioned community. If there is a lack of understanding, or a failure by other spheres of governments to remember that community and local government are one and the same, then we have lost the debate. But it also shows why the debate is needed. We now have a unique opportunity to take things forward, start a new thinking, and start an opportunity for our communities to have the discussion about reform.

References

Advisory Council for Intergovernmental Relations 1984, *Responsibilities and Resources of Australian Local Government*, AGPS, Canberra.

Australian Local Government Association (ALGA) 2006, *ALGA Federal Budget 2006-07 Analysis. Fact Sheet 2: Financing Local Government*. Viewed 09/04/07, http://www.alga.asn.au/policy/finance/federalBudgetAnalysis2006/factSheet02.php

Costello, P., 2006, Speech in Sydney to *The Bulletin* Top 100 Most Influential Australians Luncheon, 26 June 2006.

Dollery, B. 2005, 'A Critical Evaluation of Structural Reform Considerations in 'Rates and Taxes: A Fair Share for Responsible Local Government'', *Australian Geographer* 36 (3), pp. 385-397.

Galligan, B. 1996, 'Local Government for Twenty First Century Australia', in P. Johnstone and R. Kiss (eds), *Governing Local Communities: the future begins*, Centre for Public Policy, Melbourne University 1996.

Goss, W. 1995, *Restoring the Balance, the Future of the Australian Federation*, Federalism Research Centre, Australian National University, Canberra.

Howard, J. 2005, 'Reflections on Australian Federalism', Speech to the Menzies Research Centre, Melbourne, 11 April 2005.

IGA 2006, *Inter-governmental Agreement Establishing Principles to Guide Inter-Governmental Relations on Local Government Matters*, viewed 09/04/07, http://www.lgpmcouncil.gov.au/publications/doc/Booklet_with_parties_signatures.pdf

Local Government Inquiry (LGI) 2006, *Are Councils Sustainable? Final Report: Findings and Recommendations*. The Independent Inquiry into the Financial Sustainability of NSW Local Government (LGI), Local Government and Shires Associations of NSW (LGSA), May 2006. http://www.lgi.org.au/

McMullan, B. 2007, Speech to the Australian Fabian Society, Victorian Branch, 7 February, 2007.

Office of Urban Management (OUM) 2005, *The South East Queensland Regional Plan 2005-2026. June 2005*, Queensland Government, Department of Local Government, Planning, Sports and Recreation, The State of Queensland. Viewed 08/02/2007, http://www.oum. qld.gov.au/?id=29

Office of Urban Management (OUM) 2006, *The South East Queensland Infrastructure Plan and Program 2006-2026. May 2006*, The State of Queensland (The Coordinator General). Viewed 08/02/2007, http://www.oum.qld.gov.au/?id=315

PricewaterhouseCoopers (PwC) 2006, *National Financial Sustainability Study of Local Government*, report commissioned by the Australian Local Government Association, November 2006. http://www.alga.asn.au/policy/finance/pwcreport/pdf/PwC_Report.pdf

Rudd, K. 2005, 'The Case for Cooperative Federalism', Speech to the Don Dunstan Foundation – Queensland Chapter, 14 July 2005.

SCEFPA (House of Representatives Standing Committee on Economics, Finance and Public Administration) 2003, *Rates and Taxes: A Fair Share for Local Government*. The Parliament of the Commonwealth of Australia, Canberra, October 2003.

Wild River, S. 2006, 'The role of local government in environmental and heritage management', article prepared for the 2006 Australia State of the Environment Committee, Department of Environment and Heritage, Canberra.

Viewed 09/03/2007, http://www.deh.gov.au/soe/2006/integrative/local-government/index.html

Tripartite Partnership Agreement 2006, 'Tripartite Partnership Agreement for population Ageing in Tasmania between the Australian Government, State Government and Local Government Association of Tasmania', 28 August 2006. Viewed 09/04/07, http://www.dpac.tas.gov.au/divisions/lgo/partnerships/agreements/Tripartite_PA_for_Population_Ageing_in_Tasmania.pdf.

WorkChoices 2006, High Court of Australia, 'NSW v Commonwealth' *Australian Law Reports* Volume 231, p.1.

ENDNOTES

[1] See http://www.premcab.sa.gov.au/dpc/government_caf.html. For the Canadian model, see http://www.councilofthefederation.ca/

Chapter 12: Reforming Australian Governance: Old States, No States or New States?

Kenneth Wiltshire

Introduction

Australia's creaking federalism is back in the news, as events cause us to reflect on the appropriateness of our system of governance.

There is nothing surprising in this, since federalism is supposed to be a dynamic form of government. We see such dynamism also in the international scene. Not so long ago, Belgium moved from being a unitary to a federal country to accommodate cultural and linguistic differences. Great Britain established new regional assemblies in Scotland and Wales and devolved some central powers to them. Italy and Spain have experienced a resurgence of regionalism driven by cultural and economic forces, and the European Union itself has ignited the aspirations of regions within its member states with its generous subsidies and grants channelled directly for sub-national regions, occurring at the same time as the implementation of its general policies on subsidiarity and mutual recognition of laws. Canada fairly recently (1999) created a new self-governing territory – Nunavut – for its Inuit peoples. Countries in conflict and post-conflict situations have often turned to federalism principles as a way of combining local identity with unity, such as solutions proposed for Cyprus, Jerusalem and Kosovo. Even strong growth economies with unitary systems of government, like Japan, China, Thailand and Indonesia, experience regional tensions as they grow, and look to federal finance arrangements to address their need to share wealth creation between urban and rural or coastal regions, and to achieve a fair balance in tax and expenditure sharing between central and regional governments.

The key lesson in all of this contemporary experience is that systems of governance, to survive, need to be dynamic and not static. Change is a normal circumstance. Both unitary and federal systems alike are pursuing unity with diversity, underpinned by sound governance arrangements to protect the economic and cultural sustainability of their regions, which is now accepted as the price of nationhood.

Any attempt to rethink Australian governance arrangements would do best to revisit the approach of Henry Parkes, the key leader of the federation movement, who called the founders to that historic Constitutional Convention in Sydney in 1891. Parkes had made overtures and visits to the other colonies to engage in consultation well before that seminal event and, in his famous Tenterfield Oration, he made it clear that the achievement of national unity was his underlying motive. As he put it so eloquently, 'the crimson thread of kinship runs through us all'. When the Convention finally gathered in Sydney, Parkes began the proceedings by putting forward a set of principles for discussion and consensus before any work might begin on constitutional design and drafting (see Quick and Garran 1901; Wiltshire 1991). The two great lessons from this experience, for any ongoing reform of governance, are to ensure that the prime goal is to retain a sense of nationhood, and to agree on basic principles before becoming enmeshed in debates about maps, boundaries, functions, taxes, and roles.

The historical context

When the Constitution was being written in the 1890s, Australia was not yet a nation. The founders tended to see it as six separate economies and societies, which was natural given such a vast continent, so sparsely populated. We are told that some of the founders communicated in Morse code. The landscape of our governance, as depicted in the Constitution which was finally adopted in 1901, reflects this. The boundaries of the States, which followed those of the existing colonies, had no particular economic or social significance, although they did take some account of geographical features. The River Murray was the obvious example, serving as the border between the two main States (NSW and Victoria), along with the Queensland/NSW border in its coastal and mountain regions. But, by contrast, other boundaries simply followed latitudinal and longitudinal parallels, including the boundary of Western Australia, whose origin commenced with global lines of demarcation originally drawn between Spain and Portugal, and reinforced by Papal decree, in 1494 (see Brown 2003: 42-5; Taylor 2006: 26-31). Even the more natural boundaries have since proved inappropriate, giving rise to no end of disputes over riparian rights of one kind or another from that day to this – an aspect well known to the good citizens of Corowa where the key original Constitutional Convention was held in 1893 to kick start the path towards federation, from which the politicians had strayed after their initial bursts of drafting in 1890-91.

The Australian Constitution is a blend of the Westminster model of government to delineate the separation of powers, and the American federal design for the division of powers between the Commonwealth and the States. Switzerland provided the inspiration, if not the actual model, for the process of amending the Constitution, which is by referendum of all the people – a testimony to the importance of people power in the continual evolution of our governance. Indeed Australia is one of the few nations in the world which came into existence by a vote of its people.

In designing the federal aspects, the founders were following thought processes similar to those of the American founders, who saw the federal design as a 'layer cake' with each level of government separate and sovereign to the maximum extent, each with its own list of revenue sources and expenditure functions, despite some inevitable concurrent powers. Like the Americans, the Australian founders also tried to design a federal system where the national government would have a narrow paddock in which to exercise its limited jurisdiction in a list of enumerated powers, and the States would enjoy all the residual powers. A person from Mars arriving on Earth today, reading the Australian Constitution, would assume that it was the States that ran this country.

Of course, some modern day functions of government which were not issues in the nineteenth century are not written in the Constitution at all – for example, management of the environment. Some were curiously divided between the levels, for example in industrial relations, reflecting the six economies' slant and causing no end of confusion ever since. Still other functions were left vague, e.g. external affairs and finance. This reflected the lack of need for precision in these fields at this time, although many prescient founders predicted the turmoil this would cause in the future, the most notable being Deakin's famous vision that the States would become bound to the 'Chariot Wheels of the Commonwealth' (La Nauze 1979).

Local government was very slow in appearing in Australian history, its establishment coming mainly after that of the colonial governments, quite contrary to the experience of most nations which were built on a foundation of local government (Spann 1973). Local government was barely considered by the founders, and does not figure in the Australian Constitution at all (Aulich and Peitsch 2002; Brown 2002; Bell this volume).

However the founders were certainly familiar with concepts of regionalism. The very difficulty of getting all colonies to join the federal movement, especially Western Australia and Queensland, had alerted them to the possibility of future endeavours to fragment their creation. The famous Section 96 of the Constitution was inserted precisely to allow for the special circumstances of any State to be addressed through Commonwealth Grants, thereby anticipating threats of secession, particularly in Western Australia. Section 96 says that the Commonwealth Parliament may make grants to the States on such terms and conditions as it sees fit. It was intended solely as an emergency measure to bail out a State in financial difficulties through no fault of its own, but has become one of the most entrenched powers for the Commonwealth, now enjoying a general application (Commonwealth Grants Commission 1995). It also laid the foundation for the principle of Horizontal Fiscal Equalisation, based on the seminal Australian interpretation of 'equity', to the effect that every Australian is entitled to similar standards of government services no matter where they live. Thus the concept of unity in diversity was born.

The founders also had to accommodate other elements of regional fragmentation. Section 7 of the Constitution, allowing for states to divide themselves into regions for Senate elections (but since effectively rescinded by Parliament), was a condition of securing the support of North Queensland, and perhaps other regions, for federation. Finally, in Chapter VI, the Constitution also contained a built-in mechanism for the creation of new states, recognising the pressure not only from North and Central Queensland but other regions like New England, the Riverina and the Western Australian Goldfields for their own identity.

The regionalism trail

Since 1901 there have been numerous initiatives to introduce regions into various aspects of Australia's governance. For the most part these have been 'top-down' attempts by state governments, and occasionally the Commonwealth Government, to establish regions for their own service delivery, accompanied by some decentralisation of their financial, human, and physical resources to those regions. Rarely have these measures been accompanied by any real devolution of power to the regions; mainly they have been just administrative arrangements. Local governments have, from time to time, swelled up into regional groupings for some purpose/ program, in a bottom up approach, but where this has happened it has been predominantly in response to some financial carrot being offered by one or both of the other two levels of government and their enthusiasm for regional perspectives has withered when the carrot was taken away.

Australian local governments do not spontaneously think *regionally* (see e.g. Jones 2003). This is somewhat understandable given their often unviable size and shape, their narrow and precarious revenue base, and the exponential growth in their responsibilities. More recently they have become victims of cost shifting to them by the other levels of government which are adept at transferring functions to local government but usually without compensatory funding or revenue-raising capacity. State governments look upon them with disdain, giving true feeling to the maxim that, constitutionally, local government is the 'creature' of state governments – many state governments have established Quangos of their own rather than allow local governments deliver a service on a regional basis. Local government also did itself a great disservice through its disunity in the referenda of 1974 and 1988, which presented the possibility of local government being recognised in the Australian Constitution, but which were lost. Furthermore, Australian local government was never a formal partner in the nation's intergovernmental relations until the advent of the Fraser Government's New Federalism which saw local government given a strong role on the Advisory Council on Intergovernmental Relations, and the Hawke Government's New Federalism which saw local government win a place in the

Council of Australian governments (COAG). Local government also received strong encouragement from the Constitutional Centenary Foundation, a non-government body established in 1991 to ascertain the need for constitutional reform leading up to the Centenary of Australian federation in 2001.

The two great Australian experiments in regionalism during the twentieth century were during the post-war reconstruction period (1944-49), and the period of the Whitlam government (1972-75) which took the Commonwealth into urban and regional issues in a new venture beyond conventional thinking about the role of the national government. The approach of the Whitlam government is particularly instructive as it involved ventures into functions not normally the constitutional preserve of the Commonwealth Government, including urban and regional development, the environment, distribution of funding on a regional basis, some by-passing of state governments by extra-constitutional means to give funding directly to local governments, and an enhanced role for local government with a new Horizontal Fiscal Equalisation scheme for local government alone. Considerable research went into designing a new regional structure based on criteria for the definition of regions and their suitability for government policy (see e.g. DURD 1973).

Apart from these two major initiatives, which really did see regional governance in play in Australia, there have also been many other proposals put forward by political parties and interest groups to divide Australia into regions for various purposes, usually accompanied by suggestions that state governments should be abolished. The number of regions proposed has usually varied between 35 and 65, but their constitutional status and the implications for the composition of the Australian Senate, have rarely been spelt out.

Towards new thinking on regions: recognising federal centralism

For any new and serious approach to contemplate the creation of regions in Australia, there are a number of necessary steps in the design process. First of all, it is essential to acknowledge the profound centralisation which has occurred in the Australian federation. The modern reality of the governance landscape is quite the opposite of the intention of the founders of the Constitution, and the Commonwealth Government dominates the scene. This has occurred through at least six means.

First, there has been amendment of the Constitution itself. Although only eight out of 46 referendum proposals have been passed, at least three of these have given significant powers to the Commonwealth – the 1927 Amendment to Section 105 on public loan raising, the 1946 amendment to Section 51 giving the Commonwealth social welfare powers, and the largest 'yes' vote in Australian history (90%), in 1967, to give the Commonwealth a role in indigenous affairs.

Secondly, there have been High Court judgements. Especially in the interpretation of taxation powers and the use of the corporations and external affairs powers, the Court has progressively handed significant powers to the Commonwealth Government. This has been due not so much to the leanings of the judges themselves, as the body of conspiracy theory would suggest. It has more to do with the recognition by the judges of the impact of two particular trends: globalisation, which requires Australia to speak with one voice in international forums, and national development, in which the sheer existence of a national economy, transport and communications system, and mobile populations and resources, sees the need for stronger national solutions and approaches. Both these trends have portended stronger powers for the Commonwealth Government. They have also seen the judges prepared to adopt less fundamentalist approaches to the wording of the Constitution and embrace the need for dynamic interpretation, despite the oft-heard criticism that this is creative law making by the judiciary and hence outside its proper role.

Thirdly, Commonwealth power has grown as a result of the nature of federal financial relations. This is the arena where the greatest centralisation has been evident. As a result of the 1927 amendment on loan raising, the uniform tax arrangements entered into during World War II, and several High Court judgements involving indirect taxation, the Commonwealth Government now collects over 70% of all the taxation revenue in Australia – including control of income tax, GST, and all the main indirect taxes. It also has had the dominant role in loan-raising powers and monetary policy. So the States, which are responsible for about half of all public expenditure in Australia, raise less than 20% of public revenue from a very narrow tax base. As a result, they are extremely dependent on grants from the Commonwealth Government. This is the situation known as Vertical Financial Imbalance, and it is worse in Australia than in any other federation in the world. It means that, on average, the States are dependent on Commonwealth transfers for half of all their revenue (higher for smaller States like Tasmania and the Territories). To make things worse, the Commonwealth attaches conditions to half of all those grants it gives the States. Local government is in an even more precarious position, raising only around 5-6% of all public revenue, and being highly dependent on transfers from state and Commonwealth Governments to survive, with most of those transfers having conditions attached.

Fourthly, 'executive federalism' has also contributed to the growth of Commonwealth influence. Executive federalism is a product of the era of 'co-operative federalism', the foundation of which was laid in the aftermath of the Great Depression, as all levels of government struggled together to revive the nation. In modern Australia, the majority of public functions now involve at least two levels of government (e.g. education) and often three levels (e.g. health, transport). As a result, the 'layer cake' model of federalism desired by the founders has long since ceased to exist, just as today it does not exist in any federal system. In Germany, for example, the constitution was rewritten after World War II, with a heavy shaping hand from the Allied powers, to recognise this design fault in older federal systems and instead lay much emphasis on Joint Tasks and continuous sharing of revenue and expenditure functions, under the strong supervision of the *Bundesrat* (which is a true States' House).

In Australia, too, it is no longer possible to assign whole functions of government to just one level of government. Rather, federalism is more like a 'marble cake' where the functions of government swirl around, engulfing two or three levels. Geoffrey Sawer (1976) called it 'organic federalism', a reminder to us once again of the prescience of those founders who predicted that once the omelette had been cooked, the eggs would lose their identity. Today, the effort to make this work has led to the concept and industry of executive federalism, manifest in over 350 intergovernmental agreements, watched over by meetings of some 41 Ministerial Councils across all fields of government, at the apex of which stands COAG, mentioned earlier. Executive federalism covers over one-third of all public sector activity in Australia. It has generally increased the power of the Commonwealth Government, especially by giving it access to constitutional areas not normally its terrain, including school education, hospitals, roads, agriculture, and the capacity through its fiscal supremacy to drive public policy in these arenas.

The reasons why these intergovernmental agreements have been initiated are instructive. They include:

- to achieve uniformity in the administration of a common functional area;
- to avoid overlapping in the provision of administrative services;
- to respond to the situation of vertical fiscal imbalance whereby the Commonwealth has the funding but the States have the functional power;
- to cope with the mobility of resources, human and financial, across state boundaries;
- to ensure accessibility to public resources for all Australians, no matter where they live;
- to disseminate information, or even exhortation, on vital areas of public interest, including where national solidarity is essential; and
- to pool resources between governments for challenges too big for one level to undertake, including major research efforts and, potentially, involving complementary action between the levels (as with the handling of emergencies. See Wiltshire 1977, 1980; ACIR 1981).

Although this plethora of activity, with its labyrinth of Councils and Committees and funding agreements, may well have begun under the rubric of 'co-operative' federalism, the tone is now quite different. Almost all of these arenas are now hot beds of dispute and wrangling, where the States fight the Commonwealth over funding and policy directions, occasionally even refusing to accept funding from the Commonwealth, which in turn accuses the States of mismanaging the funding they are given and not honouring the terms of the agreements.

A fifth influence has been the emergency powers and 'overrides' possessed by the Commonwealth. All federal constitutions make provision for national emergencies whence the national government is able to assume significant additional powers, including from state governments. This has happened in Australia in war time, and in other instances. Less formal but similar effects have come when Australia has faced major challenges which have given legitimacy to the national government in accumulating more power. Examples have included rampant inflation, energy crises, and terrorism.

Finally, unconstitutional action contributes to the strength of central power. From time to time governments stray into territory which is not really their preserve, but nobody mounts a challenge. The CSIRO is an example since the Commonwealth does not really have constitutional power in its domain. The same is true for the various international activities undertaken by state governments, including their elaborate trade and migration offices around the world.

The greatest evil of these trends towards centralism, especially the fiscal and executive federalism aspects, is the way they have distorted accountability in the Australian federal system. It has become extremely difficult for the citizen to apportion credit or blame to the appropriate level of government, thus creating a recipe for constant buck-passing from one level to another.

From 1996 to 2007, the centre of gravity in Australian politics also continued to shift towards Canberra through a most unexpected influence: the centralism of the Howard Coalition government. Once upon a time the Liberal Party was the champion of states' rights and decentralisation of power. The Howard government completely reversed this ideology, and became arguably at least as centralist as any Labor government has been. This phenomenon was facilitated to some extent by the fact that all the State and Territory Governments came to be held by Labor governments during the past decade, but that is not the only explanation. Enjoying the fruits of office and burgeoning revenue, with each successive re-election the Howard government rigorously pushed through its long-held ideological and policy agenda, even if this meant overriding state governments. After unexpectedly gaining control of the Senate at the 2004 election, the momentum quickened even further. In 2006, even before the definitive 'WorkChoices' High Court decision enabled the Commonwealth Government to override state industrial relations powers using the corporations power, the Commonwealth Attorney-General made it plain that if successful, this power would be employed in a similar manner to override other state powers.

The tactics of the Howard government have included pleas for uniformity, accountability and choice, which have fallen on fertile ground in an electorate which has grown tired and wary of state governments who deliver none of these goals and have proven inept at delivering their basic responsibilities of health care, school education, law and order, water, and infrastructure. Little wonder recent surveys show considerable disdain amongst both rural and urban citizens regarding their perceptions of state governments (for the NSW position, see Gray and Brown this volume). The modalities of 'Howard centralism' have included:

- conditional funding;
- bypassing states;
- overriding states;
- treating states as service deliverers rather than policy partners; and
- introducing purchaser/provider models where states would be just one of the bidders for Commonwealth funding.

So, as Greg Craven has said, every major Australian political party is centralist now (Craven 2005, 2006). The trend will be almost impossible to reverse. This is the context in which any new moves towards regionalism will take place.

Components of an effective federal-regional response

The centralising trend in Australian federalism, while sensible in some arenas, means that a whole new approach is needed towards rebuilding a sensible system of government, including reviving the advantages of federalism. This could be by refashioning traditional ideas of states' rights, by substituting a viable new national framework of regional devolution, using central power to more effectively *de*centralise. Given the recognised limitations of state and local government in the existing system, it is not simply a matter of trying to wind back the clock, or redistribute resources among existing institutions.

Instead, what is needed is a coherent national approach, the heart of which must be a viable, effective framework of regional governance. If we are serious about federalism, this should include 'general-purpose' regional government which is large enough to be viable and adaptive in fulfilling a wider range of policy needs than current local government, but operating at a scale more aligned with the real communities of interest of constituents, than can ever be the case with most present state or territory governments. To truly rebuild an effective federal system, of course, the fact that Australians live, work and govern themselves using these regions should also be recognised and legally protected in the Constitution. Whether or how the other existing levels of government would need to be reformed, to work in with an effective regional governance system, are secondary issues to consider once the primary need for a new framework is accepted.

The design of any new regional governance framework would have three fundamental components: (1) the functions or tasks which such regions would perform; (2) the determination of the boundaries of those regions; and (3) measures to ensure that the regions are sustainable.

Approaching the first issue of tasks, it is instructive to turn to previous endeavours which have been made in Australia to unscramble the omelette of federalism and identify the functions which are appropriate for each level of government. The most comprehensive attempt was by the Australian Advisory Council on Intergovernmental Relations (ACIR 1981) which scoured the economic and political/administrative literature, and global experience, to identify criteria which would help in the assignment of functions to levels of government. The research was aided by similar efforts which had been made in Canada (the Rowell Sirois Commission 1940), and the USA (the Kestnbaum Commission 1955) as well as two seminal Australian reviews – the 1927-29 Royal Commission on the Constitution, and a 1958 Parliamentary Committee Review of the Australian Constitution (Australia 1929, 1958).

The key lesson from this exercise was that it was no longer appropriate to try to assign whole functions to particular levels of government. Rather it has to be accepted that most of the functions would continue to be shared and the appropriate task was to identify the *roles which each level of government would play in those shared functions*. Nearly a decade later the movement known as Prime Minister Hawke's New Federalism adopted this approach as part of its sweeping reform of intergovernmental relations, especially as a result of three Special Premiers Conferences which were the forerunner of COAG (EPAC 1990; Wiltshire 1992). The research identified criteria which would point to the role of each level, as shown in Table 12.1.

Table 12.1. Criteria for Roles and Responsibilities

Favouring higher levels	Favouring lower levels	Indeterminate
International responsibilities	Subsidiarity – allocating the task to the level closest to the delivery point	Recognising sovereignty
Tasks which are indivisible and achieve universality of coverage	Achieving responsiveness to clients	Alignment with revenue sources
Attainment of uniformity and catering for mobility	Capturing local knowledge and expertise	Capacity to deliver
Addressing equity and accessibility	Speedy implementation and service delivery	Efficiency
Catering for portability and spillovers	Monitoring of results	Effectiveness
Achieving national standards	Preserving uniqueness and diversity	Accountability
Acting as an initiator / stimulator		Linking policy to delivery

Source: Wiltshire 1977, ACIR 1981

The second element of the regionalism imperative is to define the regions and their boundaries. Once again there have been some well established criteria employed in the past. The best known is the concept of *community of interest*, which is the paramount criterion. A region which does not share a community of interest is not worth a 'brass razoo'. Another well-known phrase, often used in relation to local government boundaries, is that a region should be *large enough to achieve economies of scale, but small enough to be responsive and encourage civic participation*. A third important aspect which often appears is *identity*. People living in a region must feel that they share a common identity.

These may sound like theoretical concepts, but they are given reality every day in our current system of governance. Bodies such as the Electoral Commissions, Telstra, Australia Post, the Australian Bureau of Statistics, and most government agencies, employ these concepts to define their boundaries for service delivery, civic participation or community engagement. The measures which these bodies all use to delineate their regions, based on these concepts, include:

- geographical features especially rivers and mountains;
- patterns of communication;
- patterns of transport;
- degrees of remoteness;
- socio-economic homogeneity;
- cultural affinity; and
- ecology and sustainability.

Given the strong current recognition of the importance of environmental sustainability, the 'eco'-criteria will most likely dominate this list in the foreseeable future.

Once the roles of the regions and their boundaries are determined, the third fundamental stage is to consider what policy measures need to be taken to ensure their continuing viability, in order to carry out these roles. This is where genuine devolution occurs as a solution to the major problems of the existing system. With many local governments currently financially unviable, properly-resourced regions can ensure that local and regional services do not simply disappear. With state government often too remote and pre-occupied to effectively coordinate and push through new policy solutions, such properly-resourced regions can do this. However we know from the existing experience of state and local governments that some or all of the following will be required:

a. tax-sharing with the other level(s) of government, since it will never be possible to assign unique revenue sources to regions to enable them constantly to fulfil their responsibilities;
b. provision for such tax-sharing arrangements to be flexible and capable of rational review – such as in the German federation, which has a process for regular reviews of the share of taxation to go to each of the three levels of government based on rational assessment of the needs of each level;

c.   grants and subsidies, where appropriate, from other level(s) of government;

d.   Community Service Obligations (CSOs) employed by government agencies of other level(s) of government should recognise the regions and where possible be delivered through them;

e.   incentives from other level(s);

f.   taxation allowances by other level(s) for regions where appropriate;

g.   exemptions from other level(s) to relevant regions, including inappropriate regulatory arrangements; and

h.   Horizontal Fiscal Equalisation to ensure all regions have the same capacity to deliver services at the same standard, at similar levels of taxation.

Conclusion: identifying some models

Given the case for a new national framework of regions, what are the options? The historical context, and trend to federal centralisation described above, now mean there are three broad models by which the creation of Australian regions could take place: within old states, by abolishing the old states, or by creating new states.

Old states

Regions would have to be created within existing state boundaries. Local governments could also be amalgamated, realigned, or grouped for this purpose. State and Commonwealth Governments would have to devolve some tasks to regions and decentralise others. Regional elected assemblies could be established with powers over resource allocation and possibly revenue-raising. This model requires minimal disruption to Australian constitutional arrangements. It would provide a new framework for coordinating and, perhaps, rationalising a growing range of existing regional governance initiatives. In particular, it could simplify the current complex system of regional governance and make it more directly accountable and responsive to the needs of each region's community. However, this model also effectively creates a fourth tier of government in the federation. If 'co-operative federalism' is relied on to develop this model, then existing experience also suggests the pace of reform may be so slow and cumbersome that the end results might never be achieved.

No states

Under this model, all the current states would be abolished. Regions and regional governments would be created in their place, most likely by amalgamation or realignment of local governments. Most public perceptions of this model see it as resulting in only two main levels of government – Commonwealth and Regions – although in practice, the Regions might still retain or re-create some form of local government (see e.g. Hurford 2004). The model would require reconfiguration of the Senate to become a House of the Regions. This model requires considerable constitutional change and redesign resulting in a major national referendum. Sections 123 and 128 of the Constitution mean that a majority of the electors in *every* State would need to support the reform in this referendum, not just a majority of electors in a majority of States. On one hand, public attitude surveys indicate a fair groundswell of opinion in both rural and urban Australia for a governance design of this kind (see Gray and Brown, this volume). On the other hand, many commentators point to the existing record of constitutional amendment in Australia, to argue that even if the reform was desirable, the divisions and uncertainties provoked by the debate might make it very difficult to achieve.

New states

Constitutionally, it is easier to pursue a third model – that of creating new states rather than abolishing old states. Under the Australian Constitution, Chapter VI (sections 121-124) deals with new states and territories. Section 124 is the operative section – it reads: 'A new State may be formed by separation of territory from a State, but only with the consent of the Parliament thereof, and a new state may be formed by the union of two or more states or parts of states, but only with the consent of the Parliaments of the States affected'. In formal terms it is the State Parliament which would decide, but a referendum would be most likely. Given the centralism trends in Australian federalism described earlier, it is important that under section 123 of the Constitution, it could also be the Commonwealth Government who initiates this referendum. Once a region is recognised by popular vote as having been separated from the existing State (to form in effect a New State), the Commonwealth Parliament then simply votes to admit that region as a new entity in the existing federal system. The Senate would also have to be reconfigured under this model but only to the extent of accommodating more states. Essentially this model involves gaining the consent of a majority of citizens in the region where the new state is to be formed, and the consent of the citizens in the State from which the new state is to be withdrawn. A virtue of using the existing constitutional provisions is that even if a referendum is used, citizens are being asked to vote directly on the substantive question – the creation of new regional governments – rather than changes to the rules in the existing Constitution.

In fact, the creation of at least some new states will in all likelihood happen naturally throughout the 21st century. Likely candidates which have already identified themselves previously through Australian history include New England, the Riverina and North and Central Queensland. The two mainland Territories are already quasi-new states, and it is almost inevitable that the Northern Territory will be converted to full statehood, having only narrowly declined this opportunity in a referendum in 1998. Other potential regions as new states for the longer term include North-Western Australia, and much of

Central Australia also embracing remote areas of New South Wales and Queensland.

Under this scenario the new states and/or territories effectively become the primary regions in the federal system, perhaps swallowing the local governments within their boundaries or, more likely, creating a different institutional form of local service delivery and civic involvement. This model therefore revives the original logic of federalism, with all its potential advantages.

Towards a new option

Change is upon us, as can and should be expected in any federal system. The founders intended to create a dynamic, not static, system of governance. Even if we accept that this is taking place incrementally, in line with the first model, it is important to decide where this would take us and how new regional institutions are to be reconciled with our existing system. However, there are clear reasons, based on public policy and public attitudes, for taking a longer-term view and embracing more substantial and better planned reform. The existing state governments are not viewed very favourably by their own citizens. Moreover there is a demonstrable recognition that the existing state boundaries currently make little sense. Add to this the current unassailable centripetal momentum in the Australian federation occurring through natural domestic and international economic and social trends, as well as policy drivers from all the major political parties which are now all centralist. The result is that mere variations on the status quo are not likely to deliver substantial improvements in the quality of governance under our federal system.

Taken together these factors would suggest that options based merely on the 'old States' are history. There is now both a policy logic, and a popular logic, behind a configuration of Australian governance involving two main levels: an ever-stronger national government, and regional governments which combine some policy determination and much service delivery. For this model to be saleable and feasible the result must be an Australia whose system of government appears simpler and perhaps even cheaper to its citizens, based on sustainable regions with realistic boundaries. Calculating the economic and financial benefits of such reform, and addressing any costs, are crucial. However the less constitutionally painful path to achieve this system of governance is clearly through new states rather than no states. Indeed, this approach would restore the original logic of federalism itself, while also addressing the primary concerns of federalism's greatest critics.

To be worth pursuing, this model must be seen as a substantially new option. A criticism of past proposals for new states is that they have been piecemeal, with the creation of each new state compounding rather than relieving the complications of the federal system. But there is no reason, in principle, why the machinery for creating new states cannot be used to bring about a substantially new, comprehensive, national system of regions, undertaken not in a piecemeal way within one or two existing states, but as part of a national reform program. This would be led by the Commonwealth Government, and undertaken with state cooperation. The new regions would employ many former state public servants, and deal directly with Canberra on most issues of funding, taxation and national regulation – a simplified, more efficient and more accountable version of what is increasingly happening now.

Why hasn't it already happened? The history of federation itself shows that the road can be a long one. In the Australian colonies, federation was widely supported, if not assumed as far back as the 1840s and 1850s, even though it took until 1901 to be secured. The momentum for the next phase of comprehensive reform to Australia's system of governance has again been growing for several decades, informed by experience. With vision and a focus on the basic principles, there is no doubt that it can be achieved.

References

Advisory Council for Intergovernment Relations 1981, *Towards Adaptive Federalism, A Search for Criteria for Responsibility Sharing in a Federal System*, Information Paper No. 9, AGPS, Canberra.

Aulich, C. and R. Peitsch 2002, 'Left on the shelf: local government and the Australian Constitution' *Australian Journal of Public Administration,* Vol. 61 (4): 14-23.

Australia, 1929, Royal Commission on the Constitution 1927-29, *Report,* Government Printer, Canberra.

Australia, 1959, Joint Committee on Constitutional Review, *Report*, Government Printer, Canberra.

Brown, A. J. 2002, 'Subsidiarity or subterfuge? Resolving the future of local government in the Australian federal system' *Australian Journal of Public Administration,* Vol 61 (4): 24-42.

Brown, A. J. 2003, *The Frozen Continent: the Fall and Rise of Territory in Australian Constitutional Thought 1815-2003*, PhD Thesis, Griffith University.

Commission on Intergovernmental Relations (Kestnbaum Commisson) 1955, *A Report to the President for Transmittal to the Congress*, Washington DC.

Commonwealth Grants Commission 1995, *Equality in Diversity*, AGPS, Canberra.

Craven, G. 2005, 'The New Centralism and the Collapse of the Conservative Constitution', Senate Occasional Lecture, Department of the Senate, Canberra, 14 October 2005.

Craven, G. 2006, 'Are We All Centralists Now?', Address to Gilbert and Tobin Centre Constitutional Law Conference, Sydney, 24 February 2006.

Department of Urban and Regional Development 1973, *Regions*, AGPS, Canberra.

Economic Planning Advisory Council 1990, *Towards a More Cooperative Federalism, Discussion Paper No. 90/04*, AGPS, Canberra.

Hurford, C. 2004, 'A republican federation of regions: reforming a wastefully governed Australia', in W. Hudson and A. J. Brown (eds), *Restructuring Australia: Regionalism, Republicanism and Reform of the Nation-State*, Federation Press, Annandale NSW.

Jones, S. 2003, *Beyond the Boundaries: The Contribution of Regions to Queensland's Economic Development*, Information paper No. 79, CEDA, Melbourne.

La Nauze, J. 1979, *Alfred Deakin: A Biography*, Angus and Robertson, Sydney.

Quick, J. and R.R. Garran, 1901, *The Annotated Constitution of the Commonwealth of Australia*, Angus and Robertson, Sydney.

Sawer, G. 1976, *Modern Federalism*, Carlton, Pitman.

Sirois J. (Chairman) 1940, Royal Commission on Dominion-Provincial Relations, *Report*, Government Printer, Ottawa.

Spann R. N. et al 1973, *Public Administration in Australia*, NSW Government Printer, Sydney, Chapter 11.

Taylor, D. 2006, *The States of a Nation: The Politics and Surveys of the Australian State Borders*, NSW Department of Lands, Bathurst.

Wiltshire, K. (ed.) 1977, *Administrative Federalism*, University of Queensland Press, St. Lucia.

———— 1980, 'Working with Intergovernmental Agreements: The Canadian and Australian Experience', *Canadian Public Administration* 23(3), Fall, 353-379.

———— 1991, *Tenterfield Revisited: Reforming Australia's System of Government for 2001*, University of Queensland Press, St. Lucia.

———— 1992, 'Australia's New Federalism: Recipes for Marble Cakes', *Publius* 22(3), Summer, 165-180.

Chapter 13: Quantifying the Costs and Benefits of Change: Towards A Methodology

Christine Smith

Introduction

As outlined in previous chapters of this book, the current state of evolution of Australia's system of federation has been the subject of considerable criticism in recent years. This chapter narrows in on those criticisms that focus on economic factors, including the assignment of expenditure responsibilities and revenue raising powers between the federal, state and local levels. It also recognises the emergence of new regional governance and service delivery arrangements and speculates on the capacity of these arrangements to act as an alternative to more substantive change in other elements of the system. The purpose of this chapter is not to provide answers as to whether or not change to current federal structures and/or financial arrangements will generate net economic benefits. The aim here is to point to some key directions in which debates surrounding federalism and regionalism need to move, to permit the development of a more appropriate analytical framework for generating such answers.

In the next section, various calls for change based on economic rationales are documented, and the case is made for a shift in focus to the functions to be carried out by the various levels of government in order to address these concerns. In the third section of the chapter, the relevant public finance literature is reviewed for insights into potential reform principles. In section 4, attention shifts to the literature on the economics of local government amalgamation, since reform agendas that have been popularly espoused in the past have either explicitly or implicitly involved a reduction in the number of units at this level. In section 5, previous attempts at identifying the net economic benefits to be derived from various proposed reforms are evaluated and suggestions made as to how their methodology could be improved. The chapter concludes with directions that should be pursued for the sound economic evaluation of potential change agendas, based on a more detailed initial set of representative change proposals.

Change agendas and the need for a focus on functions by level

Recent calls for change in federal-state arrangements, based on economic rationales, include the following (emphasis mine):

> Australia's federation needs new life breathed into it for the benefit of the community and business. In just about every major policy area our approach to intergovernmental relations presents barriers and obstacles to getting sensible outcomes ... The time has come to take a more holistic approach to our system of intergovernmental relations so that our federation works for us rather than against us (Australian Industry Group 2005).

> Where two levels of government are responsible for different parts of the same system it is difficult or impossible to achieve coordination in policy and funding ... *Lack of coordination gives rise to significant overlaps and gaps ... with too much funding allocated to some types of service and not enough to others* ... poor coordination of services in areas of shared responsibility creates major problems for customers, who become confused and frustrated in their efforts to deal with a multi-layered system that shuttles them back and forth (National Commission of Audit 1998).

> Australia needs a summit on federalism ... Reform is overdue ... Instead of each tier exercising the powers that are most appropriate to it, we have governments prone to administrative duplication and buck passing. We also have a system where states cannot raise the money needed to provide the most basic services. Instead they rely on Commonwealth grants, an *economic and political dependency that is neither healthy nor consistent with the best delivery of services to the community* (Williams 2006).

> Through most of our past quarter century or more of improving government performance, we have had endless buck-passing between the two most important levels of government – in education and training, health, infrastructure, water management and other important issues. *The States depend on the Federal Government for funding, Canberra relies on the States for implementation – and each relies on the other for deflecting accountability* ... Only by finally fixing federal state-relations will we truly become the world leaders in public policy and economic development and be able to build on our quality of life (Devenson 2006).

Common themes that emerge are those of overlap and duplication across various functional areas and the need for greater clarification of responsibilities, as well as the need for thought to be give to the reassignment of some areas of responsibility from federal to state governments and vice versa.

Recent calls for change in federal-state-local arrangements have been even stronger, recognising the inadequate level of revenue flowing through to local governments relative to the growing importance and array of functions for which they have become responsible. These criticisms are demonstrated elsewhere in this book (see Brown, Head, Bell, and Wiltshire this volume). Other such calls include:

> Getting better results out of areas where Federal-State activities intersect is vital. Inconsistencies, duplication and additional costs associated with poorly coordinated or conflicting State-Federal (and local) government policies and regulations affect virtually every area ... (Access Economics 2004).

> Cost shifting is, ultimately, a symptom of what has become dysfunctional governance and funding arrangements. It is time to combine the best efforts of governments and choose a better way. There have been many *demands for the three spheres of government to work more closely and eliminate duplication and wasted resources.* In a shrinking and increasingly competitive world, the luxury of three spheres of government, with often different agendas, in a country of nearly 20 million people is straining our resources (House of Representatives Standing Committee on Economics, Finance and Administration 2003).

> The problem of *over-government* has long been identified, and the solution offered is the same: the abolition of the States ... they no longer manage their affairs in their own way ... most of the power to do that has already leached back to the Commonwealth through its control of the purse strings...its not going to flow back ... yet though states' rights are outdated, the States are entrenched facts ... *reformers should seek to economise elsewhere – in the third tier, local government* ... NSW comprises an intricate patchwork of tiny fiefdoms. Nearly 40 councils run services for one city – Sydney. Though some share services, the unnecessary duplication is a drain on resources ... *The amalgamation of local councils should be the first step towards a two-tier system of government in Australia* (Sydney Morning Herald 2006).

Recognition that important areas such as natural resource management and economic development may be better dealt with at a level that crosses current local (and, in some cases, state) boundaries has led to the emergence of an ever-expanding array of regional bodies. Such bodies could be argued to comprise a fourth (fifth, sixth, etc.) tier within the federal system. Some writers point to these bodies as a vehicle via which existing formal levels of government can cooperate and thereby eliminate the need for more radical reform of the current federal system (Business Council of Australia 2006; Dollery, Johnson et al 2005; Dollery, Marshall et al 2005; Marshall et al 2003). However the costs associated with these bodies have not been fully documented and neither have the benefits of their achievements relative to their costs. More substantively there has emerged a set of concerns about these regional arrangements that deserve further serious investigation before they could be seen as a viable way forward. For example:

a.   Beer et al (2003) highlight empirical research pointing to regional bodies afflicted by inadequate organisational size, low (usually non-existent) recurrent funding, 'third world'-style birth and death rates, poorly directed central funds and duplication and coordination problems between and within governments;

b.   the Regional Business Development Panel (2003) reported:

We were struck by the sheer number of (organisations) operating at a regional level with the objective of supporting regional and business development ... There is overlap, duplication and at times competition between the layers of government ... There are *too many bodies trying to achieve common outcomes for the same area.* As a result public money is spread too thinly and resource-starved organisations spend considerable time chasing additional funding... One region we visited has around 20 different development agencies, employing around 40 people. Five are Commonwealth bodies, five are state organisations, local government runs seven and business groups manage the rest ...

c.   and the Regional Implementation Working Group (2005) recommended with respect to natural resource management (NRM) that:

... the Australian and State/Territory governments *clarify and articulate their respective roles and responsibilities* in regard to the provision of support for regional NRM bodies ... *and determine the base level of core funding* required to maintain an appropriate corporate governance framework to enable a regional body to meet conformance, performance and administrative requirements ...

The themes that emerge in this area suggest that hopeful initiatives at non-traditional scales of policy and governance have tended to be unsupported by legal, administrative, financial, relevant professional expertise or other capacity. They also tend to rely excessively on the time of volunteers and to be short-lived when they fail to live up to expectations or when policy fashions change.

With such widespread dissatisfaction with various elements of the current system, it is not surprising that recent public opinion surveys by Brown and his colleagues indicate that the majority of residents in Queensland (Brown 2002a, b) and New South Wales (Brown et al 2006; Gray and Brown this volume) prefer a scenario different than the current system. In particular, a two tier system based on regional governments is the single most preferred option in both cases. Unfortunately, as yet the pilot research in this field has not provided details of the various options for change presented to respondents prior to asking them to rate these options; rather, broad descriptors were provided such as 'same system as today', 'three-tiered, more states', 'two-tiered, regional governments', and 'four-tiered'.

This is not surprising since a scan of the relevant literature reveals multiple reform agendas, albeit with scant details on the specifics (Jaensch 2003). There are calls for the abolition of states and a move to a two tier system of government, but no consensus on what replaces them at the sub-national level (e.g. how many regional governments, with what boundaries, which current state government expenditure responsibilities and taxing powers would divert to the Commonwealth and which would be assigned to the new regional governments, and the system to be put in place to ensure horizontal and vertical fiscal equalisation). Similarly, there are calls for new states, but no consensus on how many or where they would be located. There are calls for local government amalgamations, but no consensus on which ones or on what criteria they might be selected. There are calls for a new or reformed set of regional institutions, but not what powers, functions, resources or reporting mechanisms they would be given from whom.

In order to move the debate on from speculation by a broad range of well-meaning reformers, consensus needs to be developed around a concrete reform agenda (or small set of such agendas). More importantly, however, in order for such agendas to be developed in a way that net costs or savings from change can be estimated, details are required with respect to how the functions of government would be distributed in any one of these agendas. That is, to be able to be costed, any given scenario needs to specify what functions (or components of functions):

a. currently *exclusively federal, state or local* would be better assigned to other level(s);

b. currently *overlapping in terms of responsibility* would be better allocated to a single level exclusively;

c. *necessarily overlapping* but in need of better co-ordination between levels to avoid duplication; and

d. *fall between gaps* with our current levels of government leading to the need for formation of regional bodies.

A substantial amount of relevant data is available in the Australian context at a functional level of disaggregation that would provide insights into an analysis aimed at providing such details – for example, from government finance statistics and from State and Federal Government Grants Commission reports. It is important to recognise, however, that when advocating revised assignment of expenditure responsibilities between levels of government, it is necessary to also address the machinery for shifting taxation and other forms of revenue sources necessary to carry out these responsibilities.

Insights from fiscal federalism literature

The fiscal federalism literature provides some useful principles that could be invoked when fleshing out alternative reform agendas and, in particular, the proposed (re)assignment of functions (expenditure responsibilities and taxing powers) between levels of government. These principles relate to: expenditure responsibilities; taxation powers; and intergovernmental grants.

Expenditure responsibilities

The first principle that deserves mention is that of *subsidiarity*, which has been interpreted in a federal system of government as implying that provision of goods and services should be administered at the lowest level feasible within the national interest (see Brown 2002b; Brown, Podger, Head this volume; Access Economics 2004; Twomey and Withers 2007). The rationale appears to be that this permits such provision to most closely match the preferences of the people.

The second principle to emerge is that of *correspondence*, which argues that where consumption or use of a particular good or service is limited to the boundaries of a particular jurisdiction, then its provision should be allocated to a sub-national government whose boundaries are defined by the spatial benefit (or market area) boundaries associated with this good or service (Oates 1972, 2005; Warren 2005; Williams 2005b). The resulting allocation generates economic efficiency since it allows for a matching of local demand and supply, with voters able to move between jurisdictions in search for an optimal mix of provision and associated taxes and charges given their individual needs. An obvious difficulty confronted when putting flesh around this principle is that, carried to the extreme, each good or service provided by governments could conceivably have a different set of spatial benefit (or market area) boundaries leading to a need for a multitude of overlapping levels of government (Access Economics 2004; Productivity Commission 2005, 2006). Clearly, common sense is needed when interpreting this principle if only three (or at most four) levels of government are being considered.

The third principle involves giving due *recognition to economies of scale* in the provision of goods and services, with a case generated for movement of provision to a higher level where it costs less if produced or provided by single jurisdiction rather than separate smaller ones (Access Economics 2004; Williams 2005b). It has been argued more recently that possibilities for separation of production from provision should be exploited where feasible, since this may permit provision to be retained with smaller units, while at the same time allowing them to take advantage of mutually agreed co-operative production arrangements at a scale sufficiently large to generate maximum cost savings (Dollery 2005 b,c).

The fourth principle recognises the constraints imposed by existing jurisdictional boundaries and argues for the need for a *mechanism to resolve inter-jurisdiction spill-overs or spill-ins of benefits (and/or costs)* of a particular good or service. In the absence of such mechanisms, economic inefficiency in the form of under- (or over-) provision of such goods or services would result. The case is thereby created for responsibility for these goods or services to be either transferred to a higher level of government, or for it to remain at the lower level but for intervention by a higher level through system of tied grants aimed at providing 'compensation' to those lower level jurisdictions disadvantaged by the nature of the observed spill-overs (or spill-ins). The tied grant solution is preferred where location-specific or individual-specific cost differences occur between jurisdictions and/or where economies of scale are exhausted at comparatively low population levels and/or geographic spreads (Oates 1972, 2005; Productivity Commission 2005, 2006).

The fifth principle recognises that inter-jurisdictional differences in the nature, cost and/or level of provision of particular goods or services could generate negative *impacts on the mobility of factors of production,* resulting in economically inefficient locational choices. The literature suggests that where significant transaction costs are imposed on labour or firms from movement across jurisdictions, then a case can be made for minimum standard setting at higher levels and the introduction of a system of compensating grants for lower level jurisdictions for which this imposes cost increases (National Commission of Audit 1996; Productivity Commission 2006).

The final principle suggests that *accountability is strengthened if responsibility for a particular function is tier-specific* (Brogden 2006; National Commission of Audit 1996; OECD 2006; Selway 2001). For many important functions this is not a realistic option, with most analysts acknowledging that assignment of responsibilities will most often resemble a marbled not a tiered cake (see Wiltshire this volume). What is necessary, then, is to ensure that the nature of this marbling is not randomly generated but rather emerges from a process of careful deliberation (and is the subject of periodic renegotiation as economies of scale and other characteristics of production or provision change over time). If expenditure responsibility in a broad area (e.g. education or health) is necessarily shared, then respective roles in segments of this area need to be agreed and mutually understood, with cooperative arrangements put in place to ensure appropriate ongoing coordination between these segments to ensure they mesh well together at key transition points (Warren 2006; Wilkins 2004).

Taxation powers

The *principle of fiscal equivalence* implies that each level of government should finance its assigned functions with funds it raises itself. However carried to extreme this would lead to significant inefficiencies in tax collection from many revenue sources and distortions to locational choices of individuals and firms. The latter concern has also led to arguments suggesting that taxes on highly mobile tax bases should be allocated to higher levels of government, as should taxes on tax bases that are uneven across jurisdictions (Access Economics 2004; Dahlby 2001; Productivity Commission 2006).

The resulting lack of alignment of expenditure responsibilities and tax assignments leads to a situation of *vertical fiscal imbalance* – where revenue raising capacity of at least one level of government exceeds its expenditure needs whilst the reverse is the case for the other levels. In general there is support for tax sharing rather than reassignment of tax bases and rate schedules in this situation, implying the need for a system of intergovernmental transfers or grants. Such a system needs to be managed carefully – in particular, a high level of autonomy over expenditure priorities and service management is required by the recipients in order to ensure that the efficiency benefits of competitive federalism are not constrained (Allen Consulting Group 2006; Grewel and Sheehan 2003; Hancock and Smith 2001; Saunders 2002; Warren 2006).

Intergovernmental grants

The current level of vertical fiscal imbalance in Australia has been a cause for concern, with the Commonwealth Government's revenue collections exceeding its expenditure needs by up to 40% (House of Representatives Standing Committee 2003). While transfer by the Commonwealth of GST revenues to the States has made significant inroads into addressing the latter's own-source revenue shortfalls, a similar arrangement remains elusive for local government (Access Economics 2004; Productivity Commission 2006).

Australia's current system of intergovernmental grants includes horizontal fiscal equalisation (HFE) payments administered by the Commonwealth and various State Grants Commissions (Commonwealth Grants Commission 2006a, b; Local Government Grants Commission South Australia 2005, New South Wales Local Government Grants Commission 2005, Northern Territory Grants Commission 2005, Queensland Local Government Grants Commission 2005, Tasmania State Grants Commission 2005, Victoria Grants Commission 2005, Western Australian Government Grants Commission 2005). These payments are aimed at ensuring that jurisdictions at each sub-national level of government receive funding from the Commonwealth, such that if each made the same effort to raise revenue from its own sources and operated at the same level of efficiency, then each would have the capacity to provide services of the same standard to their constituents (Morris 2002; Williams 2005a).

These HFE payments currently involve correction for disadvantage on both revenue and expenditure sides, but some concern has arisen over the efficiency effects of the latter (Hancock and Smith 2001; McLean 2004; Petchey and Levtchenkova 2004; Usher 1995). Nevertheless, various attempts at estimating the size of such efficiency effects have concluded that they are small, and possibly worth incurring for the gains they generate in terms of equity (Dixon et al 2002, 2005; Harding et al 2002; Williams 2005b).

Clearly there is a need to evaluate the implications of various change options for the magnitude and nature of both vertical and horizontal equalisation payments – with a recognition that the order of magnitude of such payments may need to involve both a one-off compensation for past inadequate service provision in some newly emerging jurisdictions, and a steady state set of payment schedules for such jurisdictions in the future.

Insights from local government amalgamation literature

As mentioned earlier in the chapter, there exists a widespread notion in both the popular media and government and business reports that economies of scale exist in the provision of goods and services within the level of local government, such that economic benefits can be derived from the elimination of numerous small local government authorities through a process of amalgamation (forced or voluntary). It is also widely assumed that attempts to redress the poor financial position of this level should await resolution of this structural problem (Business Council of Australia 2006; Department of Transport and Regional Services 2005; House of Representatives Standing Committee 2003; State Chamber of Commerce (NSW) 2005; Sydney Morning Herald 2006).

In addition, many of the more radical proposals for reform of the federal system involve the elimination of the current state and local levels of government and their replacement by a single regional level of government (e.g. Hall 1998; Soorley 2004). This in turn implies both the devolution of most, if not all, current functions allocated to the States to the new regional level, and the amalgamation of a large number of the current local government authorities into larger regional units. It is of considerable interest then to examine the empirical evidence available relating to the economics of local government.

Overseas empirical evidence suggests that while total costs do vary with population size, it is not the case that a decreasing cost curve prevails for all population sizes (Byrnes and Dollery 2002; Dollery and Fleming 2005). That is, while there is evidence that costs do decrease up to a certain population size, after this point these costs generally begin to rise again – with suggestions that for large metropolitan areas the best solution is for a body charged with ensuring co-ordination of policy and implementation across key areas (such as transportation systems) but that this body be complemented by a series of smaller local government units responsible for ongoing service delivery (Sancton 2005). In addition, the results of various studies point to the population range associated with the lowest per capita costs being different depending on the type of service being investigated. This in turn highlights the fact that much of the overseas research in this area is of limited relevance to the Australian context, since local governments in our federal system have responsibility for a different range of services than those in other countries – for example, police and schools in the United States and public housing in the United Kingdom.

Empirical evidence from Australia is extremely limited in terms of volume, and mixed in terms of its results. However the majority of studies conducted to date suggest an 'optimum size' from an economic viewpoint as in 30-80,000 population range (Byrnes and Dollery 2002; Marshall 1998; Soul and Dollery 2000; Soul 2000) – a size exceeding many of our current local government jurisdictions. At the same time, the results obtained from these empirical studies have been criticised (Allen 2003; Dollery and Crase 2004; Dollery, Crase et al 2005; Woodbury et al 2002) for ignoring the variable nature of local government services and the presence of differentiated economies of scale – a fact confirmed from a detailed reading of the reports of the various state grants commissions referred to above as well as by studies focussing on particular local government services (for example, Worthington and Dollery 2000; Woodbury et al 2002). Labour intensive customer-oriented services would generally be expected to generate lesser economies of scale than capital intensive services (such as water and sewerage) where benefits can be obtained from spreading fixed costs across a larger number of service points (Dollery and Fleming 2005).

Many of the empirical studies conducted based on the Australian experience have also been criticised for employing single- rather than multi-variate analysis with omitted variables (demographic/geographic characteristics) such that the true impact of population size has, in general, been overestimated (Byrnes and Dollery 2002). It is not surprising then that local government grants commissions introduce variables such as population density, remoteness, ethnicity, indigenous status, age structure, non-resident service provision, climate and terrain into their analysis of the appropriate size of their equalisation grants, rather than distributing them on a strict per capita basis (Department of Transport and Regional Services 2005). This in turn suggests that the optimal size of a local government jurisdiction may differ for rural and remote communities than those based around provincial centres and metropolitan areas (Soul and Dollery 2000), but investigation of this hypothesis in a rigorous manner has yet to be undertaken.

Given the mixed results and the methodological flaws discussed above, it is not surprising that evaluations conducted post-amalgamation have almost invariably reported that the economic benefits actually experienced have been considerably lower than those estimated by the proponents of the change prior to amalgamation (Allen 2003; Dollery, Crase et al 2005) – and that this experience has been replicated overseas as well (Dollery, Keogh et al 2005; Frontier Centre for Public Policy 2003; Rouse and Putterill 2005). This in turn has led to some commentators suggesting that alternative means exist for achieving economies of scale in key functions without amalgamation (eg. ROCs, strategic alliances for joint provision, tendering) (Dollery 2005a; Dollery and Crase 2004; Dollery, Crase et al 2005; Dollery and Johnson 2005). However, little if any evaluation has been conducted with respect to the cost effectiveness of these alternative arrangements.

Previous attempts at evaluating net benefits of change

Alongside this specific, albeit incomplete, research into the economics of current structures of governance, some effort has been made to estimate the full range of net benefits that might be expected to be derived from reform of the federal system. Numerous government publications, consultancy reports, popular media analysts and non-economics academic papers quote various estimates made by Drummond as to the costs of duplication and coordination inherent within the current federal structure (for example, Access Economics 2004; House of Representatives Standing Committee 2003; Parliament of Victoria 1998). These estimates vary from $10-$40 billion dollars per annum, depending on which calculation is chosen for quotation. The most often quoted figure, however, is the $20+ billion claimed to be able to be saved from moving to a two tier system that abolishes the States (Drummond 2002).

By contrast, a study commissioned by state and territory governments, which focuses only on the direct and indirect overlap costs associated with special purpose payments, argues that the cost savings are more like $1 billion (ACIL Economics and Policy Pty Ltd 1996; Tredbeck and Cutbush 1996). A more recent study using Commonwealth Grants Commission data produces a similar order of magnitude estimate, namely $0.8m, for the cost of overlap and duplication between the Commonwealth and state levels (Garnaut and Fitzgerald 2002; Allen Consulting Group 2006). Yet another recent report estimates these costs to be $8.92 billion (Access Economics 2006).

These are vastly different estimates, suggesting the need for a careful examination of the underlying methodologies in order that we might be able to move towards development of a framework capable of resolving these differences and in so doing get a better handle on the real order of magnitude of potential savings (and/or costs) from various reform options. This is especially important given flaws inherent in the Drummond and Access Economics (2006) approaches, and the narrow focus of the alternative estimates. Some of these flaws have already been commented on by others (e.g. Twomey and Withers 2007).

Drummond's (2001, 2002) approach commences with the assumption that government expenditure associated with any jurisdiction can be divided into a fixed cost component and a single variable cost component. The single variable cost component is calculated as a function of the aggregate population level in the jurisdiction; while the fixed cost component is assumed to be associated with overheads or administration of the level of government in question, and hence able to be avoided or eliminated if this level of government is phased out. Since the variable cost component is solely a function of population levels, it is argued that such costs will remain unaltered in magnitude should responsibility for that population shift to another jurisdiction. The sizes of these two components are estimated by fitting a simple linear regression model to pooled time series/cross-section data relating to three consecutive years (1998-99 to 2000-01) and eight jurisdictions (states and territories) – that is a total of 24 observations. The derived regression equation is:

$$E = 1.5883 + 6.6152\ P$$

where E = total public sector expenditure ($ billion in 2000-01 dollars), and P = population (in millions).

The fixed cost estimate is $1.5883 billion and the variable (or marginal) cost estimate is $6,615 per head of population. It is this fixed cost estimate which it is argued to be saved if a particular jurisdiction is merged with another. Abolition of seven of the eight States (with the remaining one absorbing the responsibilities of those abolished and in effect administered by the Commonwealth) is argued to yield cost savings of seven times the fixed cost estimate – namely $11.12 billion (= 7 x 1.5883). Drummond also assumes that individual state deviations around the estimated regression line were accounted for by higher or lower variable costs per head of population and hence able to be eliminated through horizontal amalgamation. An algorithm was developed for achieving these mergers in ascending population size order. Application of this algorithm resulted in an almost doubling of the estimated cost savings from abolition of the States, namely $20.22 billion.

A number of serious criticisms can be made with respect to this aspect of the Drummond approach:

a. 24 observations is too small a number of observations to support the findings reported, especially given the comparative lack of variability in the total level of government expenditure in any given jurisdiction over successive years and the use of pooled time series and cross sectional data – a longer time series of observations is available, even though the recent shift from cash to accrual accounting within government finance statistics may generate the need for care to be exercised in splicing relevant time series together;

b.   The assumption of a single variable cost component based on population levels ignores a large volume of available data relating to determinants of inter-jurisdictional variations in costs. For example, federal and state grants commissions have long recognised in their horizontal equalisation grants that aggregate population size is only one relevant factor that needs to be taken into account when seeking to understand inter-jurisdictional expenditure requirements. Other factors of relevance include population composition, population dispersion, and geography including climate and terrain. Ignoring these other factors leads to an overestimation of the fixed cost component. In technical terms the regression equation is inappropriately specified due to omitted variables, such that at the very least there is a need to move to a multiple regression equation that includes other variable cost terms;

c.   In Drummond's estimation the effects of all these other variable cost factors are being inappropriately attributed to the fixed costs component, leading to its overestimation. Given the importance of this fixed cost component to the remaining steps in the Drummond approach, this represents a serious problem;

d.   While Drummond reports the coefficients related to his fixed and variable cost components, he does not report the associated standard deviations or t test statistics, such that the statistical significance of his parameter estimates related to these two components cannot be determined. In addition he does not report results of any regression diagnostic tests conducted – yet previous modelling experience in this area suggests that the equation as estimated has problems that require it to be re-specified and re-estimated in a different format. In particular, as other critics (Access Economics 2004; Parliament of Victoria 1998) have pointed out, it is more usual to estimate models relating to government expenditure in per capita terms because of serial correlation between total expenditure and population;

e.   The assumption that functions carried out by a state government could be transferred to a national body without altering either the fixed cost or variable cost component is simply unrealistic. In particular it ignores the coordination costs that could be expected to result from attempts to manage population-oriented services such as education, health and policing from a single centralised location in a nation as large as Australia with its vast areas of sparsely dispersed populations. It also ignores research relating to economies/diseconomies of scale in provision of the services for which our state governments are currently responsible – which for many functions have resulted in regionalisation of service provision rather than the adoption of a one size fits all model within many states;

f. The implied assumption that population is the only determinant of variable or marginal costs of service provision suggests, for example, that transfer of responsibility for providing state level services to a particular area within Queensland would not involve any increase in per capita costs if this provision was administered from say Perth rather than Brisbane. This is clearly unrealistic.

g. By using pooled time series/cross-section estimation the assumption is being made that *all* state governments host equal fixed and variable costs – so that amalgamation of any two states is argued to liberate cost savings equal to an identical quantum of fixed costs. This assumption too is unrealistic. For example it ignores the geography and demographic composition of the various states, as well as differences in the level and nature of the services that they currently provide in each major area of responsibility which would inevitably need to be bought into alignment following a merger. More significantly this assumption would be able to be dispensed with, if the regression exercise was to be redone with the underlying data collected over a longer time period;

h. The assumption that individual state deviations around the regression line were accounted for by higher or lower fixed costs and not higher or lower variable costs could also be readily tested via use of a more extended time series of expenditure data and the introduction of a series of dummy variables for the different states.

Drummond (2001, 2002) explored cost savings associated with change options other than abolition of the States, for example a new states option and an option that eliminated local rather than state governments were developed. However, the cost savings estimates derived were based on the same regression methodology underlying the abolition of the States option, and so most of the criticisms outlined above continue to apply. Some additional unrealistic assumptions were introduced when these options were explored. In particular:

a. the new states option assumed that data and associated parameter estimates derived from Tasmania would be representative of any new state likely to be introduced. This is patently not realistic given the geography, economy and demography of Tasmania compared with potential mainland new states (such as the New England region of NSW and the Northern regions of Queensland, as mentioned by Wiltshire, this volume).

b. the elimination of local governments option assumed that the Australian Capital Territory (ACT) could be regarded as representative of all other 'reformulated states' – on the basis that the ACT government performs a mixture of both state and local government options. Again this is simply not realistic given the geography, economy and demography of the ACT compared with the rest of Australia. The ACT, for example, has the vast majority of its population employed in the public sector on incomes significantly higher than the national average, it has only one major urban centre which was centrally planned and administered from its inception, and it covers a very small geographic area. The costs of local government service provision under these circumstances are vastly different to those in either major metropolitan areas or remote rural regions elsewhere in Australia.

Despite the problems inherent in the Drummond (2001, 2002) analysis, he did attempt to estimate the full range of net benefits that might be expected to be derived from reform of the current federal system. Accordingly, this work has provided a significant departure point for ongoing work and significant stimulation to further debate and more targeted research. In addition, most alternative estimates also suffer their own problems. Most of the alternative estimates that have been published focus on only a narrow subset of potential savings (e.g. from reducing the Commonwealth Government's reliance on specific purpose payments as a form of intergovernmental grants) and/or ignore the role of local governments in the federation.

The most comprehensive alternative analysis to date, by Access Economics (2006), focuses on a large range of possible categories of cost savings that could be argued as able to be derived from reform. These categories were classified into two groups: (a) costs associated with spending-related efficiencies (including cost of administering intergovernmental grants and costs of coordination across different levels of government when overlap of functions exists) estimated at $5.1 billion, and (b) costs associated with taxation-related efficiencies (including the use of inefficient taxes by the States) estimated at $3.8 billion.

However, in the Access Economics (2006) analysis, the dollar values placed on these various categories of costs have not been derived from detailed economic or statistical analysis but rather from a set of assumptions or educated guesses. For example 10% of the dollar amount associated with special purpose payments to the States is argued to be associated with states spending above the efficient level due to lack of adequate coordination and/or oversight by the Commonwealth. No justification is given for why 10% represented a reasonable assumption. Similarly it was assumed that 3% of the expenditure by states was on activities that represented 'overlap and duplication' with the Commonwealth. In arriving at this 3% figure, no specific areas of overlap or duplication were identified or costed, nor was any insight provided as to why 3% was a reasonable figure to select from the 99 other possibilities between one and 100. In terms of cost shifting, the area of pharmaceuticals and public hospitals was singled out, and state governments accused of shifting costs on to the Commonwealth in the order of 3% of Commonwealth expenditure in this area. Cost shifting in other areas or from the Commonwealth to states were ignored; and even in the restricted area of pharmaceuticals and public hospitals, no reasoning was provided to justify the selection of 3% rather than 2% or 5% or some other percentage. In addition, the focus of the Access Economics (2006) report was purely on inefficiencies argued to be associated with current federal-state relations – local government and various regional organisational arrangements discussed earlier in this chapter are not mentioned.

As a result, there remains considerable scope for further research in this area.

Conclusion: towards a sound evaluation framework

In moving forward from this point in terms of economic evaluation of potential change agendas, one could proceed with analysis of aggregate expenditure for each level of government and in so doing improve on the econometric methods employed in the Drummond type of analysis. However, using this approach it is difficult to accurately estimate possible costs and savings of reform with a detailed focus on the distribution of government functions (expenditure responsibilities and taxing powers), argued as necessary at the beginning of the chapter. Accordingly, examining the strengths and weaknesses of existing methodologies leads to a new preferred approach. Rather than continuing in the tradition of aggregate forms of analysis, a sounder approach would:

a. take a particular function, analyse the costs of current mode(s) of delivery across various levels of government, and then identify potential net cost savings from a small set of change proposals;

b. repeat this for a selected subset of functions at each level;

c. sum the results across this subset of functions to identify the order of magnitude of savings for each change proposal; and

d. develop a ranking of these change proposals on the criteria of net economic benefits.

Not all government functions need be the subject of detailed analysis in this approach. Rather, a case can be made for narrowing attention in the first instance to only major functions (that is, ones accounting for a significant proportion of total expenditure at any given level) or ones seen as problematic (that is, ones subject to potentially significant overlap and duplication problems or ones that have been suggested in the literature as possibly being assigned to the wrong level currently).

In order for the proposed approach to work well, the change proposals to be evaluated in the first instance also need to be reasonably detailed (in terms of number of levels of government, which levels of government, how many units at each level and ideally their rough geographic locations). This is reinforced by public debates, noted earlier, over the feasibility of options that eliminate both the current state and local government levels and replace them with a new set of regional institutions. In addition, the public finance and local government amalgamation literature reviewed in this chapter indicates that the costs of public sector service provision by any particular level of government depend significantly on the nature of the jurisdiction in which these services are provided. Changing the demographic composition of the jurisdiction, its geography and/or its economic base can have a significant impact on these costs. This in turn suggests that when working up potential change options for further evaluation, there is a need to be specific about the number and boundaries of units at each sub-national level within each of the options. An option with 30 regional institutions, for example, will generate different results than one with 60 regional institutions. New states emerging around major metropolitan regions and the peri-urban areas in their immediate proximity will generate different results than new states emerging based around rural/mining regions remote from their current state capitals, and so on.

A separate set of research questions needs to be addressed, therefore, to producing a set of change proposals that are sufficiently specific and grounded to be usefully costed. This involves its own debates, as shown by the controversy surrounding suggestions that local government amalgamations in New South Wales may be able to be based on the concept of eco-civic regions (Brunckhorst and Reeve 2006; Dollery and Crase 2004b). However the details of the tested scenarios can be changed and refined over time, and the economic evaluations recalibrated, so the initial set of change proposals need only to be representative of possible directions rather than set in stone.

The purpose of this chapter has not been to provide answers as to whether or not change to the current federal structure, and/or the financial arrangements underpinning it, will generate net economic benefits. Rather the aim has been to point to some key directions in which debates surrounding federalism and regionalism need to move, in order to permit a framework capable of providing such answers to be developed. In doing so, it is acknowledged that economic criteria are only one class of criteria having relevance to the reform of our systems of government. Clearly, however, economic criteria are important ones given the nature of the statements extracted for quotation at the start of the chapter. The aim of the proposed new approach is to enable identification of which types of change agendas can potentially reap net economic benefits and which seem most likely to generate net economic costs. With this sort of information to hand, change proposals can be better developed and refined, thereby enabling debate to progress to a level likely to lead to the achievement of the type of improvement to our federal system that recent public opinion surveys suggest is desired by the electorate.

References

Access Economics 2004, *Commonwealth-State Funding of Local Government: An Assessment of Reform Proposals.* Report prepared for Australian CEOs Group. Access Economics Pty Limited, Canberra.

———— 2006, Appendix 2. *The Costs of Federalism. Report by Access Economics Pty Limited for the Business Council of Australia.* Access Economics Pty Limited, Canberra.

ACIL Economics and Policy Pty Ltd 1996, *Costs of Overlap and Duplication Between Different Levels of Government.* Institute of Public Affairs for State and Territory Governments.

Allen, P. 2003, 'Why Smaller Councils Make Sense.' *Australian Journal of Public Administration* 62(3): 74-81.

Allen Consulting Group 2006, *Governments Working Together? Assessing Specific Purpose Payment Arrangements.* Report prepared for Victorian Government, June.

Beer, A. et al. 2003, *Developing Australia's Regions: Theory and Practice.* University of New South Wales Press, Sydney.

Brogden, J. 2005, *Practical Federalism.* Accessible at http://www.nsw.liberal.org.au

Brown, A.J. 2002a, 'After the Party: public attitudes to Australian federalism, regionalism and reform in the 21st century.' *Public Law Review* 13(3): 171-190.

———— 2002b, 'Subsidiarity or subterfuge? Resolving the future of local government in the Australian federal system.' *Australian Journal of Public Administration* 61(4): 24-42.

Brown, A.J., I. Gray and D. Giorgas 2006, 'Towards a more Regional Federalism: rural and urban attitudes to institutions, governance and reform in Australia.' *Rural Society* 16(3): 283-302.

Brunckhorst, D. and I. Reeve 2006, 'A Geography of Place: Principles and Application for Defining Eco-Civic Resource Governance Regions.' *Australian Geographer* 37(2): 147-166.

Business Council of Australia 2006, *Modernising the Australian Federation: A Discussion Paper.* Business Council of Australia, Melbourne.

Byrnes, J. and B. Dollery 2002, 'Do Economies of Scale Exist in Australian Local Government? A Review of the Research Evidence.' *Urban Policy and Research* 20(4): 391-414.

Commonwealth Grants Commission 2006a, *Report on State Revenue Sharing Relativities 2006 Update.* Commonwealth Grants Commission, Canberra.

———— 2006b, *Relative Fiscal Capacity of the States 2006.* Commonwealth Grants Commission, Canberra.

Dahlby, B. 2001, *Taxing Choices: Issues in the Assignment of Taxes in Federations.* UNESCO, Paris.

Department of Transport and Regional Services 2005, *Local Government National Report. 2003-04 Report on the Operation of the Local Government (Financial Assistance) Act 1995.* Australian Government, Canberra. Accessible at http://www.dotars.gov.au

Devenson, I. 2006, 'One step from best in the world.' *The Australian,* 14/07.

Dixon, P.B., M.R.Picton M.T. and Rimmer 2002, 'Efficiency Effects of Inter-governmental Fiscal Transfers in Australia.' *The Australian Economic Review,* 35(3):304-15.

———— 2005, 'Efficiency Effects of Changes in Commonwealth Grants to the States: A CGE Analysis'. *Australian Economic Papers* **44** : 82-104.

Dollery, B. 2005a, 'The State of Play in Australian Local Government' *Working Paper Series in Economics,* No. 2005-5, University of New England, Armidale.

———— 2005b, 'A Critical Evaluation of Structural Reform Considerations in 'Rates and Taxes: A Fair Share for Responsible Local Government'. *Australian Geographer,* 36(3): 385-397.

———— 2005c, 'Alternative Approaches to Structural Reform in Regional and Rural Australian Government' Paper presented at Dean's Lecture Series, La Trobe University, November.

Dollery, B. and L. Crase 2004a, 'Is Bigger Local Government Better? An evaluation of the economic case for Australian municipal amalgamation programs' *Working Paper Series in Economics,* No. 2004-4, University of New England, Armidale.

———— 2004b, 'A Critical Note on 'Eco-Civic Regionalisation as the Basis for Local Government Boundaries in Australia.' *Australian Geographical Studies* 41(3): 221-236.

Dollery, B., L. Crase and S. O'Keefe 2005, 'Improving Efficiency in Australian Local Government: Structural Reform as a Catalyst for Effective Reform.' *Working Paper Series in Economics,* No. 2005-16, University of New England, Armidale.

Dollery, B. and E. Fleming 2005, 'A Conceptual Note on Scale Economies, Size Economies and Scope Economies in Australian Local Government.'

Working Paper Series in Economics, No. 2005-6, University of New England, Armidale.

Dollery, B. and A. Johnson 2005, 'Enhancing Efficiency in Australian Local Government: An Evaluation of Alternative Models of Municipal Governance.' *Working Paper Series in Economics,* No. 2005-1, University of New England, Armidale.

Dollery, B., A.Johnson, N. Marshall and A. Witherby 2005, 'ROCs Governing Frameworks for Sustainable Regional Economic Development: A Case Study.' *Sustaining Regions,* 4(3): 15-21

Dollery, B., C. Keogh and L. Crase 2005, 'Alternatives to Amalgamation in Australian Local Government: Lessons from the New Zealand Experience.' *Working Paper Series in Economics,* No. 2005-15, University of New England, Armidale.

Dollery, B., N. Marshall and T. Sorensen 2005, 'An Analytical Evaluation of New Models for Local Government Service Provision in Regional New South Wales.' *Working Paper Series in Economics,* No. 2005-12, University of New England, Armidale.

Drummond, M.L. 2001, 'Updated Estimates that Provide Stronger Support than ever for the Abolition of State Governments and a Move to a Better System of Government can Improve Australia's Situation to the Value of some $30 billion per annum.' Accessible at http://www.asc.org.au/cost.htm

———— 2002, 'Costing Constitutional Change: Estimating the Cost of Five Variations on Australia's Federal System.' *Australian Journal of Public Administration* 61(4): 43-56.

Frontier Centre for Public Policy 2003, *Reassessing Local Government Amalgamation.* Accessible at www.fcpp.org

Garnaut, R. and V. Fitzgerald 2002, Review of Commonwealth – State Funding. Final Report. Accessible at www.reviewcommstatefunding.com.au

Grewel, B. and P. Sheehan 2003, *The Evolution of Constitutional Federalism in Australia: An Incomplete Contracts Approach.* CSES Working Paper #22, Victoria University, Melbourne.

Hall, R. 1998, *Abolish the States! Australia's Future and a $30 Billion Answer to our Tax Problems.* Pan-Macmillan, Sydney.

Hancock, J. and J. Smith 2001, *Financing the Federation.* South Australian Centre for Economic Studies, Adelaide.

Harding, A., N.Warren, G. Beer, Phillips and K. Osei 2002, 'The Distributional Impact of Selected Commonwealth Outlays and Taxes and Alternative

Grant Allocation Mechanisms.' *The Australian Economic Review* 35(3): 325-34.

House of Representatives Standing Committee on Economics, Finance and Public Administration 2003, *Rates and Taxes: A Fair Share for Responsible Local Government*. Parliament of the Commonwealth of Australia, Canberra.

Jaensch, D. 2003, 'Reforming Federalism?: A Discussion Paper.' Paper presented to Annual National Republican Convention. Accessible at http://www.republicans.org.au

Local Government Grants Commission South Australia 2005, *Annual Report 2004-2005*. Accessible at www.localgovt.sa.gov.au

Marshall, N. 1998, 'Reforming Australian local government: efficiency, consolidation – and the question of governance.' *International Review of Administrative Sciences* 64(4): 643-662.

Marshall, N., B. Dollery and A. Witherby 2003, 'Regional Organisation of Councils (ROCs): The Emergence of Network Governance in Metropolitan and Regional Australia?' *Australasian Journal of Regional Studies* 9(2), 169-187.

McLean, I. 2004, 'Fiscal Federalism in Australia.' *Public Administration* 2(1), 21-38.

Morris, A. 2002, 'The Commonwealth Grants Commission and Horizontal Fiscal Equalisation.' *The Australian Economic Review* 35(3): 318-24.

National Commission of Audit 1996, *Report to the Commonwealth Government*. Accessible at http://www.finance.gov.au/bubs/ncoa.htm

New South Wales Local Government Grants Commission 2005, *2004-05 Annual Report*. Accessible at www.dlg.nsw.gov.au

Northern Territory Grants Commission 2005, *Annual Report 2004-05*. Accessible at http://www.grantscommission.nt.gov.au

Oates, W.E. 1972, *Fiscal Federalism*. Harcourt Brace, New York.

Oates, W.E. 2005, 'Towards a Second Generation Theory of Fiscal Federalism.' *International Tax and Public Finance* 12: 349-373.

Organisation for Economic Cooperation and Development 2006, *Economic Survey of Australia 2006: Fiscal Relations across Levels of Government*. OECD, Paris.

Parliament of Victoria 1998, *Report on Australian Federalism: The Role of the States*. Accessible at http://www.parliament.vic.gov.au/fdrc/report

Petchey, J. and S. Levtchenkova 2004, 'Fiscal Equalisation in Australia: Proposals for An Efficiency-Based System.' *Economic Papers* **23** (2): 189-200.

Productivity Commission 2005, *Annual Report 2004-05*. Productivity Commission: Canberra.

———— 2006, *Productive Reform in a Federal System: Roundtable Proceedings*. Productivity Commission: Canberra.

Queensland Local Government Grants Commission 2005, *Report for 2005*. Accessible at www.qlggc.qld.gov.au

Regional Business Development Panel 2003, *Regional Business: A Plan of Action*. Report to the Department of Transport and Regional Services, Canberra.

Regional Implementation Working Group 2005, *Regional Delivery of NRM – Moving Forward*, March.

Rouse, P. and M. Putterill 2005, 'Local Government Amalgamation Policy: A Highway Maintenance Evaluation' *Management Accounting Research,* **16**: 438-463.

Sancton, A. 2005, 'The Governance of Metropolitan Areas in Canada' *Public Administration and Development* **25**, 317-327.

Saunders, C. 2002, 'Collaborative Federalism.' *Australian Journal of Public Administration* **61**(2), 69-77.

Selway, B. 2001, 'The Federation – What makes it Work and What Should we be thinking about for the Future' *Australasian Journal of Public Administration* **60**(4): 116-122.

Soorley, J. 2004, 'Do We Need a Federal system? The Case for Abolishing State Governments', in W. Hudson and A. J. Brown (eds) *Restructuring Australia: Regionalism, Republicanism and Reform of the Nation State*. Federation Press, Sydney.

Soul, S.C. 2000, *Population Size and Economic and Political Performance of Local Government Jurisdictions*. Unpublished PhD thesis, Southern Cross University, Lismore.

Soul, S. and B. Dollery 2000, 'An Analysis of Criteria Used by Australian Government Amalgamation Inquiries Between 1960 and 1992' *Working Paper Series in Economics,* No. 2000-9, University of New England, Armidale.

State Chamber of Commerce (NSW) 2005, *Local Government Enquiry Submission*. State Chamber of Commerce NSW, Sydney.

Sydney Morning Herald 2006, 'Editorial: The time has come to shed a tier.' *Sydney Morning Herald* 10/2: 10.

Tasmania. State Grants Commission 2005, *Annual Report for 2005-06*. Accessible at www.treasury.tas.gov.au

Tredbeck, D. and G. Cutbush 1996, 'Overlap and Duplication in Federal-State Relations.' Proceedings of the Seventh Conference of the Samuel Griffith Society, Adelaide, June. Accessible at http://www.samuelgriffith.org.au

Twomey, A. and G. Withers, 2007, *Australia's Federal Future: Delivering Growth and Prosperity,* Federalist Paper 1, Council for the Australian Federation.

Usher, D. 1995, *The Uneasy Case for Equalization Payments*. The Fraser Institute, Vancouver.

Victoria Grants Commission 2005, *Annual Report 2004-05*. Accessible at www.dvc.vic.gov.au

Warren, N. 2006, *Benchmarking Australia's Intergovernmental Financial Relations*. Interim Report to New South Wales Treasury, March.

Western Australian Local Government Grants Commission 2005, *Annual Report 2005*. Accessible at www.dlgrd.wa.gov.au/lggc/

Wilkins, R.B. 2004, 'Federalism: Distance and Devolution.' *Australian Journal of Politics and History,* **50**(1): 95-101.

Williams, R.A. 2005, 'Federal-State Financial Relations in Australia: The Role of the Commonwealth Grants Commission.' *The Australian Economic Review* **38**(1): 108-18.

———— 2005, 'Fiscal Federalism: Aims, Instruments and Outcomes.' *The Australian Economic Review* **38**(4): 351-69.

Williams, G. 2006, 'Federal System needs a new Deal.' *The Courier Mail,* 24/02

Woodbury, K., B. Dollery and P. Rao 2002, 'Local Government Efficiency and Management in Australia.' *Working Paper Series in Economics,* No. 2002-1, University of New England, Armidale.

Worthington, A. C. and B.E. Dollery 2000, 'Productive Efficiency and the Australian Government Grants Process: An Empirical Analysis of New South Wales Local Government.' *Australasian Journal of Regional Studies* **6**(1), 95-121.

Chapter 14: Where To From Here? Principles for a New Debate

A. J. Brown and Jennifer Bellamy

As the chapters in this book have demonstrated, the relationship between subnational regionalism and federalism remains an enduring dilemma in Australian public policy. In response to globalisation and increasing demands for social, economic and environmental sustainability, the role of local and regional governance has re-emerged as an important practical and political issue for the restructuring of the federal system of governance. This is not as a result of some 'high theory' of regionalism as a sociological construct, nor political activism for devolutionary change based on particular constitutional ideologies. While both sociological theory and constitutional ideology form part of our history of debate about the place of local and regional governance in the federal system, the rationale for reform that emerges from this book commences with more immediate public policy considerations.

Seen from different spatial, policy and governmental perspectives – rural, urban, coastal, environmental, economic, social, state, local and national – the place of Australia's regions in the federal system raises some practical questions about the quality of governance including its impacts and outcomes. The first point of consensus between these different perspectives is that the evolution of state, regional and local institutions is a vital issue for the future of the federal system. In other words, making federalism work is not simply a matter of continual improvement in public administration, or fine-tuning intergovernmental relations between the Commonwealth and existing state governments, but a question of structural reform involving the distribution of roles, responsibilities and governance capacities throughout our system of government.

In this sense, 'reform' is not necessarily seen by all contributors to this book as something that need involve change to written constitutional arrangements in a formal sense. However, all agree that it does require new approaches to devolution, collaboration, power-sharing and institutional capacity-building which are quite fundamental in their implications. While there is a range of views as to how these new approaches are best to be supported – administratively, legislatively, or by existing or new constitutional arrangements – there is agreement that reform needs to be based on a systemic 'top to bottom' view of federalism rather than simple variation on the existing federal-state compact. It emerges as axiomatic that our national understanding of our 'regions', both in socio-demographic terms and for public policy purposes, is something very different for the most part to the six States and two Territories that form the membership of our federation. This fundamental disjunction is not about to be willed away by those who might wish it were otherwise.

How, then, is this enlarged reform task to be approached? History demonstrates that building effective local and regional governance within the federal system, and using this focus on devolution to improve the effectiveness, legitimacy and efficiency of the entire system, are not things that can be left to chance or 'natural selection' in the process of our political evolution. These elements of the federal reform agenda need to be addressed in a conscious and concerted way, through a program of informed restructuring. This is a process that needs to engage all policy sectors and all existing levels of government. Many questions arise about the form that the reform of regional governance should take, and how it will fit in the Australian federal system of governance. But more important than a specific institutional prescription is a debate based on the common principles that the reform proposal needs to address, in order to establish a more coherent direction.

Five principles about how to progress this debate emerge from the papers in this volume, as well as the rich discussion on the floor of the Symposium. The first is that it is a debate that needs to be open and inclusive, but informed by better and more targeted research on the challenges and opportunities that face our system of governance. Recent experience shows that good research – social, economic, historical and, wherever possible, empirical – can help dramatically narrow the points of divergence and strengthen the points of consensus on what exactly needs to be reformed in the federal system, and why. The debate in the Symposium revealed that there is often divergence in the understanding of the governance 'problem'; whether one starts from an institutional/political, economic, environmental or social perspective, a common disconnect exists for many people between the understanding of the 'reality' of practical problems at the regional level, and the possible sources or causes of the problem within the system of governance – if, indeed, the problem lies with the system at all. As a consequence, the reality of the human and social impacts of our governance system is easily a source of conflict among the many people with an interest in reform. Closing these gaps and disconnects in knowledge is critically important. Many of the chapters point to specific research needs. Chapters 10-13 also underscore the importance of more precise research into the financial and economic costs and benefits of various reform scenarios, to take the debate forward. All this needs to take place within a framework in which the goals, or perceived advantages, of alternative approaches to governance are made explicit. Such a framework is set out in the Appendix to this volume, in the form of the discussion paper commissioned by one stakeholder, the NSW Farmers' Association, as background to the Symposium.

The second principle is the need for continued recognition – and cataloguing – of the extent to which the governance challenges that need to be addressed by reform exist in common across a diversity of policy contexts and sectors. It may be that the perceived dysfunctions of current systems of governance are unique, in varying degrees, to particular types of regions and policy areas. However the contributions to this book demonstrate that the drivers for reform are strikingly similar, and call for similar devolutionary solutions, even if the problems to be solved may often be different.

The clearest example of this, demonstrated in the Symposium, is the extent to which the present deficit in regional governance capacity afflicts not only rural regions, but urban ones and, indeed, regions in varying stages of transition between rural and urban. Chapters 4, 5 and 6 set out problems that are locally specific, but in which an agreed framework for devolution of governance functions, autonomies and capacities to the regional level represents a common solution. Chapters 7, 8 and 9 similarly demonstrate that while there may be differences in different contexts and policy sectors in the understanding and interpretation of sustainability, the rationale for governance reforms that would help better achieve it remains comparable, if not common. This lends considerably to both the appropriateness and feasibility of generalised reform of the federal system to support strengthened regional governance, on a national basis – reinforced by the evidence in chapter 3 that public opinions and preferences with regard to the federal structure seem to vary only marginally between urban and rural communities, at least in NSW. The need for stronger local and/or regional governance is not just an urban issue, nor just a rural issue, but a truly national one.

What type of reform are we talking about in practice? The remaining principles can help ensure that the investigation of options becomes more focused, but still remains productive. The third principle to emerge from the debate is the need for clarity as to when we are talking about reform of government structures, and when we are talking primarily about reform in the configuration of government functions. There is substantial consensus that, if local and regional governance could be strengthened in tangible and enduring ways, without major reform of the political structures of federalism, that would obviously be desirable. Following theories of collaboration and 'whole of government' cooperation, and by simply devolving functions and resources to local government, such strengthening should also be achievable – at least in far greater measure than currently occurs. The question 'what structural reform?' arises as a secondary consideration, when turning to a frank assessment of the institutional requirements that are needed for the desired functional reform to indeed prove tangible and enduring. Although reform often tends to work backward from institutional options ('wouldn't it be better if we did it this way ...'), the fact is that institutional restructuring in and of itself does not necessarily lead to enhanced governance. Particularly if one objective is more adaptive, flexible governance systems, then creating new institutions may only lead to new points of constitutional inertia, inflexibility and atrophy.

This need for clarity in the relationship between functional and structural reform is brought into sharp relief by the question of the 'fourth tier' – the development of an increasing array of regional institutions, not constitutionally recognised and with wildly varying roles and accountabilities, but whose continuing growth demonstrates that functionally, a lot more of the 'real' work of governance is now being done at regional levels. This 'fourth tier' or 'sphere' of governance is not a hypothetical entity – it is a political, functional and institutional reality within our current federal system. While many citizens might like to move towards a more two-tiered federal-regional system of government if given the choice, the simple fact is that we are increasingly operating with a four-tiered one. The evidence is that this is more good than bad, given that each new regional body or strategy clearly arises in response to a perceived need. However, there is equally clearly a larger need for real policy debate, supported by robust research, about the nature and future of these institutions, based on wider appreciation of the reasons for their growth and proper long-range planning of the functional demands likely to continue to exist at the regional level.

A fourth principle, as a corollary to this, is that we must avoid over-simplification of the idea of 'regional governance'. The complexity of regional governance is well demonstrated by the existing political and institutional landscape. The lack of uniformity on the one hand and the diversity of approaches on the other, together with the overlap and duplication of different regional policy strategies being pursued by different jurisdictions, all raise a plethora of issues for any program focussed on strengthening governance capacity at the regional level. As revealed at the Symposium, these include issues of policy coherence and alignment; clarity in roles and responsibilities; resourcing capacity (e.g. skills, financing, knowledge); communicativeness and connectedness; devolution and sharing of power; and cost of compliance and burdens of bureaucratic red tape.

Perhaps most dramatically, it is impossible to talk about strengthening regional governance without recognising the importance of existing local governments in the reform process. Local government exists. Often it provides the only tangible or enduring institutional support, 'on the ground', for the program and policies of other levels of government, including regional programs. The presence of local government as an elected, general-purpose tier of government means that, politically, the deficits in regional governance capacity cannot be addressed unless the public legitimacy of regional institutions and strategies is faced squarely in their design – including issues of fairness in participation or process, and equity in outcomes. The under-resourced state of local government means that there are short-term gains to be made in the devolution of a greater share of public resources to this level, irrespective of how longer term institutional reform might unfold. Given the already centralised nature of the political system, forced amalgamation of local governments is not a logical strategy for building stronger regional capacity – it runs the risk of not just 'robbing Peter to pay Paul', but killing Peter in the process. A more sophisticated approach is needed to building local and regional capacity *together*, reinforcing the need for this to be undertaken as a coherent national strategy, and not a piecemeal, state-based one.

Finally, there is a need for specific reform options to be more clearly articulated, in sufficient detail to enable these to be evaluated and costed. Imagining the alternatives can easily be dismissed as 'high theorising', of no practical relevance – if we assume that there are no practical prospects of change. However, as this volume demonstrates, there is already plenty of change underway and on foot in the federal system, and the demands and needs of regional governance are not hypothetical questions. In the quest for a more informed debate about an improved federal system, specific, costable scenarios for reforms that would also strengthen local and regional governance are vital, because they will yield important lessons to help shape the reality of reform, even if any single given scenario is unlikely to provide all the answers. Most importantly, the papers in this volume confirm that we should not compromise our short-term decisions by dismissing the relevance of long-term options, any more than we should ignore short-term realities when imagining what might eventually unfold. As several contributors have argued, federation itself was a case of fundamental and systemic change which did not happen overnight, but rather incrementally over time.

Federalism is a reality; and so is regionalism. They are both vital and positive forces in all elements of our system of governance. These are the immediate starting points for a new debate about how these forces are best to be reunited and reconciled in Australian constitutionalism, political practice, and public policy.

Appendix - Reform of Australia's Federal System: Identifying the Benefits

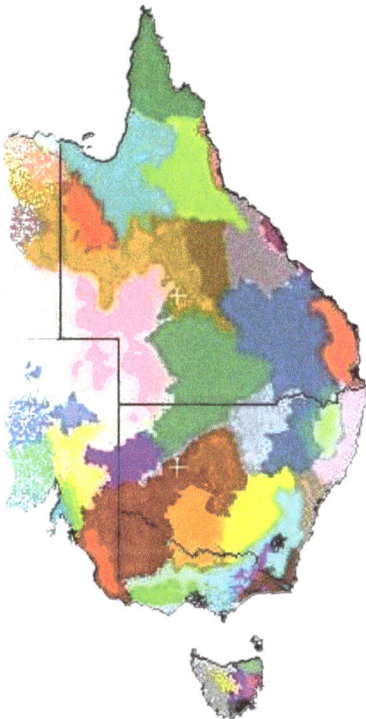

Reform of Australia's Federal System Identifying the Benefits

A Discussion Paper

Produced for the NSW Farmers' Association by The Federalism Project

Griffith University
www.griffith.edu.au/federalism

May 2006

(This abridged version: May 2007)

Growing the Business of Farming | NSW Farmers ASSOCIATION

Griffith UNIVERSITY

Published by

NSW Farmers' Association

Level 10, 255 Elizabeth St

Sydney NSW 2000

Reform of Australia's Federal System: Identifying the Benefits

1. Federalism—Australia. 2. Regional planning—Australia.

I. Brown, Alexander Jonathan.

Acknowledgements

This paper was prepared by **Dr A.J. Brown**, Senior Lecturer and Senior Research Fellow in the Socio-Legal Research Centre, Griffith Law School, Griffith University, and visiting fellow at the Australian National University College of Law. Many thanks to the following for ideas, input and comments: **Ian Gray**, Centre for Rural Social Research, Charles Sturt University; **Frank Stilwell**, Professor of Political Economy, University of Sydney; **Mal Peters**, NSW Farmers' Association; **Christine Smith**, Professor of Economics, Griffith University; **Jenny Bellamy**, University of Queensland; **Ken Wiltshire**, University of Queensland; **Suzanne Lawson**, Urban Research Program, Griffith University; **Stephen Welstead**, New States for Australia <newstates.com.au>; **Ian Mott**, New Farm States Australia; and **Amy Keenan-Dunn**, Griffith University.

The Federalism Project is a national program of research into federalism, regionalism and forces of stability and change in the structure of Australia's political institutions

www.griffith.edu.au/federalism

Table of Contents

Reform of Australia's Federal System Identifying the Benefits: A Discussion Paper Summary

Introduction

This discussion paper sets out a draft framework for the evaluation of different options for the future of Australia's federal system of government.

In 2004, the NSW Farmers' Association established a taskforce to investigate the feasibility of creating one or more new states from within the present boundary of New South Wales. In 2005, the Association commissioned Griffith University's Federalism Project to advise on a suitable contemporary methodology for assessing the costs and benefits of federal reform.

This paper represents the first step in the development of this larger evaluation methodology. It provides a framework for a larger program of research to assess the potential costs and benefits of a range of options for structural and administrative reform of Australia's federal system.

NSW Farmers' Association and Griffith University welcome feedback on the framework to inform the evaluation program, and invite expressions of interest from organisations and researchers interested in supporting and conducting the research involved.

Australian federalism – a troubled history

Australia's federal system of government is in a crucial state of change. As the nation adjusts to globalisation and new approaches to governance, questions surround how the three-tiered federal system can best adapt to serve the needs of an integrated economy, while also serving the needs of diverse communities spread over a vast continent.

Despite the great achievement of federal union of the Australian colonies in 1901, the last century has seen ongoing debate about the need for greater federal power over matters of national importance, as well as for stronger frameworks for devolution of decision-making and services to local and regional levels in many public policy areas.

These ongoing debates reflect the problem that Australia's federal system has become unusually centralised, in an ad hoc, largely unplanned way. Greater Federal power and national uniformity have been achieved in some areas, but in many important areas the gains are incomplete or constitutionally fragile.

Federal, state and local governments are also agreed on the economic, social and environmental importance of strengthening governance capacity at the local and regional levels. The pressure for such strengthening is not new. It is reflected in longstanding calls for reforms such as the creation of new states, abolition of the States in favour of new provincial or regional governments, and/or expansion and national constitutional recognition of local government. However, despite its renewed importance since the 1990s, regional governance remains fragmented and weak, lacking the resources, funding and institutional support needed for any realistic form of devolution.

Options for reform

Preliminary research demonstrates that Australian citizens have a high level of interest in long-term reform of the federal system. However opinion varies on the optimum type of structural reform, ranging from:

- creation of new states, as contemplated by Australia's federal founders under Chapter VI of the 1901 Constitution, to
- restructuring and amalgamation of existing state and local governments into a new 'second tier' of regional government, to
- abolition of state governments and redistribution of their functions between existing federal and local governments.

The renewed interest of federal, state and local governments in regional governance has also given currency to the option of developing stronger regional institutions as a 'fourth tier' of government, as the number of regional programs and organisations grows.

At the same time, governments are experimenting with new forms of administrative collaboration designed to more effectively deliver nationally coherent programs to target communities at local and/or regional levels. These new spatial approaches represent alternative responses to the same pressures, also demonstrate that the system is in a state of flux, and similarly require evaluation for their longer term significance.

Evaluating the options – the need for a framework

Despite the importance of these reform debates, no single comprehensive model exists for evaluating current trends and alternative options for the federal system. The lack of an accepted framework for analysing different reform options, combined with the political partisanship surrounding some options in previous decades, has made it difficult for the feasibility of these options to be objectively compared and assessed.

More recently new frameworks have been proposed for identifying the political, economic and policy issues that need to be considered when evaluating the effectiveness of new spatial approaches to governance, in both rural and urban contexts.

This paper brings together some key lessons of these proposals to present a new, comprehensive framework of 20 evaluation principles associated with the five key governance elements and/or outcomes implicit in our changing federal system (Table 1). Each principle identifies, in broad terms, a key intended benefit of reform, enabling the relative merits of reform options to be compared with each other and with the status quo.

Preliminary discussion of many of these principles indicates the feasibility, and importance, of productive research in these areas. In particular, it suggests:

- There is no reason to doubt the financial viability of most new state or similar regional government options, within Australia's system of federal public finance;
- There is good reason to believe that options for stronger regional governance can be found that will deliver improved financial efficiencies in public administration;
- There is good reason to believe that reform based on regional devolution can also contribute to greater national policy coherence, if accompanied by a commitment to a stronger culture and institutions for intergovernmental collaboration; and
- There is good reason to believe that stronger regional governance within the federal system will deliver long-term social, economic and environmental benefits.

Where to from here

This evaluation framework provides a basis for further, more detailed interdisciplinary research into the costs and benefits implied by current or potential options for the future of the federal system.

A future paper in this series will set out more specific examples of reform scenarios, for the purposes of comparison, evaluation and further public debate.

NSW Farmers' Association and Griffith University welcome feedback on the framework to help inform the evaluation program. We also invite expressions of interest from other organisations interested in supporting any area of this research, and from researchers interested in carrying it out.

A framework for evaluation

Table 1. Evaluation framework for federal reform in Australia

Governance element/outcome		Evaluation principle
A. Political power	A1.	Accountability/representativeness of leaders is ensured
	A2.	Legitimacy deficits are addressed (inc. re: non-elected decision-makers)
	A3.	National political identity/citizenship is strengthened
	A4.	Regional political identity/citizenship is strengthened
B. Policy responsibility and development	B1.	Roles and responsibilities are defined based on 'subsidiarity'
	B2.	Resources and funding are allocated and available at appropriate spatial level(s) ('subsidiarity' in practice)
	B3.	Greater policy coherence is achieved; collaboration and integration across and between governments is strengthened
	B4.	Capacity for regionally diverse policy responses is negotiated and institutionalised
C. Public administration	C1.	Complex policy issues are addressed (see also D)
	C2.	Public service delivery is improved
	C3.	Financial efficiencies of administration are improved
	C4.	Transparency in revenues, outlays, transfers and financial responsibility is improved
D. Citizen and expert engagement	D1.	Knowledge integration is supported and maximised
	D2.	Participation (or capacity for participation) of citizens is improved; partnerships facilitated and strengthened
	D3.	Socially inclusive participation is ensured
	D4.	Equity and procedural fairness are ensured
E. Long-term outcomes	E1.	Regulation, compliance and participation costs are reduced
	E2.	'Triple bottom line' sustainability is realised
	E3.	Sustainable economic innovation is fostered
	E4.	Long-term systemic and structural change is supported; communities' adaptive capacity for governance is improved

Reform of Australia's Federal System Identifying the Benefits: A Discussion Paper

1. Introduction

This discussion paper sets out a draft framework for the evaluation of different options for the future of Australia's federal system of government.

In 2004, the NSW Farmers' Association established a taskforce to investigate the feasibility of creating one or more new states from within the present boundary of New South Wales. This proposal, which has a 150-year history, reflects the renewed importance of regionalism within the Australian federal system and the extent to which Australian federalism is again subject to change.

In 2005, the Association resolved to continue its assessment of the social, economic and political case for new states, and commissioned Griffith University's Federalism Project to advise on a suitable contemporary methodology for assessing the costs and benefits of federal reform.

A key feature of past reform debates has been the presence of a wide range of institutional options for development of the federal system. As well as different constitutional options, such as the establishment of new states, many policy practitioners argue for a range of sub-constitutional, administrative reforms based on increased intergovernmental collaboration in priority policy areas.

Another feature has been lack of clarity over the criteria for categorising and assessing the potential benefits of different reform options. Even when a particular scenario can be identified as offering clear benefits, uncertainty about the overall effect of reform, possible unidentified costs and the presence of alternative options has prevented general consensus from emerging – leaving a federal system that most Australians appear to regard as less than optimum.

This paper represents the first step in the development of an evaluation methodology which can provide an agreed basis for comparing and assessing different proposals for reform. It takes as its starting point that reform is not purely theoretical or hypothetical – Australia's federal system has been subject to change over the past 105 years, and continues to change as citizens and policymakers strike new balances between the global, national, state, regional and local imperatives confronting Australian society.

The paper provides a framework for a larger program of research to assess the potential costs and benefits of a range of options for structural and administrative reform of Australia's federal system to meet current challenges. NSW Farmers' Association and Griffith University welcome feedback on the framework to inform the evaluation program, and invite expressions of interest from organisations and researchers interested in supporting and conducting the research involved.

2. Australian federalism – a troubled history

Federalism: '... a system of government in which authority is constitutionally divided between central and regional governments.'

James Gillespie, 'New federalisms' in *Developments in Australian Politics*, J. Brett, J. Gillespie and M. Goot (eds) (1994), pp.60-87; Blackshield and Williams (2004), p.241.

Australia's federal system of government is in a crucial state of change. As the nation adjusts to globalisation and new approaches to governance, questions surround how the three-tiered federal system can best adapt to serve the needs of an integrated economy, while also serving the needs of diverse communities spread over a vast continent.

Despite the great achievement of federal union of the Australian colonies in 1901, the last century has seen ongoing debate about the need for greater federal power over matters of national importance, greater simplicity and consistency in national regulation, and stronger frameworks for devolution of decision-making and services to local and regional levels in many public policy areas.

Pressures for centralisation

Questions about the right framework for governing the Australian continent have been part of Anglo-Australian political debate ever since colonisation in 1788, and establishment of the first civilian governments in 1823 (NSW) and Van Dieman's Land (Tasmania, 1825).

At the same time as they created the six Australian colonies between 1823 and 1859, British policymakers vacillated between federal and unitary theories for establishing a national system of government (Brown 2004a, b; 2006). By the time nationhood was achieved in 1901, a federation of the largely independent colonies was almost inevitable (Galligan 1995).

Nevertheless, much of Australia's federation debates, and much of its first 105 years of federal history have seen conflict over barriers to the federal government's ability to act on issues of national importance. In particular, since the 1940s debate has surrounded the need for greater uniformity, consistency and simplicity in regulation affecting the economic welfare of the nation, and the ability of the federal government to efficiently manage the national economy.

Since the 1980s, pressure for the federal government to take on a stronger regulatory and policy role has extended further into the province of state governments:

- Transport and infrastructure planning, including roads and ports;
- Environmental regulation and natural resource management (including Landcare, biodiversity, vegetation and water);
- Secondary and tertiary education;
- Health services and aged care;
- Industrial relations.

Since the 1940s, federal governments have used their constitutional power over taxation to assume *de facto* control of many policy areas through financial inducement and pressure. This was extended in 1999 by the establishment of the federally-collected Goods and Services Tax (GST), described by some as a 'stealth missile' for state governments (Wood 1999).

Much national standardisation of laws and regulation has also occurred collaboratively, through 'cooperative federalism', particularly in the 1920s-1930s and 1990s (Wilkins 1995; Painter 1998). Nevertheless this has been an ad hoc process, with Australia's mechanisms of intergovernmental relations remaining informal and weak.

These ongoing debates reflect the problem that Australia's federal system has become unusually centralised, in an ad hoc, largely unplanned way. Greater federal power and national uniformity have been achieved in some areas, but in many important areas the gains are incomplete or constitutionally fragile. For all these reasons, a range of national interest groups have continued to advocate the need for review of Australia's federal system as the nation confronts the 21st century (see e.g. Business Council of Australia 1991, 2004).

Pressures for decentralisation

Federal, state and local governments are also agreed on the economic, social and environmental importance of strengthening governance capacity at local and regional levels within Australia's federal system. The pressure for such strengthening is also not new, having taken at least four different forms. The first pressure for regional strengthening can be seen in longstanding calls for the creation of new states – the philosophy that saw creation of Tasmania (1825), South Australia (1836), Victoria (1851) and Queensland (1859) (Ellis 1933). This process was re-endorsed by Australia's federal founders through inclusion of Chapter VI 'New States' of the Constitution, as well as by official constitutional review commissions in the 1920s and 1950s (e.g. Peden et al 1929).

While there have been no formal efforts to create new federal territories or new states since the 1920s, popular support for structural devolution of this kind has at times remained strong. In an official NSW referendum in 1967, for example, 46% of electors in north-east NSW voted in favour of the proposed new state of New England, including 66% of all electors outside the Newcastle/Hunter region.

A second, parallel pressure for regional strengthening is found in repeat proposals for replacement of state governments with new provincial or regional governments, in a more general constitutional restructure. These have also occurred since the 1840s (Brown 2006), but are more commonly associated with ideas for 'unification' or total abolition of the States (e.g. Macphee 1994, Hall 1998), although they could also be consistent with retention of a federal system (Hurford 2004).

A third pressure for regional strengthening can be found in the campaign of local government since the 19th century for stronger formal powers, a fair share of public revenues, and at times, federal constitutional recognition (Chapman and Wood 1984). International comparisons routinely show Australia to have an unusually centralised subnational structure due to the weakness of local government (Watts 1996; OECD 1997: 77; Winer 2002). Local government's recent campaign against public 'cost-shifting' (Commonwealth 2003), requests for a direct share of GST revenue, and a new Intergovernmental Agreement on local government finance (2006) all reflect moves towards this form of strengthening.

The 'New' Regionalism?

Finally, since the 1940s all levels of government have proposed and invested in various regional programs as an administrative strategy. Since the 1990s, such programs have expanded considerably, particularly in non-metropolitan areas (Pritchard and McManus 2000; Beer et al 2003; Eversole and Martin 2005). Today a proliferation of new regional governance institutions and strategies cut across the key policy areas of all existing levels of government:

- regional economic development and infrastructure planning;
- natural resource management and environmental regulation; and
- community engagement and new strategies for integrated social service delivery based on management of 'places' and 'regions'.

The recent renewal of interest in stronger regional programs has been boosted by international theories about 'new regionalism' or 'glocalisation' as a response to increased global economic integration and competition (see Markusen 1987; Courchene 1995; Keating 1998; Rodriguez-Pose and Gill 2003). In Australia, 'new regionalism' has also been taken up as a platform for improved government-community reengagement or 'associational governance' based on communities' own social capital – i.e., the capacity of communities to organise themselves (e.g. Smith et al 2005).

Nevertheless complex questions surround the 'new regionalism' in Australian circumstances (Beer et al 2003: 248-264; Rainnie and Grobbelaar 2004).

Historically, regional development programs have often been revealed to be 'palliatives … entertained for political consumption rather than for substantive outcomes' (Wanna and Withers 2000: 85). By comparison with overseas examples such as British devolution, Australian governments have still made little or no public investment in political or administrative institutions to support the new regional programs (Gleeson 2003; cf Jones et al 2005).

The Commonwealth's recent Regional Business Development Analysis called for a major rationalisation and strengthening of regional bodies on this basis, describing local governments as 'generally too small', state governments as 'too large', and complaining of 'poor regional planning, inadequate coordination between the three levels of government, duplication and wastage' (RBDA 2003: 5, 30). There remains no coherent, national response to this call.

Similar questions surround the long-term sustainability of new regional programs for natural resource management. Despite being promoted and legitimised through rhetoric of decentralisation and public involvement within an integrated policy framework, 'institutional capacity for these new collaborative approaches however is often lacking' (Bellamy et al 2005).

In the development of 'associational governance' at local and regional levels, important questions similarly surround 'matters of administration and governance' – the 'organisational changes and advances in skills and capacity' needed 'to turn good rhetoric into reality.' Without these, the new strategies remain 'fragile', pursued with little enduring institutional support and despite the 'realities of local politics and Australia's federal system of governance' with its 'ambiguous and contested' accountabilities, legitimacies and relationships (Reddell 2005: 9, 73, 198-201).

Together, the history of these unresolved pressures for local and regional strengthening confirms the benefit of holistically re-evaluating the different options for reform of the federal system. Despite its renewed importance since the 1990s, regional governance remains fragmented and weak, lacking the resources, funding and institutional support needed for realistic devolution. Despite the rural focus of many regional programs, these basic challenges also extend to governance of the urban regions in which the vast majority of Australians work and live.

As the Prime Minister, John Howard has noted, the troubled history of Australian federalism does not mean that, *in principle*, it is not the best system of government for Australia. Federalism continues to promote the dispersal of power, and continues to hold the potential to deliver services closer to peoples' needs, more clearly than alternative non-federal political systems. The problems with

Australian federalism lie in the way in which these principles are currently institutionalised:

> The trouble is that, in practice, there is often less to these arguments than meets the eye. For instance, the view that State governments have benign decentralist tendencies has always been something of a myth … (Howard 2005).

How is Australian federalism likely to evolve in response to these continuing pressures for further centralisation of federal government control over many key areas of public policy, *and* further decentralisation of institutional capacity for more adaptive, response governance at local and regional levels?

What options for reform are currently being explored by Australian governments? What options are possible, and how should we as a community assess the relative benefits and costs of these different options?

3. Options for Reform

In the past, solutions to the structural challenges of the Australian federal system have often conflicted. As discussed in the previous section, there have been a variety of options proposed for reforming the system, with experts and policymakers often disagreeing on where reform is needed, and the type and extent of any reform.

Nevertheless, even among experts and policymakers there is widespread consensus that mechanisms can and should be found for developing a better federal system. Generally speaking, commentators tend to divide their focus between short-term administrative options, medium-term legislative options, and long-term constitutional options.

Short-term options (administrative)

Australian governments are already experimenting with new forms of administrative collaboration designed to more effectively deliver nationally coherent programs to target communities at local and/or regional levels. Similarly, informal systems of intergovernmental collaboration – and coercion – continue to be used to shape more coherent national responses to public policy challenges across a range of areas.

As discussed earlier, these new spatial approaches represent alternative responses to current pressures for centralisation and decentralisation within the Australian federal system. They demonstrate that the system is in a state of flux, and require evaluation for their longer term significance.

In relation to devolution options, many of the key questions surround whether, and how, increased public funding will flow to support the 'new regionalism', and what type of administrative bodies will continue to develop as vehicles for stronger regional programs. Given the increasing importance of federal policy involvement, and reliance on federal funding, other questions surround whether and how Commonwealth Governments will pursue more nationally coherent strategies for the development of regional institutional capacity to support federal-regional initiatives. Similar questions surround more effective use of administrative strategies such as regional budgeting by state and federal governments.

Medium-term options (legislative)

The Commonwealth continues to rely heavily on legislative strategies for pursuing greater uniformity and consistency in economic and regulatory areas, such as in industrial relations. While sometimes cooperative, this is also done through use of section 109 of the Constitution to override inconsistent state laws, depending on the High Court's approach to constitutional interpretation.

The renewed interest of federal, state and local governments in regional governance has also seen increased focus on legislation to support the growing number of regional programs and organisations. While no federal legislation of this kind exists, many of the institutions on which strengthened regional governance relies – including in response to federal-regional initiatives – have their basis in state legislation, including local government and catchment management agencies. Continuing federal support for reform and strengthening of local government finance, and for more permanent collaborative funding strategies under programs such as the Natural Heritage Trust and Roads to Recovery, are also likely to demand more stable legislative frameworks.

As the number of programs relying on regional bodies grows, along with recognition of the need for durability, accountability and adaptive capacity on the part of regional organisations, the more likely it appears that Australia is gradually developing a 'fourth tier' of regional government. Many questions surround this trend, including whether and how it can – or should – be given a clearer, more coherent legislative basis. Key questions surrounding devolution of the 'political and administrative resources such as mandate, authority, legitimacy and funding' necessary to support these responses have been well-known since the 1970s (Power and Wettenhall 1976; Reddell 2005: 192).

Long-term options (constitutional)

Where is Australia's federal system ultimately headed? As highlighted by the previous section, the need for formal adaptation of the federal system has always been part of Australian political debate, and was incorporated in the present federal constitutional design. Constitutional reform via referendum has been used, albeit sparingly, to extend Commonwealth power in areas of national consensus, principally when proposals have received bipartisan political support.

Convictions also continue to run strongly among Australian citizens that the federal system should – and will – ultimately include formal structures for general-purpose regional government, as opposed simply to administrative or legislative strategies. The general principle of regional government has received renewed support on economic, environmental and social grounds (Stilwell 2000; Gray and Lawrence 2001). Depending on its precise form, constitutional devolution of this kind is also potentially more consistent with federalism than the present system, providing for constitutionally-entrenched regional governments that more closely align with the socio-economic structure of daily life and governance needs than existing institutions.

However opinion also continues to vary on the optimum type of reform:

Creation of new states

As outlined earlier, this option was contemplated by Australia's federal founders under Chapter VI of the 1901 Constitution.

Even within this option, views may vary on the number of states that would be desirable or feasible. Figures 1-3 contrast how NSW would look if divided into just two states (coastal and inland), four states (the traditional position of NSW new state movements), or a new state for 'every major region' (Blainey 2004). Nevertheless this option is likely to be utilised in the short to medium-term, when the citizens of the Northern Territory (population 198,544 people in 2003) next request the opportunity to be admitted to statehood.

A two-tiered system based on regional government

This option is perhaps most consistent with the 'unification' option referred to in the previous section, but could be established either through abolition and replacement of the existing States under a new constitution *or* through the creation of 'regional states' using the Constitution's new state provisions (figure 3).

While constitutionally more complex, this option is widely seen as most consistent with more general rationalisation and simplification of the federal system. This scenario formed part of the Business Council of Australia's recent predictions for how the federal system might evolve over the next 20 years (BCA 2004).

A two-tiered system based on local government

This option involves the simplest form of 'shedding a tier' and would see abolition of existing state governments, and constitutional entrenchment of Australia's 700 local governments and/or transfer of legislative control over them to the federal government. This option is least consistent with federalism due to the disproportionate degree of central power that would be wielded by the national government, even though local government may well also be substantially stronger than at present. It would be constitutionally most difficult to achieve.

Figure 1

Figure 2

Figure 3

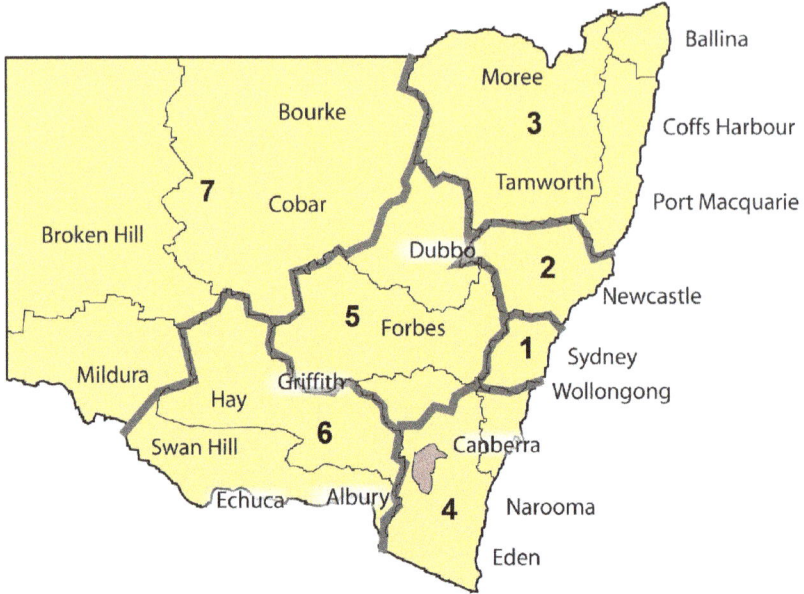

Notes accompanying figures 1-3

		Population (2003)	Av tax income (2002) ($)	Total pers income (2001) ($m)	Per capita pers income ($000)
Figure 1. A Single Inland State					
1	Coastal NSW	5,752,218	42,548	122,541.6	21.30
2	Inland NSW	929,835	35,411	15,854.4	17.05
Figure 2. Traditional New States					
1	New South Wales	5,176,243	43,755	114,477.2	22.12
2	New England	718,484	32,533	10,539.1	14.67
3	Riverina	465,592	35,661	8,037.5	17.26
4	Macquarie	321,734	35,630	5,342.2	16.60
Figure 3. Regional States					
1	Greater Sydney	4,198,543	45,040	97,411.2	23.20
2	Hunter	599,575	38,137	10,465.7	17.46
3	New England	688,838	32,292	9,965.8	14.47
4	Koszciusko	583,758	37,689	10,166.9	17.42
5	Macquarie	289,813	35,597	4,860.5	16.77
6	Riverina	257,154	35,338	4,506.5	17.52
7	Outback	64,372	34,891	1,019.4	15.84
For comparison					
	Tasmania	477,305	34,221	7,931.0	16.62
	South Australia	1,526,301	36,405	27,695.6	18.15

Data source: Australian Bureau of statistics National Regional Profiles (www.abs.gov.au)

What do Australians think about these options?

Preliminary research in Queensland and NSW demonstrates a high level of popular interest in long-term reform of the federal system. In this research randomly selected samples of Queensland and NSW adults responded to key questions about the future of the federal system when surveyed respectively in 2001 (Brown 2002a, b) and 2005 (Brown et al 2006 in press).

Although a substantial majority of citizens profess satisfaction with the way democracy works in Australia, a much lower proportion express satisfaction with the three-tiered federal system. When presented with several of the options outlined so far in this paper, a significant majority – 74.2% in NSW – expressed a preference for a constitutional scenario in another 50-100 years other than the system they have today.

Importantly, there is relatively little difference between urban and rural citizens of NSW when it comes to their opinion of existing levels of government, or their preferred system in the long-term.

While these surveys indicate a two-tiered system based on regional governments to be the single most preferred option in Queensland and NSW, they also indicate this is clearly not just a simplistic choice. In the NSW survey, government employees (61.6%) were among the most likely to favour this form of restructure, with state government employees the most likely of all (66.7%).

This research also reinforces the importance of local institutions in the thinking of many Australian citizens, with 36.3% of respondents preferring retention of existing local government as the second tier in a restructured federation, even though 52.6% would favour restructuring local government into new regional governments.

The high degree of public interest in long-term reform provides a reminder that, even if constitutional change is a longer-term process, constitutional theory can and should help inform the choice of short and medium term options.

Recognising the range of options raised by debates over the future of Australian federalism, also helps emphasise the challenge of developing a more informed and productive public discussion about the costs and benefits of any given reform. In the past, assumptions about particular options have been used to dismiss others, even when they have been based on similar principles and could in fact have delivered complementary benefits.

History suggests that the potential benefit of reforming the Australian federal system is frequently less in dispute than *which types* of reform are necessary or sufficient. In the 1970s, for example, new initiatives in 'regional planning' and 'new regional entities' were seen as the final nails in the 'collective coffin' of new state movements (Kidd 1974: 57), even though this phase of regional programs did not prove any more successful as a long-term response to the problems of the federal system.

In fact experts in constitutional theory and public policy have emphasised the need to approach the assessment of different options with an open mind. For example Professor Ken Wiltshire has noted that the most viable reforms may lie in a combination of principles previously associated with different competing options, through the marriage of federalism's principles of divided sovereignty with notions of 'pure regionalism' to produce a 'realistic alternative design' (Wiltshire 1991: 12).

Despite the importance of these reform debates, until now no single comprehensive model has existed for evaluating current trends and alternative options for the federal system. The lack of an accepted framework for analysing different reform options, combined with the political partisanship surrounding some options in previous decades, has made it difficult for the feasibility of these options to be objectively compared and assessed – despite the high level of agreement that Australian federalism needs to evolve to address this range of problems. This paper is intended to help establish a framework for a program of research to more effectively fill this gap.

4. Evaluating the options – the need for a framework

The evaluation of existing reform initiatives, and objective assessment of potential benefits and costs of other reform options, both require clear and agreed criteria against which the effects of reform can be measured or estimated.

In broad terms, it is clear that all the reforms discussed in the preceding sections are aimed at creating more legitimate, effective and efficient systems of governance. They also assume that governance will not improve through goodwill and intent alone. Tangible administrative and institutional change is required to support new efforts in more responsive and adaptive governance, and deliver the type of federal system needed by Australia in the 21st century.

The international experience confirms that any assessment framework must necessarily be holistic. By their nature, the political, economic, social and environmental effects of governance reform are unlikely to be easily separated, instead being interwoven.

Nevertheless, while no single comprehensive framework for evaluating these options has existed until now, starting points are provided by recent experience. Internationally, although devolutionary reforms are usually undertaken as 'acts of faith' without comprehensive prior planning, governments are usually then forced to evaluate these reforms against *ex post facto* descriptions of their intentions (Kay 2003; Jones et al 2005: 401).

Closer to home, Australian public policy contains a number of proposals for new frameworks for identifying the political, economic and policy issues to be considered when evaluating the effectiveness of new spatial approaches to governance. In NSW, for example, the need for effective evaluation of state government-funded 'place management' projects led to an illustrative framework for estimating the effects of projects against six dimensions: Change, Capacity, Governance, Learning, Cost-benefit, and Sustainability (Stewart-Weeks 2002).

This framework provides an example of key themes for evaluating particular projects or programs, but a wider process is needed to holistically evaluate the governance approaches lying behind the project. Examples can be found in both rural and urban contexts.

Recently increasing effort has gone into evaluating the complex and changing planning processes for regional natural resource management (NRM) around Australia, another key focus for federal-regional governance reform. Results include 20 criteria, or principles, to guide the evaluation of these diverse regional planning approaches, taking into account Context, Structure, Process, and Outcomes (Bellamy et al 2005).

These criteria provide a strong basis for evaluating a wide range of new spatial approaches to governance, particularly at the regional level where in fact, natural resource management, sustainable economic development and effective social programs are closely interlinked. Since these governance arrangements are not 'project-specific' but rather intended to support long-term programs and structural economic and social change, they provide a good guide to what is increasingly sought from regional governance more generally.

This framework also compares favourably to new suggestions for the content of evaluation frameworks for the new spatial approaches to governance increasingly deemed necessary in Australian urban contexts.

The resonance between rural NRM and urban planning evaluation is one good indicator that these frameworks share fundamental criteria, important to any area of governance reform. It also provides a salient reminder that the challenges of policy effectiveness, social sustainability, community engagement and 'democratic deficit' implicit in Australia's current federal system are not confined to rural regions but span the urban-rural divide (Gleeson and Low 2000; Gray 2004; Lawson and Gleeson 2005). Figure 4 sets out an overall approach to evaluating new spatial approaches in urban contexts, based on recognition of the different governance 'elements' involved in any such program, and articulation of key principles against which these might be judged (Lawson and Gleeson 2005: 90).

Table 4. Evaluation principles for spatial approaches (Lawson and Gleeson 2005)

Governance element	Evaluation principle
Political power	Ensure accountability of political leaders – representation
Policy development	Achieve greater policy coherence
Public administration	Improve service delivery – financial efficiencies. Address complex issues
Citizen engagement	Improve participation of citizens – partnerships. Social inclusion.
Institutional arrangements	Build collaboration across government – integration and coordination. Lead to long-term systemic and structural change.

Together these existing frameworks provide alternative structures, but common and complementary criteria and principles to guide the evaluation and assessment of complex new governance options.

Drawing on these efforts, the next section of this paper presents a new, comprehensive draft framework of 20 evaluation principles associated with the five key governance elements and/or outcomes implicit in our changing federal system (Table 5). It is framed principally in terms of the governance elements suggested by Lawson and Gleeson, recognising that the main foci of evaluation are the alternative structural and institutional options discussed earlier. However as the evaluation criteria/principles show, these elements overlap strongly with the structure and process themes identified by Bellamy et al (2005).

Further, in considering the actual or likely effects of new governance arrangements, it is important to consider overall outcomes to which a high level of consensus attaches, and which no one specific governance element can achieve on its own but which remain the goal of the governance system as a whole. Within this framework, each principle identifies, in broad terms, a key intended benefit of reform, guiding the evaluation of existing approaches and enabling the relative merits of reform options to be compared with each other and with the status quo.

Table 5. Evaluation framework for federal reform in Australia

Governance element/outcome	Evaluation principle		Evaluation methods			
			Political / social science (qualitative)	Political / social science (quantitative)	Public finance / inst economics	Economics
A. Political power	A1.	Accountability/representativeness of leaders is ensured	✓	✓		
	A2.	Legitimacy deficits are addressed (inc. re: non-elected leaders)	✓	✓		
	A3.	National political identity/citizenship is strengthened	✓	✓		
	A4.	Regional political identity/citizenship is strengthened	✓	✓		
B. Policy responsibility and development	B1.	Roles and responsibilities are defined based on 'subsidiarity'	✓		✓	
	B2.	Resources and funding are allocated and available at appropriate spatial level(s) ('subsidiarity' in practice)	✓		✓	
	B3.	Greater policy coherence is achieved; collaboration and integration across and between governments is strengthened	✓	✓		
	B4.	Capacity for regionally diverse policy responses is negotiated and institutionalised	✓	✓		✓

C. Public administration	C1.	Complex policy issues are addressed (see also D)	✓			✓
	C2.	Public service delivery is improved	✓	✓		✓
	C3.	Financial efficiencies of administration are improved	✓	✓	✓	
	C4.	Transparency in revenues, outlays, transfers and financial responsibility is improved		✓	✓	
D. Citizen and expert engagement	D1.	Knowledge integration is supported and maximised	✓	✓		
	D2.	Participation (or capacity for participation) of citizens is improved; partnerships facilitated and strengthened	✓	✓		✓
	D3.	Socially inclusive participation is ensured	✓	✓		
	D4.	Equity and procedural fairness are ensured	✓	✓		
E. Long-term outcomes	E1.	Regulation, compliance and participation costs are reduced		✓	✓	✓
	E2.	'Triple bottom line' sustainability is realised		✓	✓	✓
	E3.	Sustainable economic innovation is fostered		✓		✓
	E4.	Long-term systemic and structural change is supported; communities' adaptive capacity for governance is improved	✓	✓	✓	✓

5. A framework for evaluation

This section of the paper explains briefly, in relation to each principle within the above framework, the type of evaluation involved in holistically assessing the advantages and disadvantages of different reform options. In this way the framework provides an overall guide to the types of research and research methods than can be usefully deployed in evaluating the types of options outlined earlier.

The section concludes with a brief preliminary assessment of the lessons from existing research, and priority areas for further work.

A. Political power

Evaluation principles:

A1. Accountability/representativeness of leaders is ensured

This principle identifies a particularly important potential advantage of reform. In a democratic system, clear systems of political representation remain the cornerstone of ensuring the ultimate accountability of federal and regional governance actors.

Federalism is particularly predicated on the principle that each of the nation's major regions should receive direct representation in the national parliament, as well as delivering systems of subnational representation at scales conducive to effective accountability. This principle provokes analysis of the extent to which existing or reformed institutions can deliver enhanced political representation.

For example, section 7 of the present Constitution guarantees each existing state a minimum of six Senators (currently 12), and federal legislation provides for two Senators from each federal territory. Section 24 of the Constitution requires that 'as nearly as practicable' the number of Senators must be maintained at half the number of Representatives. If the principle of equal Senate representation is maintained, then the admission of one NSW new state (figure 5a above) would require a total increase of 38 Commonwealth politicians, or 17% of the Parliament. If variable Senate representation were introduced for new states, as provided for by section 122 of the Constitution, then Australia could be subdivided into 25 states and 5 territories with an increase of only 11 Commonwealth politicians (4.8% of the Parliament).

Can a given reform option also enhance regional and local-level democracy? Currently the relative weakness of local government mitigates against this, particularly as local representation is poorly remunerated, regional representation is typically indirect, and while state representation occurs at too high a scale. This principle calls for analysis of the democratic qualities of alternative regional bodies, including, in the case of regional governments, the potential for unicameral legislatures such as proposed for the new states of New England (1967) and the Northern Territory (1998), as well as the potential for greater use of regional-level proportional representation as used in some local governments, Tasmania, the ACT and New Zealand.

A2. Legitimacy deficits are addressed (inc. re: non-elected decision-makers)

This principle identifies that as well as providing reapportioned representation within existing institutions, an important potential benefit of reform is to provide accountability where this is currently lacking. It helps distinguish decentralisation options based on administrative or appointed regional bodies, and devolution options in which regional bodies are directly constitutionally accountable (e.g. via election) to the community.

Today many regional programs rely on short-term administrative arrangements (boards, committees, forums) in which participation is based on unrealistic levels of 'volunteerism', and/or whose legitimacy remains dependent on appointment from 'top down'. In regional natural resource management, for example, the call for stronger devolution of resources and authority to non-democratic institutions (Wentworth Group 2002) has been criticised for displaying a dangerous 'utopian localism' (Lane et al 2004). In many policy areas where outcomes are dependent on effective design and implementation at local and regional levels (e.g. education, health, community policing, natural resource management), the main implementation strategies remains classic departmental bureaucracies, even when open to 'engagement' at community levels.

This principle also helps identify that whereas many Australians are concerned that the nation may be 'over-governed' (in terms of numbers of politicians per capita), the real problem may be imbalance between the representation afforded at different levels. Indeed compared to many countries, Australia is over-governed in terms of parliament-based legislators (Commonwealth and state) but under-governed in terms of overall numbers of representatives in local and/or regional government.

A3. National political identity/citizenship is strengthened

This principle recognises the indirect advantages of a political system which citizens understand, support and with which they have a minimum level of political and cultural identification. Australians place a high value on nationhood and expect the Federal Government to be able to act in the national interest, particularly on economic matters.

Devolutionary reform also provides an opportunity for constitutional renewal, allowing communities to rebuild their relationship with the political institutions on which they depend, so contributing to national cohesion as envisaged by the Business Council of Australia's *Aspire Australia 2025* scenarios (BCA 2004).

A4. Regional political identity/citizenship is strengthened

In Australian public culture, one of the most prevalent criticisms of the nation's political geography is that it remains dependent on colonial-era decisions and defaults. Whatever the inputs to the decisions at the time, they predated European settlement in most regions and bear little relation to many of the fundamentals of Australian economic, environmental and social geography. The development of subnational governance frameworks based more clearly and strongly on the regions with which citizens have most direct affinity, stands to better support the social and political sustainability of communities as well as the responsiveness of regional level programs. Today geographers, social scientists and public policy practitioners are equipped with a more detailed understanding of the country in which we live, as demonstrated by new techniques in 'social surface modelling' (Brunckhorst et al 2004). While these approaches are still open to criticism (e.g. Dollery and Crase 2004b), there are advantages to be expected from a national political system in which a higher proportion of citizens identify with the nation's 'first order civil divisions' (state or regional government) more strongly than they do with current state governments.

B. Policy responsibility and development

Evaluation principles:

B1. Roles and responsibilities are defined based on 'subsidiarity'

'Subsidiarity' is the policy principle that government functions and services should be administered at the lowest level of government that can feasibly exercise that function, 'to the maximum extent possible consistent with the national interest' (Australian Premiers and Chief Ministers 1991, quoted in Galligan 1995: 205; Wilkins 1995). In the 1990s it was adopted by Australian governments as one of the four key 'pillars' of modern intergovernmental relations.

Subsidiarity is an internationally recognised principle, particularly associated with the benefits of federal systems (Grewal et al 1981; Bermann 1994). Its economic benefits are derived from the theory that each public good should be provided at the smallest scale of government consistent with no spatial spillovers into adjacent regions (Dollery 2002).

'Pure' public goods with nationwide benefits, such as defence and monetary policy, are best administered nationally, while services which are more direct or 'private' goods, with geographically limited benefits, are best administered locally.

'Fiscal federalism' based on this principle has long been promoted as a mechanism for maximising financial responsibility and allowing local governments the flexibility to respond to the preferences of their 'customers' or electorates (Tiebout 1956; Musgrave 1969; Oates 1972, 1999; Rodriguez-Pese and Gill 2003). Subsidiarity provided a strong economic argument in support of Australian new state movements (Clark 1952; 1955). Recent arguments for 'enterprise zones', in which taxation regimes are used to provide incentives for businesses or citizens to move between regions or states, are borne out by the way in which existing States such as Queensland Government have used their control over at least some financial instruments to attract population.

More recently, subsidiarity has been given only limited use as a rationale for not transferring further policy responsibilities from state governments to the Federal Government. In other words, it has been used as a principle to stop some responsibilities from being further centralised, but not as a guide to which responsibilities would be better devolved by federal and state governments to more local or regional levels.

Evaluation against this principle allows current and proposed reforms to be tested for economic efficiency and maximum responsiveness in the formulation of policy and deliver of services. Areas in which benefits might accrue from further centralisation to the Commonwealth include economy-wide management and regulation. Areas in which benefits can be expected from stronger local and/or regional governance include many of the current core areas of state responsibility, from the 'classic' regional policy areas identified earlier, to community justice, policing, health and human service delivery, and primary and secondary education.

B2. Resources and funding are allocated and available at appropriate spatial level(s) ('subsidiarity' in practice)

This principle requires assessment of the (a) intended and (b) actual distribution of public resources in support of the apportionment of responsibilities described above. Many problems associated with Australia's current version of federalism flow from the fact that even when local and regional governance capacity exists formally, or in theory, control over the necessary resources remains highly centralised. The problem of vertical fiscal imbalance (VFI) also relates to this issue (see C4 below).

Since the 1930s, Australia's federal system has developed a strong theoretical capacity for ensuring that the public resources collected by the Commonwealth (now the vast bulk of revenues) are redistributed to lower levels, through the Commonwealth Grants Commission. Under principles of horizontal fiscal equalisation, the different economic and demographic challenges faced by different states (and different regions within the different states) play a role in calculating the 'relativities' for distribution of revenues, now including the estimated $45 billion per annum in GST and Health Care Grants (HCGs) (2005-06). These relativities detail the proportion of revenue returned to each state, relative to the amount collected from within that state – as made controversial in recent years by the NSW government (see Table 6).

Table 6. Per Capita GST Relativities (Commonwealth Grants Commission 2005)

New South Wales	0.86846
Victoria	0.87552
Western Australia	1.02500
Queensland	1.04389
Australian Capital Territory	1.14300
South Australia	1.20325
Tasmania	1.55299
Northern Territory	4.26682

Clear potential exists for extending these principles to ensure more effective devolution of resources to sub-state levels. Although the less wealthy regions of all states are taken into account in calculating these relativities, there is currently no direct method of ensuring that resources are actually distributed regionally, within states, according to that need. Most regions of NSW would have a relativity between Tasmania and South Australia if considered in their own right, e.g. if they were constituted as states.

Short and medium-term options also exist for addressing this principle. Currently the main mechanism of sub-state equalisation is the system for federal grants under the federal *Local Government (Financial Assistance) Act 1995*, which amount to only $1.617 billion (2005-06). Enlarged shares of revenue could be directed to local government or to other regional bodies by increasing this share, direct-funding from what would otherwise be the statewide share of GST, other compensatory strategies under the new Intergovernmental Agreement on cost-shifting, and other direct-funding programs such as Roads to Recovery I and II

(R2R, R2R2) to increase the likelihood of resources being spent in the regions and localities where they are most needed.

B3. Greater policy coherence is achieved; collaboration and integration across and between governments is strengthened

This principle recognises the need for political and institutional frameworks that deliver greater coherence ('seamlessness') in policy outcomes at a variety of levels – local, regional and national. Proposals for strengthened federal power in key areas clearly address this principle. At local and regional levels, this principle currently drives initiatives in 'joined up' or 'whole-of-government' approaches, aimed at overcoming the extent to which policy responses are constrained by different institutional 'silos'.

This principle also recognises that improved policy coherence is not likely to be efficiently and sustainably achieved in the long-term, unless supported by institutional reforms to promote intra- and inter-governmental collaboration. A range of short, medium and long-term options can promote more effective 'whole-of-government; outcomes at the regional level, from regional managers' forums, to regional budgeting, to general-purpose regional government.

Most importantly, this principle emphasises the importance of more formal, durable system of intergovernmental relations. While the recent renewed focus on regional solutions is often the product of collaboration between governments, stronger regional governance also ensures the need for ongoing horizontal collaboration to maintain coherence between an increasing number of formal governance actors. Governance is increasingly a shared activity in which multiple levels of government, as well as non-government actors, all play a role. As a result, governance is now understood as much in terms of 'networks' (Rhodes 1997) as 'structures'.

In the 1950s, the risk that new state proposals would only further fragment and complicate national processes of government made it 'very questionable whether the creation of new States ... within the existing federal system would not exacerbate more of the problems of federalism than it solved' (Parker 1955: 16). More recently, devolution in Britain has raised new questions about how the policy decisions of 'the centre' and the devolved institutions are best coordinated (Jones et al 2005: 400).

Although Australia has experimented strongly with intergovernmental collaboration, this often appears to remain the exception rather than the rule, with mechanisms such as the Council of Australian governments (COAG) notoriously informal and weak. Any reform option must be evaluated for its likely contribution to mechanisms and capacity for collaboration and policy integration at both national and regional levels.

B4. Capacity for regionally diverse policy responses is negotiated and institutionalised

When greater policy coherence and national collaboration have been sought in Australian federal experience, this has usually been with a focus on forging more uniform national responses and making up for deficiencies in federal power. While this process can be expected to further benefit from reform options in a range of policy areas, in others it is important to build capacity for maximising the opportunity for greater diversity in regional policy responses.

Strengthened regional governance, even in the form of new states, is unlikely to ever provide a mechanism for regaining the 'autonomy' of regions in the form once enjoyed by the original states. For example, even with strong general-purpose regional governments, regions would only become more subject to externally-influenced (federal) environmental regulation, and national systems of commercial law and industrial relations. Nevertheless, any reform must be evaluated for the extent to which it provides regions with increased 'agency' to experiment and innovate with policy and services within the broad national framework, particularly in respect of innovations that would have been more difficult to pursue at the central or federal level (Rodriguez-Pese and Gill 2003). This principle reinforces these objectives.

C. Public administration

Evaluation principles:

C1. Complex policy issues are addressed (see also D)

This principle recognises that governance at all spatial levels involves the identification and solution of complex problems. Improved problem-solving capacity is also an intended benefit of reform in relation to other governance elements – including policy coherence and collaboration (above). However overcoming institutional divides does not in itself guarantee better problem-solving capacity, if for example all policy actors still see the problem in the same way.

Clearer federal government authority and resources, and more effective scales of state/regional government can both potentially lead to improved technical capacity in complex problem-solving. Local decision-makers are often considered to be more in touch with communities and are better placed to identify and react to issues. The different technical and policy knowledges relevant to understanding and solving major problems are more likely to be forced to be integrated, at a scale where direct evidence of the problem and of the feasibility of proposed solutions is better able to be assessed by experts, decision-makers and those affected (see also D below). Finally, the resources needed to efficiently harness the best expertise are more likely to be available if aggregated at a more appropriate level.

C2. Public service delivery is improved

This principle recognises that as well as better-adapted policy, proposed reforms need to be assessed for their capacity to better deliver government services – whether uniform or similar services to those delivered elsewhere, or regionally-specific ones.

In any given service area, will reform provide: an enhanced ability to vary and tailor services in line with regional needs; greater freedom to innovate in the development of services; and more direct accountability for services? Will it provide heightened and more rapid feedback systems, through the proximity of elected representatives to their electors and reduction in the numbers of layers of administration between citizens and decision-makers? In evaluating reform options, answers may be found in either the form or content of services, i.e. in regional tailoring or simplification of simple administration of programs as well as in substantive criteria, goals and outputs.

C3. Financial efficiencies of administration are improved

This principle emphasises the importance of ensuring public resources are not unnecessarily wasted in administration, overlaps or duplication, that could otherwise be devoted to substantive services or used to relieve the burden on Australian taxpayers.

Regional institutional reform is sometimes presumed to be financially efficient, even when in fact this may not necessarily be so. For example, in some states assumptions about optimum economies of scale for administration have been used to support local government amalgamation programs which have since been criticised for the 'crass simplicities' of their financial rationale (Vince 1997: 151; Dollery and Crase 2004a).

Questions about the financial effects of reform tend to revolve around two questions: whether or how stronger regional governance can be made financially viable; and whether reform will remove wastage or overlap, and offer savings in the cost of government that might then be redirected to existing services or new programs.

Current initiatives raise questions regarding the financial efficiency of multiple, fragmented regional programs and bodies, including regional economic agencies noted for their 'third world' birth-and-death rate (Beer et al 2003). The financial viability of such programs is problematic, given their frequent reliance on non-government or quasi-non-government organisations, and questions over the ability of many types of regional bodies to reliably manage large resources even if available. By contrast, medium-to-long term options for formal regional government raise fewer questions of viability, given that regions have long ceased to operate with the economic and financial independence once experienced by Australia's original states. Today new state or regional governments would form new financial units within Australia's integrated system of national public finance, supported by horizontal fiscal equalisation.

Could options for reform of the federal system lead to greater efficiency in the cost of government overall? A theoretical model for calculating the possible different overall costs of government, relative to the current cost, based on a variety of different constitutional reform scenarios, was developed by Drummond (2002).

On this analysis up to $30 billion per annum (or about 10% of total public expenditure) could be saved if state governments were simply abolished, leaving national and local governments. Other scenarios are extrapolated from this baseline, the known cost of the existing system, and the known costs of Tasmanian-sized state governments and the ACT government (which combines both state and local government functions). On this graph, 'new states' assume retention of a three-tiered system of government, while 'regional states' assume the new regional governments would exercise both state and local functions. In both cases, the 'simplified' scenarios are variations in which some existing State government functions are also reallocated to the Federal Government.

While superficially this model suggests it would be expensive to create more states on a three-tiered model, in fact this is only true if all new states or regional states were to have the same fixed and marginal costs as today's Tasmanian or ACT governments.

The value of this model is in setting up outer boundaries within which more in-depth analysis of the net costs and benefits of reform can occur, using more specific, 'ground-truthed' options for alternative frameworks of regional governance. Even with its existing limitations, the model identifies up to 6-7% of current public expenditure (approx. $20 billion per annum) as realistically capable of being saved through federal reform of the federal system, through a combination of centralisation and devolution.

C4. Transparency in revenues, outlays, transfers and financial responsibility is improved

Australian public administration has long been characterised by a complex and opaque system of interregional and intergovernmental transfers, with negative implications for both efficiency and accountability. This principle recognises the value of greater transparency in the financial basis of public administration.

The aggregated nature of state finances mean there is currently low transparency in the spatial collection and redistribution of public resources, and in decision-making regarding what could genuinely be considered 'equitable' for given regions (rural or urban). Reform options can be assessed for their contribution to clearer general-purpose regional budgeting, providing administrative and accountability benefits.

Similarly substantial criticism has surrounded the striking degree of vertical fiscal imbalance (VFI) embedded in the current federal system. Currently the Federal Government collects over 90% of all public revenue, even though it is directly responsible for only about 50% of all public expenditure. According to some economists, the divorce between financial 'or 'fiscal' responsibility (who levies the taxes) and electoral accountability (who spends the money) raises economic and political problems. On this analysis, governments feel less responsible for how funds are spent, and unlikely to spend these funds as wisely and efficiently as if they bore the political pain of collection themselves. Local government is somewhat better off, because while it receives federal funds laundered through the States, it is also directly responsible to the community for property rates decisions.

On other analyses, VFI is not really a problem in its own right, but rather can be accepted as a longstanding element of Australian administration. One Canadian political economist found little evidence that governments are more wasteful with transferred funds, primarily because 'the provincial voter, who is also the federal voter, sees through the circular route taken by his or her taxes' (Winer 2002: xi). Others argue that decisions about taxing *should* be separated from spending, because the efficiencies of each are different at different levels (Dollery 2002).

The key question is not whether federal reform can or should relieve VFI as such, but whether it can contribute to greater transparency in the flow of resources. In particular, reform options can be assessed for the extent to which they make it easier for administrative and resource needs to be identified, and for resources to be efficiently transferred to where they are most needed (see 'subsidiarity' above).

D. Citizen and expert engagement

Evaluation principles:

D1. Knowledge integration is supported and maximised

This principle is the first of four principles dealing with the governance processes offered by different reform options, particularly in relation to the involvement of non-government actors in federal and regional governance.

As discussed above, a key evaluation principle in relation to public administration is capacity to address complex issues, including by overcoming institutional 'silos'. The corollary of this principle is the need for reform that better overcomes knowledge-based 'silos' by integrating different types of expert or technical knowledge, and community knowledge and experience in the design and implementation of new policy solutions.

D2. Participation (or capacity for participation) of citizens is improved; partnerships facilitated and strengthened

This principle recognises that improved participation of communities and businesses in public decision-making is a universal objective, especially where focused on improved outcomes at local and regional levels (Smyth et al 2005; Eversole and Martin 2005). In this respect, participation and engagement is pursued at all levels of the design and delivery of programs, rather than simply through political and electoral processes. While commonly framed around notions of social capital, improved participation is also noted for its economic benefits (Wanna and Withers 2000: 86; Cavaye et al 2002).

Under this principle, reforms can be assessed for their contribution to the revitalisation of relationships between communities and government, through enduring engagement mechanisms in which formal structures better align with major communities of interest. Localised governments are better placed to develop networks and involve community and local business in seeking solutions to issues confronting that community.

D3. Socially inclusive participation is ensured

This principle recognises that the effective engagement of citizens in government and community processes is a vital part of their effective inclusion in society more generally, which today is increasingly accepted as an indicator of personal and societal well-being as opposed to poverty (Saunders 2005). Some specific indicators of levels of social inclusion are already routinely collected in official e.g. ABS monitoring of the progress of Australia's society and economy. While many recent regional policy initiatives can be linked with political desires to address perceived social exclusion (Pritchard and McManus 2000), whether or not this is achieved depends on the broader economic effects of reform, and the extent to which reform better engages a broader cross-section of the community or entrenches particular elites.

D4. Equity and procedural fairness are ensured

This principle recognises that citizens and businesses have different capacities to participate in governance, but will share in the effects of decision-making and be subject to new forms of federal and regional regulation as reform occurs. It requires evaluation of the differential impacts of governance reform on different communities, individuals and industries, and of the extent to which reform options carry with them the capacity for amelioration of inequitable impacts either through alternative processes or substantive compensation.

E. Long-term outcomes

Evaluation principles:

E1. Regulation, compliance and participation costs are reduced

These final four principles identify the extent to which different governance options contribute to the major economic, social and environmental outcomes currently sought from reform as a whole.

This principle recognises as politically and economically important that reform should not increase, and ideally that it reduce, the costs borne by business and the community in dealing with government. These include the direct costs of regulation, and indirect costs such as compliance burdens and time.

Under this principle, the economic effects of different reform options would be estimated through applied general equilibrium (CGE) modelling, in effect as an example of assessing the economic consequences of whole 'alternative constitutions' (Winer 2002: 306). Evaluation would extend from estimates of national economic benefits derived from simplified, more consistent regulation in key areas, to include the regional economic effects of strengthened local and regional governance through use of regional models such as developed by Monash University's Centre of Policy Studies, Access Economics, National Economics (which produces the annual State of the Regions Report for the Australian Local Government Association), and NATSEM at the University of Canberra.

E2. 'Triple bottom line' sustainability is realised

This principle recognises environmental, social and economic sustainability as the central governance challenge confronted by Australian society as a whole, and as a unifying objective for all options for reform of the federal system of governance.

Any given reform option needs to be assessed for its capacity to directly help in the delivery of more effective governance solutions in response to the sustainability challenge. Clearer, rationalised federal policy responsibilities for the coordination of Australia's sustainability transition, and strengthened capacity for economic, environmental and social policy innovation and action at the regional level are both crucial to achieving this outcome.

New state movements of the 1920s and 1950s were at times inspired by an 'Australia unlimited' view of economic development, with stronger regional governance intended to help 'take the brake off' development by facilitating major new infrastructure projects, such as dams, hydroelectric schemes and railways. However more recent decades have seen emergence of a relative consensus that the final measure of our institutions will be whether they help place society on a more sustainable footing, measured in 'triple bottom line' terms (e.g. Gray and Lawrence 2001; Cavaye et al 2002).

Under this principle, a variety of existing economic, environmental and social indicators bear on the evaluation such as those used by the Australian Bureau of Statistics in its ongoing project *Measuring Australia's Progress,* based on 15 'headline dimensions' under four broad areas (ABS 2005).

By considering the effects of reform against an array of established indicators such as these, a holistic judgement can be formed as to whether, or how, specific reforms will contribute to the national transition. Use of expert and/or lay panels to assess options against these indicators is one useful way of describing their likely advantages and disadvantages.

Table 7. Headline Dimensions – Measures of Australia's Progress (ABS 2005)

	Individuals	The economy and economic resources	The environment	Living together in our society
1	Health			
2	Education and training			
3	Work			
4		National income		
5		National wealth		
6		Housing		
7		Productivity		
8		Financial hardship		
9			The natural landscape	
10			The human environment	
11			Oceans and estuaries	
12			International environmental concerns	
13				Family, community and social cohesion
14				Crime
15				Democracy, governance and citizenship

E3. Sustainable economic innovation is fostered

This principle recognises that within the above framework of a sustainability transition, a major objective of governance reform is to increase the capacity for economic innovation at national and regional scales, along with overall competitiveness.

Recent theories of 'new regionalism' as applied in Australia highlight the importance of governance reform for creating a more conducive environment for business to innovate and prosper in a 'do it yourself' fashion (Beer et al 2003: 248-264). Reform of the federal system to provide a simpler regulatory environment for business is one avenue. Another is improved regional-level economic coordination mechanisms such as consolidated, legislatively-backed and better funded Regional Development Agencies, involving direct community and business participation, and directly accountable to regional democratic processes, of the kind recommended by the Commonwealth Regional Business Development Analysis (RBDA 2003). Options would be analysed for their contribution towards increased 'agency' on the part of regional industries to create institutional circumstances more conducive to their own economic opportunities, and more effectively interpret, lead, influence and maximise economic events.

Under this principle, the economic modeling described under principle E1 would extend to estimation of the broader economic effects of devolution, by adapting existing modeling techniques to isolate the impact of devolved from other (scalar) influences on economic governance

(McGregor and Swales 2005). At the same time, in addition to estimating regional benefits, economic modelling under this principle would estimate the stimulatory effects of associated reforms (e.g. simplified national systems of business regulation) on the national economy.

E4. Long-term systemic and structural change is supported; communities' adaptive capacity for governance is improved

This principle recognises that many key areas of government policy are not static but aimed at achieving medium-long term change in social and economic conditions (e.g. sustainability transitions, creating sustainable employment opportunities, economic restructuring to cope with globalisation, business innovation, safer and more harmonious communities, increased community capacity to deal with an aging population). An important feature of institutional frameworks is that they themselves are not rigid, but remain adaptive, flexible and supportive of change.

Under this principle, different institutional options can be evaluated for their ability to meet these challenges. Reform options should deliver stability, continuity and durability while also allowing a high degree of adaptiveness and flexibility in their delivery of change-based programs, including further opportunity to innovate in the nature of local and regional institutions.

Preliminary conclusions

The above framework is intended to provide a structure for a program of research into the relative costs and benefits of different federal reform options, and to facilitate agreement among experts, policymakers and interested groups about the objectives of reform and how the feasibility of reform might be evaluated.

While conclusions about the feasibility and desirability of any given reform must obviously await more research of this kind, this discussion highlights the many areas in which reform of Australia's federal system – as a general principle – can be expected to deliver social and economic benefits. In particular, it suggests:

There is no reason to doubt the financial viability of most new state or similar regional government options, within Australia's system of federal public finance;

There is good reason to believe that options for stronger regional governance can be found that will deliver improved financial efficiencies in public administration;

There is good reason to believe that reform based on regional devolution can also contribute to greater national policy coherence, if accompanied by a commitment to a stronger culture and institutions for intergovernmental collaboration; and

There is good reason to believe that stronger regional governance within the federal system will deliver long-term social, economic and environmental benefits.

6. Where to from here?

This evaluation framework provides a basis for further, more detailed interdisciplinary research into the costs and benefits implied by current or potential options for the future of the federal system.

A future paper in this series will set out more specific examples of reform scenarios, for the purposes of comparison, evaluation and further public debate. These scenarios will draw on the analysis earlier in this paper. They will provide a range of tangible options to which the above evaluation framework can be applied, as a means of stimulating further debate about the most desirable directions for reform.

Reform of Australia's federal system will also necessarily involve its own direct costs. These need to be weighed against the benefits thrown up in evaluation, and include: the cost of public education associated with reform; federal compensation or financial inducement to other governments to accept territorial change; transitional costs; the start-up costs of new institutions; and adjustment assistance for localities and businesses temporarily adversely affected by change.

NSW Farmers' Association and Griffith University welcome feedback on the framework to help inform the evaluation of different reform options. We also invite expressions of interest from other organisations interested in supporting any area of this research, and from researchers interested in carrying it out.

7. References

ABS (2005). *Measures of Australia's Progress: Summary Indicators*. Australian Bureau of Statistics, Canberra.

BCA (1991). *Government in Australia in the 1990s: A Business Perspective*. Melbourne, Business Council of Australia.

BCA (2004). 'Riding the Wave', in *Aspire Australia 2025*. Melbourne, Business Council of Australia.

Beer, A. (2000). 'Regional policy and development in Australia: running out of solutions?', in *Land of Discontent: The Dynamics of Change in Rural and Regional Australia*, W. N. Pritchard and P. McManus (eds). Sydney, University of New South Wales Press: 169-194.

Beer, A., A. Maude, et al (2003). *Developing Australia's Regions: Theory and Practice*. Sydney, University of New South Wales Press.

Bellamy, J., T. Meppem, et al (2003). 'The changing face of regional governance for economic development: implications for local government.' *Sustaining Regions* **2**(3): 7-17.

Bellamy, J., Smith T., Taylor B and Walker M. (2005). 'Regional natural resource management planning arrangements: Evaluating through the regional lens', in *Regional natural resource management planning: the challenges of evaluation as seen through different lenses*, J. Bellamy (ed.), Papers from an Occasional Symposium, October 2004, CSIRO Sustainable Ecosystems and CIRM Social Dimensions of NRM Working Group. Queensland Department of Natural Resources and Mines, Indooroopilly.

Belshaw, J. P. (1955). 'The Economics of New States', in Australian Institute of Political Science (ed.), *New States for Australia*. The Institute, Sydney: 51.

Bermann, G. A. (1994). 'Taking Subsidiarity Seriously: Federalism in the European Community and the United States' *Columbia Law Review* **94** (2): 331-456.

Blackshield, T. and Williams, G. (2004). *Australian Constitutional Law and Theory*. Sydney, Federation Press.

Blainey, G. (2004). 'Why Every Major Region Should Be Its Own State', in *Restructuring Australia: Regionalism, Republicanism and Reform of the Nation-State*, W. Hudson and A. J. Brown (eds). Sydney, Federation Press.

Brown, A. J. (2001). 'Can't wait for the sequel: Australian federation as unfinished business.' *Melbourne Journal of Politics* 27: 47-67.

Brown, A. J. (2002a). 'After the party: public attitudes to Australian federalism, regionalism and reform in the 21st century.' *Public Law Review* 13(3): 171-190.

Brown, A. J. (2002b). 'Subsidiarity or subterfuge? Resolving the future of local government in the Australian federal system.' *Australian Journal of Public Administration* 61(4): 24-42.

Brown, A. J. (2004a). 'One Continent, Two Federalisms: Rediscovering the Original Meaning of Australian Federal Ideas.' *Australian Journal of Political Science* 39(4): 485-504.

Brown, A. J. (2004b). 'Constitutional Schizophrenia Then and Now: Exploring federalist, regionalist and unitary strands in the Australian political tradition', in K. Walsh (ed.), *The Distinctive Foundations of Australian Democracy: Lectures in the Senate Occasional Lecture Series 2003-2004*. Papers on Parliament No. 42, Department of the Senate, Parliament House, Canberra.

Brown, A. J. (2005). 'Regionalism and Regional Governance in Australia', in R. Eversole and J Martin (eds), *Participation and Governance in Regional Development: Global Trends in an Australian Context*. Ashgate.

Brown, A. J. (2006). 'The Constitution We Were Meant To Have: Reexamining the origins and strength of Australia's unitary political traditions', in K. Walsh (ed.), *Democratic Experiments: Lectures in the Senate Occasional Lecture Series 2004-2005*. Papers on Parliament No. 44, Department of the Senate, Parliament House, Canberra.

Brown, A. J., Gray I. and Giorgas, D. (in press). 'Towards a more regional federalism: rural and urban attitudes to institutions, governance and reform in Australia', article submitted to *Rural Society*, Special Governance Issue, 2006.

Brunckhorst, D., Coop, P. and Reeve, I. (2004). *An Eco-civic Regionalisation for Rural New South Wales: Final Report to the NSW Government*, Institute for Rural Futures and Centre for Bioregional Resource Management, University of New England, Armidale.

Cavaye, J., B. Blackwood, et al (2002). *Sustainable Regional Development: The Stalled Agenda and the Way Forward*. Rockhampton, Occasional Paper 2/2002, Central Queensland University.

Chapman, R. J. K. and M. Wood (1984). *Australian Local Government: The Federal Dimension*. Allen & Unwin.

Clark, C. (1952). *The organisation of a new state*. Australian Decentralisation and New States Movement, Sydney.

Clark, C. (1955). 'Australia's Economic and Population Capacity' *Australian Journal of Politics and History* 1: 49-58.

Commission of the European Communities (2001). *Decentralisation: Better Involvement of National, Regional and Local Actors*. Brussels, A White Paper. Report from European Governance Working Group 3b.

Commonwealth (1949). *Regional Planning in Australia: A History of Progress and Review of Regional Planning Activities through the Commonwealth*. Canberra, Department of Post-War Reconstruction.

Commonwealth (2001). *Time Running Out: Shaping Regional Australia's Future*. Canberra, House of Representatives Primary Industries and Regional Services Committee, Australian Government Publishing Service.

Commonwealth (2003). *Rates and Taxes: A Fair Share for Responsible Local Government*. Canberra, House of Representatives Standing Committee on Economics, Finance and Public Administration, AGPS.

Commonwealth Grants Commission (2001). *Review of the Operation of the Local Government (Financial Assistance) Act 1995*. Canberra, Commonwealth of Australia.

Courchene, T. J. (1995). 'Glocalization: The Regional/International Interface.' *Canadian Journal of Regional Science* 18(1): 1-20.

Dollery, B. (2002). 'A Century of Vertical Fiscal Imbalance in Australian Federalism', Working Paper Series in Economics, University of New England.

Dollery, B. and Crase, L. (2004a). *Is Bigger Local Government Better? An evaluation of the economic case for Australian municipal amalgamation programs*, School of Economics, University of New England.

Dollery, B. and Crase, L. (2004b). 'A Critical Note on `Eco-Civic Regionalisation' as the Basis for Local Government Boundaries in Australia' *Australian Geographer* 35(3): 289-300.

Drummond, M. L. (2002). 'Costing constitutional change: Estimating the cost of five variations on Australia's federal system.' *Australian Journal of Public Administration* 61(4): 43-56.

Ellis, U. R. (1933). *New Australian States*, Endeavour Press.

Galligan, B. (1995). *A federal republic: Australia's constitutional system of government*, Cambridge University Press.

Gleeson, B. J. (2003). 'Learning About Regionalism from Europe: 'Economic Normalisation' and Beyond' *Australian Geographical Studies* 41(3):221–236.

Gleeson, B. J. and Low, N.P. (2000). *Australian Urban Planning: New Challenges, New Agendas*, Allen & Unwin.

Gray, I. and G. Lawrence (2001). *A Future for Regional Australia: Escaping Global Misfortune*. Cambridge University Press.

Grewal, B. S., K. Wiltshire and C. Balmer (1981). *Towards Adaptive Federalism*. Australian Council of Intergovernment Relations, Information Paper No. 9, Canberra, Australian Government Publishing Service.

Hall, R. (1998). *Abolish the States! Australia's Future and a $30 Billion Answer to our Tax Problems*, Pan-Macmillan.

Howard, J. (2005). 'Reflections on Australian Federalism', Address to the Menzies Research Centre, Melbourne, April 11 2005.

Hurford, C. (2004). 'A Republican Federation of Regions: Reforming A Wastefully Governed Australia', in *Restructuring Australia: Regionalism, Republicanism and Reform of the Nation-State*, W. Hudson and A. J. Brown (eds). Sydney, Federation Press.

Jones, M., Goodwin, M. and Jones, R. (2005). 'State Modernization, Devolution and Economic Governance: An Introduction and Guide to Debate', *Regional Studies* 39(4): 397.

Kay, A. (2003). 'Evaluating Devolution in Wales', *Political Studies* **51**(1): 51-66.

Keating, M. (1998). *The new regionalism in Western Europe: territorial restructuring and political change.* Edward Elgar.

Kidd, G. A. (1974). 'New Cities – An End to New States.' *Australian Quarterly* 46(2)(June 1974): 57-68.

Lane, M., G. McDonald, et al (2004). 'Decentralisation and Environmental Management in Australia: A Comment on the Prescriptions of the Wentworth Group.' *Australian Geographical Studies* **42**(1): 103-115.

Lawson, S. and Gleeson, B. (2005). 'Shifting Urban Governance', in Smyth, P., Reddell, T. and Jones, A. (eds). *Community and Local Governance in Australia.* UNSW Press, Sydney.

Markusen, A. (1987). *Regions: The Economics and Politics of Territory.* New Jersey, Rowman and Littlefield.

McGregor, P.G. and Swales, K. (2005). 'Economics of Devolution/Decentralisation in the UK: Some Questions and Answers' *Regional Studies* 39(4): 477-494.

Musgrave, R.A. (1969). *Fiscal Systems*, New Haven, Yale University Press.

Neale, R. G. (1950). 'New States Movement.' *Australian Quarterly* September 1950: 9-23.

Oates, W. E. (1972). *Fiscal Federalism*, New York, Harcourt Brace Jovanovich.

Oates, W. E. (1999). 'An Essay on Fiscal Federalism' *Journal of Economic Literature* **37**: 1120.

OECD (1997). *Managing Across Levels of Government.* Public Management Committee (PUMA), Organisation for Economic Cooperation and Development, Paris.

Painter, M. (1998). *Collaborative federalism: economic reform in Australia in the 1990s*, Cambridge University Press.

Parker, R. S. (1955). 'Why New States?', in Australian Institute of Political Science (ed.), *New States for Australia.* The Institute, Sydney: 1-19.

Peden, J. B., P. P. Abbott, T. R. Ashworth, E. K. Bowden, H. P. Colebatch, M. B. Duffy and D. L. McNamara (1929). *Report of the Royal Commission on the Constitution.* Commonwealth of Australia, Canberra.

Power, J. and R. Wettenhall (1976). 'Regional government versus regional programs.' *Australian Journal of Public Administration* 35(2): 114-129.

Prescott, J. R. V. (1987). 'New state movements', in J. C. R. Camm and J. Mc-Quilton (eds), *Australians: A Historical Atlas*. Fairfax, Syme and Weldon, Sydney, vol 6: 257, 286.

Pritchard, W. N. and P. McManus (ed.) (2000). *Land of Discontent: The Dynamics of Change in Rural and Regional Australia*. Sydney, University of New South Wales Press.

Rainnie, A. and Grobbelaar, M. (2004). *New Regionalism in Australia: Limits and Possibilities*. Ashgate Publishing.

RBDA (2003). *Regional Business: A Plan for Action*. Report of the Commonwealth Regional Business Development Analysis, Australian Government, Canberra.

Reddell, T. (2005). 'Local Social Governance and Citizen Engagement', in Smyth, P., Reddell, T. and Jones, A. (eds). *Community and Local Governance in Australia*. UNSW Press, Sydney.

Rhodes, R. A. W. (1997). *Understanding Governance: Policy Networks, Governance, Reflexivity and Accountability*, Open University Press, Philadelphia.

Rodriguez-Pese, A. and Gill, N (2003). 'The global trend towards devolution and its implications', *Environment and Planning C: Government and Policy* 21.

Saunders, P. (2005). 'Social exclusion as a new framework for measuring poverty', in Smyth, P., Reddell, T. and Jones, A. (eds). *Community and Local Governance in Australia*. UNSW Press, Sydney.

Smyth, P., Reddell, T. and Jones, A. (eds) (2005). *Community and Local Governance in Australia*. UNSW Press, Sydney.

Stewart-Weeks, M. (2002). 'Assessment of evaluation strategies and tools for place management and community renewal projects', Paper presented at the 2002 Australasian Evaluation Society International Conference, October/November 2002, Wollongong Australia. www.aes.asn.au

Stilwell, F. (2000). *Changing Track: A New Political Economic Direction for Australia*. Pluto.

Tiebout, C. (1956). 'A Pure Theory of Local Public Expenditures' *Journal of Political Economy*, 64: 416-24.

Vince, A. (1997). 'Amalgamations', in B. Dollery and N. Marshall (eds), *Australian Local Government: Reform and Renewal*. Macmillan, Melbourne: 151.

Wanna, J., Kelly, J. and Forster, J. (2000). *Managing public expenditure in Australia*. Sydney, Allen & Unwin.

Wanna, J. and G. Withers (2000). 'Creating capability: combining economic and political rationalities in industry and regional policy', in *The Future of*

Governance: Policy Choices. G. Davis and M. Keating (ed.). Sydney, Allen & Unwin.

Watts, R. (1996). *Comparing Federal Systems in the 1990s*. Kingston, Queen's University.

Wentworth Group (2002). *Blueprint for a Living Continent: A Way Forward from the Wentworth Group of Concerned Scientists*. Sydney. World Wide Fund for Nature Australia.

Wilkins, R. (1995). 'Federalism and Regulatory Reform', in *Microeconomic Reform and Federalism*. P. Carroll and M. Painter (eds). Canberra, Federalism Research Centre, Australian National University: 216-222.

Wiltshire, K. (1991). *Tenterfield Revisited: Reforming Australia's System of Government for 2001*, University of Queensland Press.

Winer, S. L. (2002). *Political Economy in Federal States: Selected Essays*. Cheltenham, Edward Elgar.

Wood, A. (1999). 'Stealth missile for the States: the rise and rise of Federalism', in Waldren (ed.), *Future Tense: Australia beyond election 1998*. Allen & Unwin: 215.